SOCIAL MEDIA MATERIALITIES AND PROTEST

Far from being neutral, social media platforms – such as Facebook, Twitter, YouTube, and WeChat – possess their own material characteristics, which shape how people engage, protest, resist, and struggle. This innovative collection advances the notion of social media materialities to draw attention to the ways in which the wires and silicon, data streams and algorithms, user and programming interfaces, business models and terms of service steer contentious practices and, inversely, how technologies and economic models are handled and performed by users. The key question is how the tension between social media's techno-commercial infrastructures and activist agency plays out in protest. Addressing this, the volume goes beyond singular empirical examples and focuses on the characteristics of protest and social media materialities, offering further conceptualizations and guidance for this emerging field of research. The various contributions explore a wide variety of activist projects, protests, and regions, ranging from Occupy in the USA to environmental protests in China, and from the Mexican Barrio Nómada to the Copenhagen-based activist television channel *TV Stop* (1987–2005).

Mette Mortensen is Associate Professor at the University of Copenhagen, Denmark. She is the Principal Investigator of the collective research project "Images of Conflict, Conflicting Images" (2017–2021) and author or editor of seven books, including *Eyewitness Images and Journalism* (2015).

Christina Neumayer is Associate Professor at the IT University of Copenhagen. Her research focusses on the role of media technologies in political conflict. She has published on digital media and activism, social movements, racism, and propaganda.

Thomas Poell is Senior Lecturer at the University of Amsterdam, the Netherlands. His research focusses on digital platforms and public communication. He co-authored *The Platform Society* (2018), and co-edited *Global Cultures of Contestation* (2017) and *The Sage Handbook of Social Media* (2018).

SOCIAL MEDIA MATERIALITIES AND PROTEST

Critical Reflections

Edited by Mette Mortensen, Christina Neumayer and Thomas Poell

Routledge
Taylor & Francis Group
LONDON AND NEW YORK

First published 2019
by Routledge
4 Park Square, Milton Park, Abingdon, Oxon OX14 4RN
605 Third Avenue, New York, NY 10017

Routledge is an imprint of the Taylor & Francis Group, an informa business

British Library Cataloguing in Publication Data
A catalogue record for this book is available from the British Library

Library of Congress Cataloging-in-Publication Data
A catalog record has been requested for this book

ISBN: 978-1-138-09306-5 (hbk)
ISBN: 978-1-138-09308-9 (pbk)
ISBN: 978-1-315-10706-6 (ebk)

Typeset in Bembo
by Taylor & Francis Books

CONTENTS

ILLUSTRATIONS

Figure

Table

CONTRIBUTORS

Tina Askanius is a Senior Lecturer in Media and Communication Studies, School of Arts and Communication at Malmö University, Sweden. She holds a PhD in Media and Communication from Lund University where she defended a thesis on contemporary forms of video activism in 2012. Her research primarily concerns the interplay between social media and social movements and she has published extensively on these matters in the context of climate change and social justice movements in Europe as well as ultra-nationalist and neo-Nazi movements in Scandinavia.

W. Lance Bennett is Professor of Political Science and Ruddick C. Lawrence Professor of Communication at the University of Washington, Seattle, USA, where he directs the Center for Communication and Civic Engagement (www.engagedcitizen.org). The focus of his work is on how communication processes affect citizen engagement with politics. His publications include *The Logic of Connective Action: Digital Media and the Personalization of Contentious Politics* (with Alexandra Segerberg, Cambridge, 2013). His current interests focus on how better to align thinking about the economy, democracy and the environment in order to build more equitable and sustainable human systems on the planet.

Lorenzo Coretti is an Assistant Professor of Media and Communication at the American University of Rome, Italy, where he directs the Communication and Film & Digital Media programmes. Lorenzo completed a PhD at Communication and Media Research Institute (CAMRI), at the University of Westminster in June 2014. He has researched and published in the field of critical theory of technology and social movement theory. In particular, Lorenzo focusses on the relationship between technological design and social movement activities, such as mobilization strategies, organizational patterns, and collective identity building processes. He is also member of the Editorial Board of Westminster Papers in Communication and Culture (WPCC) where he co-edited a special issue entitled "The Role of Social Media in Arab Uprisings – Past and Present".

Sky Croeser is a lecturer in the Department of Internet Studies at Curtin University in Western Australia. Her research focuses on how activists use, and reshape, technology. Her first book, *Global Justice and the Politics of Information* (Routledge, 2014), argues that farmers' movements in India and digital liberties activists are engaged in the same global movement to challenge the power of corporations and governments. More recent research looks at anti-fascist struggles in Greece, post-revolutionary Tunisia, and feminist responses to online harassment. To find out more, visit: skycroeser.net.

Anne Kaun is Associate Professor at the Department for Media and Communication Studies at Södertörn University, Stockholm, Sweden. Her research combines archival research with interviews and participant observation to better understand changes in how activists have employed media technologies and how technologies shape activism in terms of temporality and space. In her most recent book, *Crisis and Critique* (Zed Books, 2016), she explores the role of media in the shaping of social movements and resistance to capitalism. She is currently developing her new project on prison media, tracing media practices and media work since the inception of the modern prison system.

Jun Liu is an Associate Professor in the Department of Media, Cognition and Communication and the Centre for Communication and Computing at University of Copenhagen, Denmark. His research areas cover political communication, communication technologies, and political sociology. He has articles published in *Mass Communication & Society, Social Movement Studies, Acta Sociologica,* among others. His research has won several awards, including the Best Dissertation Award, the Information Technology and Politics Section of American Political Science Association (2014). He is currently working on a book manuscript under the contract of Oxford University Press about contention and communication in the digital age.

Martina Skrubbeltrang Mahnke is a postdoctoral researcher at the University of Copenhagen, Denmark. She is currently involved in the "HumanImpact" project, which works towards mutually beneficial learning collaborations between research in the humanities and small and medium-sized companies. Prior to this project, Martina worked at the IT University of Copenhagen, Denmark in the digital design department and earned her PhD in digital media and communication from the University of Erfurt, Germany. In her research she is especially interested in exploring what constitutes the algorithm–user relationship. Furthermore, she is working on making creative (design) methods fruitful for rigorous social science studies.

Alice Mattoni is Assistant Professor in the Department of Political and Social Sciences of the Scuola Normale Superiore, Florence, Italy. Her research investigates to what extent and how different types of media intersect with what politicians, activists and concerned citizens do to participate in and mobilize on politics. She is the author of *Media Practices and Protest Politics. How Precarious Workers Mobilize* (Ashgate, 2012) and her work has been published in several international journals, including *Communication Theory, European Journal of Communication, Information Communication & Society, Journal of Information Technology & Politics*, and *Social Movement Studies.*

Stefania Milan is Associate Professor of New Media and Digital Culture at the University of Amsterdam, Netherlands. Her research explores the interplay between digital technology and participation, and activism and social movements in particular, cyberspace governance, and data epistemologies. She is the Principal Investigator of the DATACTIVE project, funded through a Starting Grant of the European Research Council. Stefania is the author of *Social Movements and Their Technologies: Wiring Social Change* (Palgrave Macmillan, 2013; released in paperback in March 2016), and co-author of *Media/Society* (Sage, 2011). Her work has appeared in a variety of peer-reviewed journals, including *Information, Communication & Society, International Journal of Communication, Policy & Internet, Internet Policy Review*, and *Social Media + Society*.

Daniele Pica is an Associate Professor of Management and Information Systems at John Cabot University, Rome, where he teaches among other courses Management of Innovation, Social Media Management, and Supply Chain Management. In 2006, he completed his Doctoral dissertation at the London School of Economics in the consequences of the introduction of mobile information technologies on Police work in the UK. He is part of the mobility@lse research unit (http://mobility.lse.ac.uk), which aims to draw together academics with an interest in the profound changes to society, organizations and individuals from mobile, pervasive and ubiquitous information technology. Since 2001, he has researched and published on how information technologies influence work and has, in the past decade, studied and consulted on enterprise mobility, digital infrastructures, systems of innovation, and information privacy and security.

Alexandra Segerberg is Associate Professor in the Department of Political Science at Uppsala University, Sweden. Prior to this, she worked at the Department of Political Science at Stockholm University and spent two years as a postdoctoral research fellow at the Center for Communication and Civic Engagement at the University of Washington, Seattle. She is founding editor-in-chief of the European Consortium for Political Research flagship open access journal Political Research Exchange (PRX). Her research focusses on communication and collective action, addressing classic issues of power and democracy as they play out in societies undergoing social and technological change.

David M. Struthers is a historian with interdisciplinary pursuits. His monograph *The World in a City: Multiethnic Radicalism in Early Twentieth Century Los Angeles* (University of Illinois Press, 2019) explores the dynamics of a city and region with a rapidly developing economy and large-scale immigration. His volume *Wobblies of the World: A Global History of the IWW* (Pluto Press, 2017), edited with Peter Cole and Kenyon Zimmer, is the first global history of the industrial workers of the World. He is currently working on a monograph on the history of activist social media before the Internet.

Emiliano Treré is a lecturer at the School of Journalism, Media and Culture at Cardiff University, Wales, UK. He has published extensively on the challenges, the opportunities, and the myths of media technologies for social movements and political parties in Europe and Latin America. He is a member of the "Data Justice Lab" that examines the intricate relationship between datafication and social justice, and the co-founder of the "Big Data from the South Initiative" that aims to interrogate the techno-cultural practices that subvert the dominant narratives of datafication as narrated by the Global North.

Julie Uldam is Associate Professor at Copenhagen Business School. In 2010 she completed her PhD following a collaboration between London School of Economics and Copenhagen Business School. She conducted her postdoctoral research at London School of Economics, Copenhagen Business School and Free University of Brussels, Belgium. Her current research explores the role of digitization in civic and corporate citizenship. Julie's work has been published in peer-reviewed journals, including *New Media & Society* and *International Journal of Communication.* Her book *Civic Engagement & Social Media* (co-edited with Anne Vestergaard) was published by Palgrave Macmillan in 2015. Julie is chair of the Communication & Democracy section at the European Communication Research and Education Association (ECREA).

INTRODUCTION

Social media materialities and protest

Christina Neumayer, Mette Mortensen and Thomas Poell

This book undertakes research at the intersection of social media and protest. Far from being neutral platforms, social media possess their own material characteristics, which shape how people engage, protest, resist, and struggle. We advance the notion of social media materialities to draw attention to the ways in which the wires and silicon, data streams and algorithms, user and programming interfaces, business models and terms of service steer contentious practices and, inversely, how technologies and economic models are handled and performed by users. Scholars have long studied media as *tools* taken up by activists and other social actors or as inherently political *determinants*. Especially with the emergence of social media platforms such as Twitter, Facebook, Instagram, Snapchat, Weibo, and YouTube, scholars have focussed either on the benefits for activists, such as accelerated processes of political mobilization, or on the drawbacks in terms of control and surveillance (for an overview, see Chapter 8 of this volume; Neumayer & Svensson 2016; Poell & van Dijck 2018).

As Raymond Williams (1974) urged us, we need to look beyond claims that the invention of new media technologies would change our world and keep in mind that "the new technology is itself a product of a particular social system" (Williams 1974: 140) and the way we use technologies is part of a more general process of social struggle. Instead, media technologies are embedded in and produced by cultural, political and social practices (see Gillespie, Boczkowski & Foot 2014). While social media do both – emancipate and control, diversify and homogenize, empower and disempower, challenge and reproduce hierarchies, give voice and silence – they are never simply tools that activists can adopt solely for their own purposes. There are numerous examples of how media technologies are appropriated for purposes of political dissent unintended by their designers, but even so these technologies always shape user activity. From this perspective, media technologies and economic models need to be considered as an assemblage of *actors* that become involved in contentious action, as they do in other social activities. As such, they become part of complex socio-cultural and techno-commercial configurations, which this edited volume aims to untangle. Ultimately, this book takes up the challenge of interrogating how contemporary protests and social media materialities mutually shape one another.

Exploring how social media materialities and activist practices become entangled, we are confronted with a conundrum. Feenberg (2010) argues that technologies reproduce existing hierarchies and systems of power but can be appropriated for subversive action to challenge power and to lead to political change. Although corporate social media platforms have not been designed for activism, they nevertheless enhance activist agency by enabling protestors to rapidly connect with one another; coordinate and report on street protests; and share protest slogans, declarations, and creative visual materials with each other and potentially also a wider public. At the same time, social media seem to undermine the long-term efficacy of contemporary protest movements. They algorithmically privilege spectacular viral images over content that may illuminate wider social and political issues (Blaagaard, Mortensen & Neumayer 2017), remove activist accounts and content that allegedly break terms of service, and disturb processes of community formation (Youmans & York 2012). The automated and manual forms of curation and moderation are in turn informed by business models focussed on maximizing user engagement without alienating the overall user population, advertisers, and other commercial partners (van Dijck, Poell & de Waal 2018). This book explores how this dynamic of empowerment and disempowerment plays out as media materialities and activist practices become increasingly intertwined.

Social media materialities matter

Taking the material serious in the study of social phenomena can be traced back to Marx's socio-political analysis of engines, factories, and factory workers as artifacts of capitalism (Marx 2008[1962]). Scholars have since studied the material as infrastructures that in relation with other actors turn into invisible structures and networks of power residing in institutions such as scientific laboratories (Latour & Woolgar 1986) or the archive (Foucault 2003[1969]). In media and communication studies, the material has largely been pushed into the background and started to matter again with science and technology studies (STS) entering the field – with the exception of the material culture of consumption in cultural studies (see Gillespie, Boczkowski & Foot 2014; or Dourish 2017: 33–60 for overviews). Social media materialities thus depart from a material culture perspective which mainly has focussed on consumption, as we cannot separate the processes of production and consumption in social media (see Ingold 2007; or Fuchs 2017b for critical discussions). Materialities in the plural form also depart from materialism – as in Horkeimer's (1982) *Critical Theory* – and refer to technologies, its uses and institutions but also economic models as well as to the discourses that legitimize these technologies and models. As Kittler (1999) contends, media have different materialities such as the materiality of the technology, of information processing and storage, of numbers and data, and the literal materiality of the letter. Just as scholars tend to understand social practices in the plural, referring to the wide variety of ways in which people develop specific activities and meanings, we also consider a multiplicity of materialities. Social phenomena (such as political protest) are then situated in the nexus of human practices and material arrangements that compose social media materialities.

Accordingly, we not only refute an understanding of technology as tools that can be freely employed, but also an understanding of technology as political *per se* and as necessarily fostering either activist emancipation or surveillance. Matter and material usually implies a physical component (Leonardi, Nardi & Kallinikos 2012), but according to Gibson's (2015[1979]) affordance theory the properties of materials are not static characteristics of matter, rather they are processual and *relational*. Hutchby (2001) includes both physical and digital artifacts when using the term "materiality". This volume is concerned with this double-edged meaning combining material and immaterial matter of social media and its implications for political contention. Materialities, then, are not stable but embedded in relationality. They are "a flux in which materials of the most diverse kinds [...] undergo continual generation and transformation" (Ingold 2007: 7). A critical analysis of social media and protest requires us to open the black box of social media materialities and follow the various actors that shape how activists voice dissent. This effectively entails developing a relational perspective on materialities and protest (Galis & Neumayer 2016; Poell, Rajagopalan & Kavada 2018). Building on actor-network theory (Latour 2005), we understand human and non-human actors as always constituted in relation with other actors. Contemporary activism is an assemblage of activists, protest practices, social media materialities, and a wide variety of other materialities. In other words, the materialities of social media begin to matter as they become part of practices. By the same token, social media are enacted as specific actors or constellations of actors as they are integrated into activist practices.

Our work thus builds on the research into social media materialities that has been conducted within platform, software, and infrastructure studies (Bucher 2018; Edwards et al. 2009; Gillespie 2018; Plantin et. al 2016). However, we note that the relationship between activists and the techno-commercial materialities of social media, in the form of interfaces, data streams, and algorithms, remains under-explored. The same can be said of the relationship between activists and the economic policies and business models of social media corporations. Political economists have critically examined the business models of social media platforms, which revolve around user profiling, targeted advertising and services, and the exploitation of labour (Fuchs 2017a; Scholz 2017; Srnicek 2017). Yet further inquiry is needed into how these commercial strategies affect activist practices through terms of use, as well as through algorithmic sorting mechanisms.

In the light of these considerations, this book is guided by the following key question: How should we conceptualize the tension between activist agency and social media's techno-commercial infrastructures? To address this question, it is vital to move beyond case study research, which typically focusses on single social media platforms during intense periods of protest in particular locations. This volume thus goes beyond singular empirical examples and focusses on the particular characteristics of protest and social media materialities, offering further conceptualizations and guidance for this emerging field of research.

By developing a relational perspective on social media materialities and protest, we hope to provide new insight into the socio-material aspects of political dissent. While social movements, activism, civic engagement, protest and (digital) media have primarily been addressed from a political communication perspective (with valuable work from e.g. Bennett 2012; Cammaerts 2012; della Porta 2011), this book takes an interdisciplinary approach to understanding how social media materialities and protest practices articulate and condition each other. We have thus invited scholars from different disciplines to track the involvement of social media in political protest. The volume comprises the work of scholars who not merely come from different perspectives, but who also cross disciplinary boundaries to critically investigate and conceptualize how social media materialities shape contemporary protest. Being concerned with an emerging field of study, the book to some extent takes an explorative route to develop and establish what constitutes social media materialities and protest from different scholarly traditions, conceptual frameworks, and theoretical underpinnings.

The chapters in this book: Space, time and platforms

The authors of this volume address social media materialities and protest along three axes: spatiality, temporality, and platformization. The notion of *space* in this volume is not limited to locations in which protests take place, such as protest camps or the streets, but also includes various social media platforms and people showing solidarity from afar through digital networks. Protest locations and multiple media-environments and platforms overlap in the complex relations of social media materialities and contentious action. The authors of this volume reshuffle questions of spatiality in contemporary protest and move towards a conceptualization of a relational perspective on social media and protest and emerging activist practices with regard to space. How do activists and the content they produce and share move between different notions of space? What spatial configurations emerge in and from today's protests?

Second, developing a relational perspective entails considering *time* not as the chronological sequencing of "moments" but instead as produced by and producing social relations and social processes. Social media, as many authors have noted, introduce new temporal relations within social interaction (e.g. Berry 2011; Chun 2011; Weltevrede et al. 2014). Much emphasis has been placed on how these media accelerate communication processes, but as several chapters demonstrate, we also see new types of memory and archival practices emerge. How do the changing temporalities of protest imposed by social media pave the way for emerging activist practices? And what new opportunities and new limitations do these temporalities involve?

Third, rather than isolated studies of intense protest events on a particular social media *platform*, we need to unpack the black box of platforms and require understanding of how social media platforms and activist practices shape one another. The authors challenge the stability of the term platform itself by unpacking their socio-technical logics (van Dijck and Poell 2013; Geiger 2014) and tracing the relations of code, algorithms, architecture, power, discourses, data, content, and protest practices. How is social protest conditioned and shaped by connected social media platforms? What are similarities and differences of activist practices across platforms? And conversely, how do activist practices shape platforms?

Along these *three axes of spatiality, temporality,* and *platformization*, the book provides a critical reflection and conceptual basis for future work on social media materialities and protest. In the following, we introduce the three axes in turn and present the chapters of the edited volume.

Part I: Spatiality

Adopting a relational perspective, we do not consider space as a 'container' of protest action but examine how spatial relations are constructed and deconstructed through processes of social interaction. Writing in 1927, Siegfried Kracauer noted a reconfiguration of proximity through the material character of photography: "Photography shows cities in aerial shots, brings crockets and figures [...] in unusual combinations that distance them from human proximity" (Kracauer 1993[1927]: 435). What is otherwise separate in space and time, is materially and spatially in close proximity through the materiality of the photograph. Today, the materialities of social media underscore the physical remoteness from political protest, yet images transmitted through screens can also create intimacy and even an experience of proximity by collapsing spatial distance. This implies that multiple spatial relations always co-exist, often competing with one other (Castells 2012; Poell, Rajagopalan & Kavada 2018; Lefebvre 1991; Massey 2005). This is particularly clear when considering protest and social media, which are usually envisioned and technologically developed as "global" infrastructures that, at least in principle, allow everyone to connect with each other (Couldry 2015). At the same time, as the chapters in this section demonstrate, despite the intensive use of social media, connecting different spatial contexts remains a complex exercise. By tracing the construction of these spatial relations at the intersection of social media materialities and protest, chapters in this section show the spatial contradictions and tensions within social movements.

These contradictions and tensions are clearly demonstrated by Alice Mattoni in her chapter on Occupy Pittsburgh, one of the key protest camps of the 2011 US Occupy movement. Mattoni observes a wide variety of communication activities, practices, and technologies. Formal assemblies and informal exchanges in the protest camp were routinely supplemented by phone calls, e-mails, Facebook and Google groups, and live streams from laptops that activists brought to assemblies, marches, and other gatherings. The intense blending of communication technologies and practices appears to engage distant publics into the actions at the protest camps. Yet in day-to-day protest communication, spatial tensions become immediately evident. While a live stream could connect to distant publics, it made some activists feel uncomfortable. To avoid exclusion of concerned activists in the protest camps, a "safe zone" was created outside the camera's reach during general assemblies. Spatiality also created tensions the other way around. While live-streaming platforms allowed distant participants at general assemblies to express their opinions through chat functionalities, these online voices were often not included in decision-making processes. The social media practices in the protest camp thus demonstrated the construction of clear spatial hierarchies of participation.

The tensions and hierarchies of different notions of spatiality become apparent not just through specific practices but also through the materialities of the social media platforms themselves. Sky Croeser critically questions the concept of networked solidarity in the global solidarity efforts surrounding the Kurdish autonomy movement. The ability to share photos and videos through platforms such as Facebook could potentially support the type of emotional connections that various theorists deem vital for developing effective solidarity (see e.g. Castells 2012; Mortensen 2015). Yet when studying actual efforts on Facebook, Croeser finds little evidence of such solidarity. This is partially conditioned by the material characteristics of social media platforms. Terms of use stipulated by these platforms discourage users from explicitly mentioning efforts to send material aid or calling for activities that are illegal in the countries in question. The tendency of social media to algorithmically privilege content that generates large amounts of engagement, creates tensions for the formation of sustainable relations of solidarity. While social media might create the potential for expressing solidarity across distance, expressions of solidarity do not always translate into – and might even prevent – political action.

In his chapter, Emiliano Treré points toward the fundamentally *hybrid* character of contemporary activist ecosystems, which also became clear in Mattoni's chapter. The media practices of the Mexican Barrio Nómada, an activist collective from Ciudad Juárez, illustrate the importance of activist tactics in navigating the instability of platform connectivity. The collective has developed what Treré calls a strategy of "total communication". This entails a rich hybrid combination of media: major social media platforms (Facebook, Twitter, and YouTube); other forms of online communication (blogs and mailing lists); alternative television and radio broadcasts via live-streaming platforms; physically distributed publications, performances, and artifacts (books, posters, graffiti, stickers, theatre, live music, circus performances). The latter media are specifically employed to combat the ephemerality of online communication. By observing these hybrid media practices, Treré emphasizes the problematic tensions arising from traditional distinctions between the spatial constructions of the digital/online, the virtual, and cyber relative to the offline, the physical, and the real. The online and offline are inextricably entangled in practice, and the digital is just as "real" and "material" as the ground itself.

Examining the spatial axis of social media activism means exploring the hybrid spaces constituted through the continuous blending of multifacetted media practices in political contention. These three chapters critically unpack how the techno-commercial architecture of platforms manifested in user- and application programming interfaces, algorithms, terms of services, and business models produce a variety of – occasionally competing and often hierarchical – spatial relations of activism. These relations should be considered fundamentally unstable. Social media do not necessarily support sustainable, frictionless global connectivity; connecting and constructing protest spaces effectively requires continuous efforts of "translation", "circulation", and "brokerage" (Poell & van Dijck 2018) – occasionally against the grain of social media materialities.

Part II: Temporality

At the intersection of social media materialities and protest, time is constructed through social interactions, centrally involving technical infrastructures for measuring and calculating time, for circulating discourses about time, for enforcing specific rules concerning the timing of interaction, and for keeping records of the past. Social media can be thought of as such infrastructures with capacities for speed, synchronicity, liveliness, immediacy, and the durability of communication through time that shape the temporal structures and rhythms of protest (Poell, Rajagopalan & Kavada 2018). Kaun (2015) captures this process as "regimes of time" imposed on social movements as they adjust their practices to the emergence of "social media time". Fuchs (2014) discusses the "capitalist regime of time" as based on the future-oriented logics of acceleration of consumption and accumulation of data for surplus value production. Barassi (2015) argues that the "temporalizing practices" of social media demand instantaneous communication by social movements to compete with the constant noise or the co-option of their political messages. While social media in particular instances enable the rapid circulation of protest materials and calls for solidarity and mobilization, these media also obscure and remove activist content. Mechanisms of personalization and virality render content invisible that fails to generate spikes of user engagement. Along similar lines, commercially informed moderation practices lead to the deletion of materials deemed in violation with terms of service (Langlois et al. 2009; Milan 2015; Neumayer, Rossi & Karlsson 2016; Poell & van Dijck 2018; Youmans & York 2012).

The chapters in this section offer a historical perspective on social media materialities and in doing so unpack the changing temporalities of protest. They provide a material perspective on the ways in which protest communication on social media becomes a means of documenting, constructing, and maintaining a record of social movements in time and over time. The authors reflect on different aspects of temporality: How social movements make sense of the material manifestations generated by their struggle, and how identity is reflected and created by "connective memory" (Hoskins 2011) enabled by analogue and digital media on their own or in combination. Even if social media are often thought to be designed for instantaneous and ephemeral communication and social movements focus on real-time communication in organizing and documenting events, the historical perspective is invariably foregrounded by the ongoing, continual accumulation of text, posts, images, videos, likes, and shares. The temporal axis accordingly emphasizes social media's archival functions, which construct and connect the material manifestations of past, present, and future. If we think of social media as archives, the spatial and temporal axes intertwine inasmuch as the physical remains of time passed or passing become visible as "a set of spatial orders" (Røssaak 2010: 12).

Tina Askanius' chapter addresses the way in which the activist television channel *TV Stop* has sought to preserve its own history while making the physical transition from analogue to digital media, from the tangible and space-consuming hardware of magnetic tapes and video cameras to keeping archives through the intangible materialities of social media. Social movements vest interest in social media archives through impulses to "*store and preserve time*; to *catch up with times* and [...] to *remember times passed*", Askanius asserts in her chapter (italics in original). In other words, they seek to systematically overcome what Still (cited after Røssaak 2010: 11) refers to as one "of the great ironies", namely that the information age has "recorded more data than any other period in history [but] will also most certainly have lost more information than any previous era". Archives emerge, writes Derrida (1995: 14), "at the place of originary and structural breakdown of the said memory". While the archive is an attempt to capture and maintain a record of time, it is also an indication of the frailty and volatility of memory, understood as the organic storytelling and collective identity of a social movement.

In their chapter, Lorenzo Coretti and Daniele Pica likewise reflect upon the ways in which the architecture of media materialities impact social movements over time, exemplified by how Facebook's communication protocols and algorithmic filters influence the lifespan and development of the Italian anti-Berlusconi movement, *Popolo Viola*. Communication protocols and algorithmic filters, Coretti and Pica contend, are spurred by profit-driven interests and lead to a "cycle of depression" for social movements because their bottom-up participatory efforts end up being incompatible with the programmability of Facebook. Processes of formalizing and institutionalizing social movements are thus ultimately obstructed by social media materialities. Processes of mobilization and forming a collective identity in social media counteract one another. This manifests itself in conflicting temporalities, as social media might foster rapid mobilization while at the same time slowing down processes of collective identity formation. Their study adds a nuanced perspective to the challenge of transforming connective action into more sustainable forms of political engagement (see Bennett & Segerberg 2013; Tilly & Wood 2015).

Christina Neumayer and David M. Struthers' chapter critically examines how social media logics generate biased online archives of social movements' communication. Social media archives are open-ended and dynamic, enduringly offering the opportunity for expansion, reconfiguration, and new patterns of meaning-making. However, algorithms and user interventions "subvert the temporal order" and sequence of data points (Milan 2015: 890–891). Neumayer and Struthers argue that this leads to processes of both "over- and underrepresentation" and activists' loss of control over data. The authors pinpoint that the archive was traditionally linked to state power and surveillance (Foucault 2003 [1969]) and served to store, preserve, classify, and access observable knowledge (Røssaak 2010: 11). In the contemporary media ecology, activists are able to create and access social media archives on demand, which seems to more evenly distribute the power involved in being able to render political issues and collectives of people visible or invisible. But still, as Neumayer and Struthers contend, the underlying techno-commercial structure imposes new and only partially discernible hierarchies, resulting in archives that are incomplete and inherently biased. As a result, social media materialities impose new temporalities that shape how the history of protests is constructed and preserved, how social movements' life cycles unfold, and how new hierarchies of representation and archiving are imposed.

Part III: Platformization

Many studies on social media and political protest focus on specific platforms. Twitter in particular has been at the centre of a large number of studies – mainly due to the accessibility of Twitter data and the availability of tools to analyze these data (Neumayer & Rossi 2016). To understand the consequences this has for social movements, it is necessary to conceptually and analytically understand platforms from a relational perspective. We must move beyond single platforms and explore how platforms become entangled in specific contentious practices and how they are connected to a wide variety of other media. The way in which social media platforms increasingly shape our social interactions is a process pointedly captured as *The Platform Society* (van Dijck, Poell & de Waal 2018). Researchers have utilized a range of concepts in their efforts to untangle the complex relationship between techno-commercial architectures of social media and protest, including "platform" and "cloud" (Milan's Chapter 8 in this volume; Poell & van Dijck 2018), "connective action" (Bennett & Segerberg 2013), "media ecology" (Treré & Mattoni 2016), and the more general concepts from the tradition of critical theory (Dencik & Leistert 2015; Fuchs 2014). The chapters in this section build upon these works to suggest conceptualizations moving beyond platforms and examining processes of platformization and their implications for activist practices and power relations.

Julie Uldam and Anne Kaun's chapter does this by developing a conceptual framework for theorizing civic engagement and social media. By drawing upon theories of platforms (van Dijck & Poell 2013), media practices (Flyverbom & Murray 2018), and discourse (Couldry 2012), they consider the technological, structural, discursive, and practice-oriented dimensions of civic engagement, going beyond a narrow focus on platforms to also consider wider power structures. Their analytical framework comprises the interrelationship between power relations (e.g. ownership, regulation, resources), technological affordances (e.g. algorithms, character limits), practices (e.g. user preferences, skills), and discourses (e.g. discourses of social justice, representation). With the illustrative example of how refugees in Sweden organize through social media, they uncover power imbalances involving platforms' techno-commercial materiality. The refugee volunteers needed Facebook for communicative purposes as the platform was widely used across the refugee community, a community that was difficult to reach through other means of communication, in part because of literacy limitations. As Facebook develops into the default social media platform, as it does in many other contexts, civic engagement becomes dependent on Facebook's sorting algorithms, policies, and interfaces whether they like it or not.

The question of how platform materialities set the horizon of possibility for online contention is systematically developed by Stefania Milan. She proposes the metaphor of 'the cloud' as a theoretical lens for understanding tensions between activist agency and the structure and political economy of platforms. Using this lens, Milan unpacks how platform infrastructures shape activists' tactics, identities, and networking strategies. She argues that three key dichotomies must be considered to gain insight into the field of tension in which activist agency takes shape within a platform ecosystem. The first and most immediate dichotomy concerns the contrast between empowerment and control, which we have also highlighted at the start of this introductory chapter. Through their particular materialities (ubiquitous data collection and user targeting), platforms offer new opportunities for activist mobilization and communication as well as for surveillance. The second dichotomy concerns the individual versus the collective dimensions of mobilization. Milan emphasizes that social media seem to primarily promote the "decentralized, atomized actions" of "single player" over the activity of social movement organizations. Simultaneously, she observes that the collective dimension is continuously mobilized at the symbolic level, as the collective "We". Finally, she considers the dichotomy of the present versus the future in as much as social media enable rapid processes of mobilization and generate media coverage but do not appear equipped to support sustainable forms of collective identities and mobilizations in the long run. These tensions are central to how social media materialities and practices mutually articulate one another. Studying contemporary protest, it is important not to collapse the opposing sides of these dichotomies into each other but to instead acknowledge that fundamental tensions are inherent to how contentious practices are shaped through platforms.

Martina Skrubbeltrang Mahnke's chapter on protesting algorithmic personalization provides an alternative approach to these issues. Taking a software studies perspective, the chapter considers how users push back against the limits that platformization imposes on user agency. In terms of the dichotomies highlighted by Milan, we can say that the users in question are seeking to overcome the tension between individual user empowerment and collectivity. Mahnke's research also makes clear how difficult it is to challenge platformization. The examined protests against algorithmic personalization on social media platforms remain (in correspondence with platform mechanisms of personalization) very much on the individual and emotional level, but they lack a collective organization. As we will see throughout this volume, social media materialities enable individual users to voice their concerns and find an audience, but these same materialities prevent users from developing sustainable collective action.

The final chapter, by Jun Liu, considers the implications of platformization from a wider societal perspective. Specifically, the chapter focusses on social media and protest in China. Bridging social movement studies and media studies, Liu draws upon Tilly's (1986) concept of "repertoires of contention" to scrutinize the long-term consequences of the growing importance of social media for contemporary protest. Liu has carried out a longitudinal study (2007–2014) across different social media platforms (such as Weibo, WeChat, mobile phones, and online encyclopedias). Evolving digital repertoires of contention can only be understood within a larger media ecology, a larger political and societal context, and over a longer period of time. Digital repertoires of contention render visible how social media materialities restrain and enable contentious performances and repertoires – and how these repertoires then alter our understanding of the actualization of social media materialities themselves. This is not least the case in China's rapidly changing media ecology.

Combined, the conceptualizations of social media materialities and protest along the axis of platformization must not only unpack the relations within platforms but also the larger consequences this entails for activists' struggles. Doing so, the authors of this volume show how the relations of social media platforms in political contention introduce new dependencies and power structures, produce fundamental tensions, threaten to undermine collectivity and collective action, but also enable, perform and constrain digital repertoires of contention.

Looking ahead

By engaging critically with the concept of social media materialities, we hope to inspire researchers to explore the ways in which social media technologies and business models shape activist practices and vice versa. As the chapters in this book illustrate, this is vital because the central involvement of social media in activism introduces new hierarchies of protest participation and triggers new concerns about the sustainability of alternative communities relying on these media for communication and mobilization. Corporate social media are obviously not developed for activism but instead for enabling communication and commodifying user activity. This creates numerous tensions that complicate processes of activist communication and mobilization. These tensions will not disappear. Consequently, activists will need to find ways of navigating the contradictions inherent in social media materialities as well as developing alternative and more sustainable modes of connecting and communicating.

To understand the specific tensions and contradictions generated by the use of social media for protest purposes, we propose to trace the connections between social media materialities and protest practices from a relational perspective. This involves studying how technologies, economic models, and users are constructed as actors through the ways in which they connect and disconnect with each other in particular contexts. Understanding protest and social media from such a relational perspective prompts us to move the inquiry beyond particular protest locations, moments, and platforms. Instead, this volume studies how spatiality, temporality, and platformization are relationally constituted in social media materialities and protest. Through such inquiries, key concerns in today's protests come to the fore, such as power relations, modes of participation, identity, and community construction.

By critically reflecting upon how social media materialities and protest practices mutually shape one another, the chapters also build bridges between disciplines. Combining insights from media and communication studies, software studies, social movement studies, and science technology studies, the authors trace in detail how activist practices and social media materialities constitute each other in complex and contradictory ways. We believe that an interdisciplinary approach is essential for gaining insight into the complexities of contemporary protest. While it might be impossible to deal exhaustively with all dimensions of social media materialities and protest in one book, the diversity of scholarship in this volume can start a productive dialogue. We hope that this volume raises questions to which further research might continue to seek answers. In so doing, we place social media materialities as a deeply social concept at the centre of our inquiry with socio-material consequences for protest. As Alexandra Segerberg and W. Lance Bennett remind us in the afterword to the edited volume, studying social media materialities and protest comes with new lessons and puzzles. With the interdisciplinarity that this edited volume opens up for we can hopefully – following Segerberg and Bennett's metaphor – build a field beyond the streetlight and start looking for keys lost in less lighted areas.

References

Barassi, V. (2015). Social Media, Immediacy and the Time for Democracy. Critical Reflections on Social media as 'Temporalizing Practices'. In: L. Dencik and O. Leistert. *Critical Perspectives on Social Media and Protests: Between Control and Emancipation*. London: Rowman & Littlefield, pp. 73–90.

Bennett, W. L. (2012). The personalization of politics: Political identity, social media, and changing patterns of participation. *The ANNALS of the American Academy of Political and Social Science*, 644(1), pp. 20–39.

Bennett, W. L., & Segerberg, A. (2013). *The logic of connective action: Digital media and the personalization of contentious politics*. Cambridge: Cambridge University Press.

Berry, D. (2011). *The philosophy of software: Code and mediation in the digital age*. New York: Palgrave Macmillan.

Blaagaard, B., Mortensen, M., & Neumayer, C. (2017) Digital images and globalized conflict. *Media, Culture & Society*, 39(8), pp. 1111–1121.

Bucher, T. (2018) *IF...THEN: Algorithmic power and politics*. Oxford: Oxford University Press.

Cammaerts, B. (2012). Protest logics and the mediation opportunity structure. *European Journal of Communication*, 27(2), pp. 117–134.

Castells, M. (2012). *Networks of outrage and hope: Social movements in the Internet age*. Cambridge: Polity Press.

Chun, W. H. K. (2011). *Programmed visions: Software and memory*. Cambridge, MA: MIT Press.

Couldry, N. (2012). *Media, society, world: Social theory and digital media practice*. Cambridge: Polity Press.
Couldry, N. (2015). The myth of 'us': digital networks, political change and the production of collectivity. *Information, Communication & Society*, 18(6), pp. 608–626.
Della Porta, D. (2011). Communication in movement: Social movements as agents of participatory democracy. *Information, Communication & Society*, 14(6), pp. 800–819.
Dencik, L., & Leistert, O. (Eds.) (2015). *Critical perspectives on social media and protest: Between control and emancipation*. London: Rowman & Littlefield International.
Derrida, J. (1995) Archive fever: a Freudian impression. *Diacritics*, 25(2), pp. 9–63.
van Dijck, J. & Poell, T. (2013). Understanding Social Media Logic. *Media and Communication*, 1(1), pp. 2–14.
van Dijck, J., Poell, T. & de Waal, M. (2018). *The Platform Society: Public values in a connective world*. Oxford: Oxford University Press.
Dourish, P. (2017). *The Stuff of Bits: An Essay on the Materialities of Information*. Cambridge, MA: MIT Press.
Edwards, P. N., Bowker, G. C., Jackson, S. J., & Williams, R. (2009). Introduction: an agenda for infrastructure studies. *Journal of the Association for Information Systems*, 10(5), p. 6.
Feenberg, A. (2010). *Between Reason and Experience. Essays in Technology and Modernity*. Cambridge, MA: MIT Press.
Flyverbom, M. & Murray, J. (2018). Datastructures – organizing and curating digital traces into action. *Big Data & Society*. Retrieved from http://journals.sagepub.com/doi/full/10.1177/2053951718799114
Foucault, M. (2003[1969]) *The Archaeology of Knowledge*. New York: Routledge.
Fuchs, C. (2014). *OccupyMedia!: The occupy movement and social media in crisis capitalism*. Alresford: John Hunt Publishing.
Fuchs, C. (2017a). *Social media: A critical introduction*. London: Sage.
Fuchs C. (2017b). Raymond Williams' communicative materialism. *European Journal of Cultural Studies*, 20(6), pp. 744–762.
Galis, V., & Neumayer, C. (2016). Laying claim to social media by activists: a cyber-material détournement. *Social Media + Society*, 2(3).
Geiger, R. S. (2014). Bots, bespoke, code and the materiality of software platforms. *Information, Communication & Society*, 17(3), pp. 342–356.
Gibson, J. (2015[1979]). *The ecological approach to visual perception*. London: Routledge.
Gillespie, T. (2018) *Custodians of the Internet Platforms, Content Moderation, and the Hidden Decisions That Shape Social Media*. New Haven, CT: Yale University Press.
Gillespie, T., Boczkowski, P.J., & Foot, K.A. (Eds.) (2014). *Media Technologies: Essays on Communication, Materiality, and Society*. Cambridge, MA: MIT Press.
Horkheimer, M. (1982). *Critical Theory*. New York: Continuum.
Hoskins, A. (2011) Media, Memory, Metaphor: Remembering and the Connective Turn. *Parallex*, 17(4), pp. 19–31.
Hutchby, I. (2001). Technologies, texts and affordances. *Sociology: The Journal of the British Sociological Association*, 35(2), pp. 441–456.
Ingold, T. (2007). Materials against materiality. *Archaeological dialogues*, 14(1), pp. 1–16.
Kaun, A. (2015). Regimes of time: Media practices of the dispossessed. *Time & Society*, 24(2), pp. 221–243.
Kittler, F. A. (1999). *Gramophone, film, typewriter*. Stanford, CA: Stanford University Press.
Kracauer, S. (1993[1927]) Photography. *Critical Inquiry*, 19(3), pp. 421–436
Langlois, G., Elmer, G., McKelvey, F., & Devereaux, Z. (2009). Networked publics: The double articulation of code and politics on Facebook. *Canadian Journal of Communication*, 34(3), pp. 415–434.

Latour, B. (2005). *Reassembling the social: An introduction to Actor-Network-Theory*. Oxford: Oxford University Press.

Latour, B., & Woolgar, S. (1986). *Laboratory life: The construction of scientific facts*. Princeton, NJ: Princeton University Press.

Leonardi, P. M., Nardi, B. A., & Kallinikos, J. (Eds.). (2012). *Materiality and organizing: Social interaction in a technological world*. Oxford: Oxford University Press.

Lefebvre, H. (1991). *The production of space*. Volume 142. Oxford: Blackwell.

Massey, D. (2005). *For Space*. London: Sage.

Marx, K. (2008[1962]). *Das Kapital. Kritik der politischen Ökonomie*. Volume 1. Berlin: Karl Dietz Verlag.

Milan, S. (2015) From social movements to cloud protesting: the evolution of collective identity. *Information, Communication & Society*, 18(8), pp. 887–900.

Mortensen, M. (2015). *Journalism and eyewitness images: Digital media, participation, and conflict*. New York: Routledge.

Neumayer, C., & Rossi, L. (2016). 15 years of protest and media technologies scholarship: a sociotechnical timeline. *Social Media + Society*, 2(3), doi: doi:10.1177/2056305116662180.

Neumayer, C., Rossi, L., & Karlsson, B. (2016) Contested Hashtags: Blockupy Frankfurt in Social Media. *International Journal of Communication*, 10(22), pp. 5558–5579.

Neumayer, C., & Svensson, J. (2016). Activism and radical politics in the digital age: Towards a typology. *Convergence*, 22(2), pp. 131–146.

Plantin, J. C., Lagoze, C., Edwards, P. N., & Sandvig, C. (2016). Infrastructure studies meet platform studies in the age of Google and Facebook. *New Media & Society*, 20(1), pp. 293–310.

Poell, T., & J. van Dijck, J. (2018). Social Media and New Protest Movements. In: J. Burgess, A. Marwick, and T. Poell (Eds.), *The SAGE Handbook of Social Media* (pp. 546–561). London: Sage.

Poell, T., Rajagopalan, S., & Kavada, A. (2018). Publicness on Platforms: Tracing the Mutual Articulation of Platform Architectures and User Practices. In: Z. Papacharissi (Ed.), *A Networked Self and Platforms, Stories, Connections* (pp. 43–58). London: Routledge.

Røssaak, E. (2010) The Archive in Motion: an introduction. In Røssaak, E. (Ed.) *The Archive in Motion*. Oslo: National Library.

Scholz, T. (2017). *Uberworked and underpaid: How workers are disrupting the digital economy*. Cambridge: Polity Press.

Srnicek, N. (2017). *Platform Capitalism*. Cambridge: Polity Press.

Tilly, C. (1986). *The Contentious French*. Cambridge: Harvard University Press.

Tilly, C., & Wood, L. J. (2015). *Social Movements 1768–2012*. London: Routledge.

Treré, E., & Mattoni, A. (2016). Media ecologies and protest movements: main perspectives and key lessons. *Information, Communication & Society*, 19(3), pp. 290–306.

Weltevrede, E., Helmond, A., & Gerlitz, C. (2014). The politics of real-time: A device perspective on social media platforms and search engines. *Theory, Culture & Society*, 31(6), pp. 125–150.

Williams, R. (1974). *Television: Technology and Cultural Form*. New York: Routledge.

Youmans, W. L., & York, J. C. (2012). Social media and the activist toolkit: User agreements, corporate interests, and the information infrastructure of modern social movements. *Journal of Communication*, 62(2), pp. 315–329.

PART I

Spatiality

1

I POST, YOU RALLY, SHE TWEETS… AND WE ALL OCCUPY

The challenges of hybrid spatiality in the Occupy Wall Street mobilizations

Alice Mattoni

Introduction

"I am not from the US, but I am here in Pittsburgh and I would like to help with the occupation". This comment, which I posted at the end of September 2011 on the Occupy Pittsburgh blog, was my first interaction with the mobilization, which was just taking off. From that moment on, I participated in the mobilization both offline and online. Occupy Pittsburgh was indeed supported through the intertwining of many physical locations as well as various technological devices and online platforms, through which people could take part in the mobilization. Many scholars who are interested in social movements have noted the importance of information and communication technologies (ICTs) for protests. They have suggested that such technologies play a key role in changing: organizational structures of mobilizations (Bennett & Segerberg 2013; Juris 2008), repertoires of contention (Earl & Kimport 2011), and the construction of shared meanings and common identities of social movements (Kavada 2015; Milan 2015a).

W. Lance Bennett and Alexandra Segerberg were probably the most influential in arguing that the rise of social media platforms changes how mobilizations are organized and represented in the public space. These changes require a novel theoretical perspective to understand how contemporary protestors act and what the socio-political consequences of protest are. Analyzing Occupy Wall Street and other recent mobilizations, Bennett and Segerberg suggest that a logic of connective action is emerging, in which people engage with mobilizations at an individual level through the personalization of interpretations of protest that are then shared on social media platforms (Bennett & Segerberg 2013). While the logic of collective action revolved around collective action frames and actors, the logic of connective action gives rise to protests in which individuals play a prominent role and personal action frames dominate (ibid). However, as Kavada (2015) already noted, the logic of connective action seems difficult to apply to those activists who are more intensely and more frequently involved in social movements. As Bennett has recognized, the analytical framework he developed with Segerberg works well when considering "organizational processes in the media crowd" situated at the periphery of mobilizations. However, this framework is less helpful when considering activists running the protest camps, as well as their relationship with more distant publics (Bennett 2015, quoted in Mercea, Iannelli & Loader 2016).

This chapter explores these connections by focussing on the specific materiality of the spatial relations that unfolded during Occupy Pittsburgh. Many scholars have claimed that protest camps have been central to contemporary mobilizations (e.g. Gerbaudo 2017, Bennett & Segerberg 2013, Castells 2012). Yet, they have not closely investigated how protest camps are intertwined with digital technologies and how they connect different geographical locations. So far, scholars have highlighted how social media intersect with key social movement activities, such as collective identity building (Kavada 2015), social movement visibility (Theocharis et al. 2015), the recruitment of new supporters (Gaby & Caren 2012), and the temporal dimension of mobilizations (Kaun 2016). However, there is still a need to develop a solid understanding of how digital technologies transform the *spatial* dimension of protest and how such transformation in turn shapes social movement activities that sustain the unfolding of mobilizations.

As outlined above, I address this topic by analyzing the participation infrastructure of Occupy Pittsburgh. This infrastructure was hybrid, offering several interfaces through which people could be included in the mobilization, allowing for the intersection of different modes of participation, as well as the encounter between the dispersed media crowd and the activists who converged daily in the protest camp. Putting the participation infrastructure of Occupy Pittsburgh at the centre of my investigation also allows me to consider social media in the broader context of the media ecology in which the mobilization was embedded (Treré & Mattoni 2016). In other words, instead of asking how one distinct social media platform changes the spatial dimension of social movements, I focus on how a broader ensemble of internet tools, web platforms, low-tech media, and physical spaces intertwined in creating a multifaceted infrastructure for political participation that was characterized by specific spatial arrangements in Occupy Pittsburgh.

Starting with such premises, I seek to answer three interrelated questions: First, what are the spatial layers that characterize the infrastructure of participation in relation to Occupy Pittsburgh? Second, what modes of participation did they enable? Third, what challenges were faced by the activists when participation in one spatial layer of mobilizations collided with participation in another? Answering these questions allows me to contribute to the current debate on how social media and other digital media are shaping the emerging spatiality of activist participation in contemporary societies. I will answer these questions by drawing on the analysis of qualitative data I gathered through an ethnographic investigation of the first two months of Occupy Pittsburgh, from its first assemblies in early October 2011 to the end of November 2011, when the protests reached their peak. I employed participant observation (Lichterman 1998), conducting fieldwork both online and offline, to grasp the interplay of physical and digital localities (Pink et al. 2015) in Occupy Pittsburgh. I participated in and took notes on the following issues: the activities that occurred on the official Occupy Pittsburgh website, the live-stream channel, the two Facebook groups, and some Google Groups; the activities that occurred at the protest camp and beyond, including general assemblies, demonstrations, working groups meetings, teach-ins and the daily life at the protest camp; and informal conversations with the activists who were at the protest camp.

The next section provides a portrait of Occupy Pittsburgh, its main phases and features. Then, I reconstruct the spatial layers that characterized the participation infrastructure of the mobilization and how it came together in three subsequent waves. The subsequent section discusses the modes of participation that were possible in the different spatial layers of the participation infrastructure. Finally, I consider two specific examples – the use of the live stream and the Facebook group – to cast light on the challenges faced by activists when the spatial layers of the mobilizations collided.

Occupy Pittsburgh at a glance

After the occupation of Zuccotti Park in New York on 17 September 2011, Occupy Wall Street quickly spread to other cities across the USA. In Pittsburgh, the Occupy Wall Street mobilizations first took shape through the creation of a website and then a Facebook group. This online presence evolved in face-to-face general assemblies aiming to prepare the occupation downtown. After three meetings with an average of 300 participants each, activists organized a demonstration on 15 October that culminated in the occupation of a public park downtown that was privately owned and managed by the Mellon Bank of New York. Before the occupation, the activists had already created several working groups that acted collectively through non-hierarchical and participatory decision-making processes to manage the many aspects involved in the establishment of a protest camp, such as the food working group, the medical working group, and the social media working group. Each working group had its own tent from which to develop its activities. In line with Occupy Wall Street mobilizations and other similar pro-democracy and anti-austerity movements that have emerged in the 2010s across the world (della Porta & Mattoni 2014), physical occupation of city space and the consequent organization of a protest camp was a defining feature of Occupy Pittsburgh. The rest of this chapter goes beyond the materiality of the protest camp to analyze its relationship with the other physical spaces and digital localities that nurtured participation in Occupy Pittsburgh, expanding the reach of the protest camp itself, well beyond the boundaries of its physical location. In doing this, I address the three research questions outlined above to explore how participation in contemporary social movements simultaneously occurs in different geographical settings, configuring a spatially hybrid participation infrastructure that poses important challenges to activists.

Participation in the hybrid spatiality of Occupy Pittsburgh

Protest camps are a longstanding feature of social movements' repertoire of contention (Brown et al. 2017, Frenzel et al. 2014, Feigenbaum et al. 2013). In such camps, four different infrastructures are usually in place, each linked to a specific spatial dimension and each providing the facilities and services to support the reaching of common goals:

1. The *domestic infrastructure* that sustains the daily life at the protest camp and includes the running of common services, including food provision and medical support;
2. the *action infrastructure* that allows the protest camp to function as a hub from which other forms of protest might develop;
3. the *communication infrastructure* that refers to the protest camp as a form of representation in which and from which activists communicate with potential supporters, bystanders and opponents; and, finally,
4. the *governance infrastructure* that sustains the decision-making process occurring within the protest camp and affecting the mobilization of which it is part.

Frenzel et al. 2014

The protest camp of Occupy Pittsburgh clearly relied on these four infrastructures. Focussing on them will allow for a reconstruction of the spatiality of the protest camp as such. However, as mentioned above, in this chapter I seek to understand how the concrete location of the protest camp intertwined with different types of media technologies, reaching beyond its physical boundaries. In particular, I am interested in reconstructing what I call the *participation infrastructure* that supported Occupy Pittsburgh, of which the protest camp was just one, although crucial, place. Drawing on Feigenbaum et al. (2013: 54), I define the participation infrastructure of a mobilization such as Occupy Pittsburgh as *all the processes, spaces and technologies that people might employ to take part in protest activities*. In past mobilizations, the participation infrastructure included media technologies that remained at the margins due to their limited ability to allow for massive long-distance and asynchronous political participation. However, today, the participation infrastructure is not only more multifaceted, but it is also more balanced between the physical experience of the protest camp and interactions with digital technologies, which expand the opportunities for participation in time and space.

To grasp the whole participation infrastructure of contemporary mobilizations, it is then necessary to adopt a comprehensive perspective that goes beyond the temporal and spatial constraints of the protest camp. On the one hand, considering protest camps from the viewpoint of their temporal dimension, it is clear that the participation infrastructure of Occupy Pittsburgh had already begun to exist when the activists gathered to decide how to set up the protest camp itself. On the other hand, considering the spatiality of the protest camp, it was clear that the spaces for decision-making related to Occupy Pittsburgh went beyond its particular location to include social media platforms, as well as physical spaces that were located in other areas of Pittsburgh. More specifically, the participation infrastructure of Occupy Pittsburgh developed in three subsequent waves that combined different places, spaces and ICTs.

The first wave began once the news about Occupy Wall Street in New York reached Pittsburgh. At that point, people living in Pittsburgh were part of the dispersed media crowd that was following the unfolding of events in New York through various social media platforms. However, soon some activists in Pittsburgh established a Facebook group and registered an internet domain on which they constructed the official Occupy Pittsburgh website. Thus, two online spaces at the core of the participation infrastructure developed in the first stage of Occupy Pittsburgh. The second wave coincided with the organization of three general assemblies that were open to the public, and convened before the actual occupation. The first and the third general assemblies occurred in the First Unitarian Church, while the second occurred in a park situated on the university campus. These waves of infrastructural development culminated with the establishment of Occupy Pittsburgh as a recognizable social movement, the organization of a peaceful demonstration on 15 October 2011, and the occupation of the downtown Mellon Bank Park where the activists established a protest camp. The third wave of infrastructural development followed, which clearly revolved around, but was not situated solely at, the protest camp. The tents in the park multiplied rapidly and, at the same time, the participation infrastructure expanded beyond its premises by combining different types of physical spaces. Due to severe weather conditions, several general assemblies occurred in the United Steelworkers building near the protest camp, and many working group meetings were held in commercial establishments that served coffee and other products, and they were also held in university buildings. Moreover, due to the widespread use of laptops and, even more importantly, smartphones, people could potentially participate in Occupy Pittsburgh from anywhere. Hence, spaces of the struggle temporarily materialized in the areas daily traversed by participants, including workplaces and habitations.

The participation infrastructure resulting from these three subsequent waves was inherently hybrid in its spatiality, since it included and integrated different types of places – public and private, online and offline, and commercial and non-profit spaces – in which people gathered to participate in the broad range of activities related to Occupy Pittsburgh. This, in turn, had the direct consequence of empowering different types of engagement in Occupy Pittsburgh. I observed how the activists devoted different amounts of time to Occupy Pittsburgh: from full-time involvement to sporadic commitment. Moreover, they engaged with the mobilization through three main entry points: the protest camp itself, its activists' working groups, and the general assemblies that sustained Occupy Pittsburgh. For each entry point, face-to-face interactions blended with ICTs in different ways. Informal chats at the protest camp and in its immediate surroundings were supplemented by phone calls and email exchanges. Furthermore, low-tech media were also used at the protest camp to engage in conversation with potential supporters, such as the "debt wall", a placard in the middle of the campsite on which anyone could declare her loan. Face-to-face interactions in working groups were complemented by the use of online Google groups and, only in one case, the use of an activist-run mailing list service. Many of the working groups continued their face-to-face conversations online, which was essential for the drafting of the proposals and documents to be discussed in general assemblies. Finally, the general assemblies were frequently complemented with live-stream technologies.

These modes of participation were not mutually exclusive, and the same activist could connect with Occupy Pittsburgh in different ways during the course of the week, hence moving fluidly between different geographical settings as well as combining online and offline forms of engagement. For instance, some of the activists began as full-time campers and then became more involved as part-time activists in other physical spaces across Pittsburgh. Others began as full-time users of online platforms and then engaged in intermittent participation at the downtown camp, for instance, going there to provide supplies. Most importantly, the grafting of online platforms onto the protest camp brought together activists who experienced Occupy Pittsburgh in different spaces and places. When this occurred, the activists had a first-hand experience of the hybrid spatiality that characterized the participation infrastructure of Occupy Pittsburgh and of the challenges that it brought with it, as will be discussed in the next section.

Facing the challenges of hybrid spatiality in the participation infrastructure.

With a participation infrastructure that also included online technologies, Occupy Pittsburgh multiplied the entry points for people who wanted to engage with the mobilization. Much of the literature on Occupy Wall Street has focussed on the opportunities that social media platforms – and other ICT-based devices – brought with them, especially to involve both the distant media crowd (Bennett and Segerberg 2013) and transnational serial activists (Bastos and Mercea 2016). We know much less about the challenges that social media platforms pose to those core activists who were involved full-time in the protest camp, the general assemblies, and the working groups. The problems faced by the activists due to the hybrid spatiality in the participation infrastructure of Occupy Pittsburgh can be better understood considering two specific aspects that were commonly present in Occupy Wall Street mobilizations: the presence of a 24/7 video coverage to air the mobilization live and the intense use of Facebook through which news related to the mobilization was continuously posted, updated and discussed online.

While the two communication technologies augmented the spatiality of the protest camp, they also affect this dimension in a rather direct way. The expansion of the protest camp beyond its physical boundaries through the constant feed of unvarnished information about daily activities contributed to blurring of the divide between the backstage and front stage of the mobilization. While the former would otherwise remain hidden to more distant protest participants, sympathizers and bystanders, the presence of live-streaming and social media platform rendered it the object of a continuous representation of the mobilization. Such representation, in turn, reinforced the sense of high accessibility to the mobilization: unlike more closed social movements, Occupy Pittsburgh – but more generally Occupy Wall Street – was presented from the beginning as a mobilization open to the contribution of anybody willing to participate. The selection and employment of specific communication technologies thus allowed activists not only to support their protests but also to make a strong statement about who they were: not a closed niche, but a welcoming movement open to include new participants at any time. While such a spirit was certainly there, the resulting spatial hybridity of the participation infrastructure challenged the activists almost on a daily basis during the peak of Occupy Pittsburgh.

Communication technologies never neutral, they "have a certain type of collective action built in [... that] configures people's options and ends up steering collective action in problematic ways" (Milan 2015b, 8). During Occupy Pittsburgh, live-streaming and social media platforms clearly shaped the mobilization; they conveyed a rhetoric of transparency, immediacy and accessibility that to some extent simplified the idea of a social movement, which is a multilayered social process often based on a fragile equilibrium. Platforms did so by accelerating the time of the mobilization (Kaun 2016), which might require a slow pace to make decisions together and resolve intra-movement disputes. In what follows, I illustrate this point in more depth through the specific tensions that I witnessed when taking part in the Occupy Pittsburgh mobilizations.

During general assemblies, marches and other informal gatherings, activists always brought a laptop equipped with a digital camera to live stream the moments in which Occupy Pittsburgh collectively made decisions or expressed discontent. Frequently, when there was no general assembly, the camera was placed in the protest camp between the food tent and the people's library to provide live footage of the daily life of the activists. This shaped the spatiality of the protest camp and partially structured the interactions that occurred there. The awareness of being live streamed made some activists uncomfortable. For this reason, after the first general assembly, an agreement was reached: those who did not want to be in front of the camera during general assemblies could gather in a safe zone outside the reach of the camera. At the same time, activists who did not want to have their chats live streamed knew they had to avoid having conversations near the food tent and the people's library, where the camera was positioned when it was not used for general assemblies.

The live stream also had a role in connecting the physical location of the protest camp with the spatiality of distant participants, sympathizers and bystanders. Through the built-in chat, the live-streaming platforms allowed them to talk with the activists who were staying at the protest camp during general assemblies. In at least a couple of instances, I attended general assemblies in which the people in the chat were able to express their opinions about the issue under discussion. However, more often, the voice of those attending the general assemblies through the live stream was not included in the conversation. In many cases, this was because there was no interest on the part of the audience to intervene; in other cases, the "voices of the live stream" – as the protest camp activists referred to them – were ignored on purpose so that they could not interfere with the decision-making process of the general assembly. While the integration of the live-streaming platform into general assemblies provided yet another mode of participation in Occupy Pittsburgh, the way in which it was actually employed made clear that the modes of participation were discernibly hierarchical. Attending the general assembly with the support of live-streaming platforms allowed those who were not on site to be up-to-date on the discussions within Occupy Pittsburgh; however, it did not grant the same "right to participate" in decision-making during general assemblies. This was also because the activists did not consider the implications that live streaming the general assemblies could have for the consensus-based method of decision-making they employed. Discussions on this topic were largely absent. The resulting decision-making process was horizontal when it concerned the activists who were physically present in the general assembly. Yet, it was rather vertical when it concerned the contributions of those online, which were easily ignored or talked over.

As noted, Facebook was particularly important for Occupy Pittsburgh. From the beginning, the official Facebook group became the online space where the minutes of the general assembly were stored, together with the proposals that had been passed during general assemblies, as well as proposals to be discussed during following general assemblies. Moreover, the activists used the Facebook page to communicate with potential protest participants, and the Facebook group with those already involved, at different levels, in Occupy Pittsburgh. As other scholars have illustrated, managing of social media platforms creates hierarchies, with "digital vanguards" that emerge in social movements claiming to be leaderless and spontaneous as was often the case with the Occupy Wall Street mobilizations (Gerbaudo 2017). In Occupy Pittsburgh, the management of the Facebook group did not reach the sophistication of coeval protests, such as the establishment of "connective leaders" in the case of the Egyptian uprising and the related Kullena Khaled Said Facebook page (Poell et al. 2016). However, the activists managing the Facebook group did find themselves trapped in struggles over control. Already a few days after it was established, haters and trolls hijacked conversations among the group members. At least one of the trolls was able to become an admin of the group, deliberately banning users and deleting comments. For a number of days, the group conversations mainly revolved around the presence of haters and trolls, and after intense debates and open insults, some activists decided to create a new Facebook group with more trusted activists as admins. Beyond the presence of trolls and haters, the conversation in the Facebook group cyclically became self-referential, with the admins under scrutiny and subjected to long debates about their conduct. The admins' role and their power to ban users and delete comments triggered several tense conversations, especially when this power was used to control the flow of information and the ability to communicate on the Facebook wall of the group. Thus, the inherent materiality of the social media platform shaped the emergence of hierarchies among the activists who participated in the Facebook group and contributed to the creation of asymmetric ties among them.

Similar to the live stream, the use of the Facebook group also brought the daily lives of the protest camp beyond its physical boundaries. Some of the activists who spent a considerable amount of time in the protest camp also posted news on specific episodes that occurred there, some of which involved acts of hate speech as well as sexist, homophobic and racist behaviours. As a result, distant participants, sympathizers, and bystanders could be updated and were enabled to express their viewpoints. Frequently, harsh, tense and long discussions on the Facebook group developed that shaped the interactions among the activists who participated on an ongoing basis in the protest camp. Without any solution, contentious discussions occurred in the Facebook group, subsequently reported to the protest camp, fed back again to online discussion, and so forth. This feedback loop made the relationships between activists more and more difficult. The meaning-making process around the protest camp often became extremely contentious. The constant chatting in the Facebook group on some occasions became a source of anxiety for the activists rooted in the protest camp. There was, thus, a mild digital divide between the activists in the protest camp and the people participating in the discussion from elsewhere. Occupy Pittsburgh relied on limited financial resources that rendered the internet connectivity of the protest camp weak, at times, and certainly discontinuous. More importantly, the activists in the protest camp did not have time to interact on the Facebook group, since they were constantly immersed in the daily life of the physical protest space, engaging in face-to-face interactions with other protest participants and focussing on the actual functioning of the protest camp. Many activists with whom I spoke, indeed, after some weeks in the protest camp were ready to get rid of the Facebook group, claiming that the "Facebook drama" that exploded at certain moments and on specific issues was draining energies and resources from the protest camp. However, other activists thought that giving up the Facebook group would exclude more distant activists. While the latter point of view prevailed, the discussions on the Facebook group continued to develop cyclically and became a structural part of the mobilization.

Conclusions

Social movements develop a variety of spatial strategies and approaches (Nicholls et al. 2013). This chapter showed that conceptually and empirically engaging with the spatiality of contemporary activism is of the utmost importance to critically address the role of social media platforms in mobilizations. When considering the role of such platforms through the dimension of space – and keeping in mind the importance that space has and always has had for social movements – it is possible to grasp the challenges that emerge when the physical spatiality of protest camps meets the less tangible locus of social media platforms. In this chapter, I discussed this with regard to patterns of participation. In other words, the ways in which people take part in and feel part of protests. In doing so, I showed that while many scholars have celebrated the role of online platforms in mobilizing and sustaining recent protests, such as Occupy Wall Street, these platforms also pose many challenges, especially to activists who devote much of their time to mobilization.

Live-streaming and social media platforms were part of a broader repertoire of communication, which included face-to-face interactions and other low-tech tools. These platforms were grafted into the many physical spaces of the mobilization, including the protest camp. These platforms were part of a participation infrastructure that allowed many entry points to Occupy Pittsburgh for potential participants, sympathizers and bystanders. Although they provided a sense of easy access to the mobilization, live streaming the mobilization and the continuous news feed in the Facebook group also posed challenges. On the one hand, the specific functions and design of the communication technologies posed challenges. The live stream enabled the continuous visibility of the protest camp and, in doing so, structured its spatiality and interactions. The activists in the Facebook group were confronted with the power assigned by the social media platform to admins. Furthermore, the use of live-streaming and social media platforms contributed to the creation of a spatial hybridity that brought together different modes of participation that sometimes were not compatible and led to physical and symbolic tensions. Moreover, online platforms triggered disputes concerning the construction of the Occupy Pittsburgh collectivity. Which participants were entitled to be fully recognized in the mobilization and have a voice? Was it fair that only those involved in the protest camp on a daily basis – knowledgeable about the problems of life in the camp – had a voice? Or, should the collective include the voices of those who were seldom, if ever, in contact with the physical space of Occupy Pittsburgh, even though they were involved in other protest manifestations, including the Facebook group? Ultimately, then, the spatial hybridity of Occupy Pittsburgh triggered questions about the definition of the boundaries of the mobilization: where it began and ended, and who was part of it. These are questions for the analysis of the role, relevance, and legitimacy of protest camps in mobilizations, especially when the protest camp is perceived as only one piece of a wider protest campaign.

On a more theoretical level, this chapter illustrates that the spatial dimension of contemporary activism goes well beyond the physical locations of protests, and it recognizes the ability of social media platforms and other digital communication technologies to augment the participation infrastructure of today's protests. Hybridity, then, is not only to be found at the level of activist media practices (Mattoni 2012), but also at the spatial level. To conclude, two methodological considerations follow from these observations. First, comparative analysis is needed to fully grasp how social media platforms affect the spatial dimension of protests in different countries. While employed by activists around the globe, social media platforms, such as Twitter and Facebook, are used in specific national settings, characterized by distinct protest cultures. Second, mixed-methods, combining big data analysis and thick ethnographic observations, should be developed to provide an encompassing reconstruction of the hybrid spatiality of contemporary social movements and the challenges that it poses to activists worldwide.

References

Bastos, M. T., & Mercea, D. (2016). Serial Activists: Political Twitter beyond Influentials and the Twittertariat. *New Media & Society*, 18(10), pp. 2359–2378.

Bennett, W. L., & Segerberg, A. (2013). *The Logic of Connective Action: Digital Media and the Personalization of Contentious Politics*. Cambridge: Cambridge University Press.

Brown, G., Feigenbaum, A., McCurdy, P. & Frenzel, F. (2017). *Protest Camps in International Context: Spaces, Infrastructures and Media of Resistance*. Bristol: Policy Press.

Castells, M. (2012). *Networks of Outrage and Hope. Social Movements in the Internet Age*. Cambridge: Polity Press.

Della Porta, D. & Mattoni, A. (2014). *Spreading Protest: Social Movements in Times of Crisis*. Colchester: ECPR Press.

Earl, J. & Kimport, K. (2011). *Digitally Enabled Social Change: Activism in the Internet Age*. Cambridge, MA: MIT Press.

Feigenbaum, A., Frenzel, F. & McCurdy, P. (2013). *Protest Camps*. London: Zed Books.

Frenzel, F., Feigenbaum, A. & McCurdy, P. (2014). Protest Camps: An Emerging Field of Social Movement Research. *The Sociological Review*, 62(3), pp. 457–474.

Gaby, S. & Caren, N. (2012). Occupy Online: How Cute Old Men and Malcolm X Recruited 400,000 US Users to OWS on Facebook. *Social Movement Studies*, 11(3–4), pp. 367–374.

Gerbaudo, P. (2017). Social Media Teams as Digital Vanguards: The Question of Leadership in the Management of Key Facebook and Twitter Accounts of Occupy Wall Street, Indignados and UK Uncut. *Information, Communication & Society*, 20(2), pp. 185–202.

Juris, J.S. (2008). *Networking Futures. The Movements against Corporate Globalization*. Durham, NC: Duke University Press.

Kaun, A. (2016). *Crisis and Critique: A Brief History of Media Participation in Times of Crisis*. London: Zed Books.

Kavada, A. (2015). Creating the Collective: Social Media, the Occupy Movement and Its Constitution as a Collective Actor. *Information, Communication & Society*, 18(8), pp. 872–886.

Lichterman, P. (1998). What Do Movements Mean? The Value of Participant-Observation. *Qualitative Sociology*, 21(4), pp. 401–418.

Mattoni, A. (2012). *Media Practices and Protest Politics. How Precarious Workers Mobilise*. Burlington, VT: Ashgate.

Mercea, D., Iannelli, L. & Loader, B. D. (2016). Protest Communication Ecologies. *Information, Communication & Society*, 19(3), pp. 279–289.

Milan, S. (2015a). From Social Movements to Cloud Protesting: The Evolution of Collective Identity. *Information, Communication & Society*, 18(8), pp. 887–900.

Milan, S. (2015b). When Algorithms Shape Collective Action: Social Media and the Dynamics of Cloud Protesting. *Social Media + Society*, 1(2).

Nicholls, W., Miller, B. & Beaumont, J. (Eds.). (2013). *Spaces of Contention: Spatialities and Social Movements*. Burlington, VT: Ashgate.

Pink, S., Horst, H., Postill, J., Hjorth, L., Lewis, T., & Tacchi, J. (2015). *Digital Ethnography: Principles and Practice*. London: Sage.

Poell, T., Abdulla, R., Rieder, B., Woltering, R. & Zack, L. (2016). Protest leadership in the age of social media. *Information, Communication & Society*, 19(7), pp. 994–1014.

Theocharis, Y., Lowe, W., van Deth, J. W. & García-Albacete, G. (2015). Using Twitter to Mobilize Protest Action: Online Mobilization Patterns and Action Repertoires in the Occupy Wall Street, Indignados, and Aganaktismenoi Movements. *Information, Communication & Society*, 18(2), pp. 202–220.

Treré, E. & Mattoni, A. (2016). Media Ecologies and Protest Movements: Main Perspectives and Key Lessons. *Information, Communication & Society*, 19(3), pp. 290–306.

2

RETHINKING NETWORKED SOLIDARITY

Sky Croeser

Introduction

Social media strengthen existing connections and help to create new networks, so we might therefore expect them to play a key role in building activist solidarity. However, social media materialities matter: social media are not, on the whole, developed primarily to connect people, but rather to make money. Nevertheless, possibilities exist for activists to repurpose social media infrastructures intended for other uses. Additionally, there are non-profit sites which, like corporate social media, are focussed on user-contributed content. These might better serve activists' purposes in strengthening solidarity efforts. This chapter explores some of the ways in which activists are using corporate and non-profit social media (Facebook and Libcom, respectively) to develop solidarity around the Kurdish movement for autonomy. In doing so, it questions how social media materialities affect these efforts.

The ongoing struggle for autonomy in Kurdistan is seen by many as a defining moment for international solidarity on the left. This moment has been constituted through contemporary accounts and, increasingly, online discussions and representations. The Kurdish movement, also sometimes called the "Rojava revolution", is inspiring attempts to join its armed resistance to Daesh, (the "Islamic State") (Oakes & Goswell 2016); solidarity actions in other countries (Jinha News Agency 2015); and numerous calls for attention to its political praxis (Goldberg 2015; Hamad 2015). This makes it a useful focus for examining some of the ways in which social media might support and reinforce – or undermine – meaningful solidarity efforts. Both non-profit and corporate social media have become places where news spreads about the movement, people discuss solidarity efforts, and specific forms of solidarity are organized or facilitated.

Over the last decade, there has been a reorientation away from the struggle for a Kurdish homeland and towards democratic confederalism, a non-state system of social and political organization based on grassroots participation (Ocalan 2011). This has also involved a broadening of the movement; as Egret and Anderson (2016: 7) note, many of those involved continue to refer to it as a Kurdish struggle – in part an act of reclamation against the ban on Kurdish identity and language – but it explicitly includes diverse ethnicities.. The shift away from a struggle for a Kurdish homeland, and a Kurdish nation in particular, has helped to draw international attention to the issue, as have the movement's efforts to develop an environmentally sustainable economic system, a more equal distribution of wealth, and gender equality.

There are many interesting and important questions to be asked about the struggle underway in Kurdistan, but my own distance (literally and metaphorically) from the region means I am better-placed to explore solidarity efforts around the movement. I am writing this chapter on maternity leave, which has both constrained the scope of my research, and focussed my interest on the questions of whether the Internet can facilitate meaningful solidarity efforts for those of us so far removed from the physical sites of such struggles, and what that solidarity might look like. As much of the literature on social movements and activism pays attention to large corporate platforms such as Facebook and Twitter, I have focussed on the possibilities independent social media sites offer for building solidarity. While corporate social media privilege the needs of corporations selling users' attention and data, independent sites offer more potential for supporting solidarity efforts. Social media also provide new forms of mediation (and different possibilities for resonance) for those directly taking part in the struggle to share their experiences, and potential to experience "new forms of transnational commonality" that do not rely on physical co-presence (Milan 2015: 6). While this sharing may be an important basis for solidarity, it is also constrained by the affordances of particular platforms.

Methodology

This chapter uses qualitative methods to explore some of the ways in which potential supporters of the Kurdish autonomous movement are enacting solidarity online, drawing particularly on feminist understandings of solidarity. This is especially appropriate given the emphasis that the Kurdish movement places on women's role, and on Jineolojî, which is based on "the reconstruction of the society and the life by questioning the existent historical framework, by taking all of the experiences of women, which existed until today, as a base" (Jineoloji 2017). This is not a representative analysis of the solidarity movement. None of the sites explored can claim to accurately represent any particular demographic, and while social media do allow for a new scale of quantitative analysis of social movement material, this can often be misleading. (For an in-depth discussion, see Croeser & Highfield 2015.) Instead, I have attempted to highlight posts or discussions which illuminate how users are negotiating solidarity online.

The main focus of this research is on Libcom (discussed in more detail below), a non-corporate site. There is also substantial material in support of the Kurdish movement available on corporate social media. Despite Facebook's limitations, its widespread reach means that it is an important platform for organizing and debate. There are a number of ethical challenges involved in using Facebook for research, even when drawing on public pages, and therefore in using these as a background to the more detailed discussion of Libcom, I have focussed on their general features rather than examining them in detail.

Libcom is a "libertarian communist" site which hosts a broad range of topics rather than being focussed specifically on the Kurdish movement. As Neumayer and Svensson have observed, corporate social media may provide possibilities for radical activism but they also have structural limitations, particularly for activists willing to engage in civil disobedience and seeking change beyond legal institutions (Neumayer & Svensson 2016: 142). This site is just one of the spaces which exists outside of the walled garden of corporate social media: the nature of independent social media (broadly conceived) means it is more diverse than corporate media, and as such it is not possible to point to a single site having the same reach or influence as Twitter or Facebook. More comprehensive research methods, such as the media ecologies model discussed by Treré and Mattoni, would be useful in developing a picture of the wide range of sites used by those building solidarity with the Kurdish movement, but as these authors note, that requires a huge amount of time and significant resources (Treré & Mattoni 2015: 303). As a starting point, this chapter discusses Libcom as an activist-run site which offers the possibility of a space not organized around the "social media logic" (van Dijck & Poell 2013) that characterizes corporate platforms. Libcom does not have the same incentives (or resources) to develop and obfuscate proprietary algorithms, and to connect users (and their data) to advertisers.

Libcom is run by volunteer administrators based in the UK and the USA. Members of the collective have chosen to reveal varying levels of identifying details, ranging from a location and full (possibly legal) name and location, through to a first name and (presumably invented) biography (Libcom 2007). As Libcom is an independent site which warns users that the site "is known to be read regularly by the police, the far right and media" (Libcom 2017), I have chosen to cite authors by their usernames, in keeping with previous work which recognizes those outside academia as active in producing theory (Yakinthou & Croeser 2016: 234). I have also avoided citing any posts or comments that directly discuss illegal acts.

Of course, the Kurdish movement is discussed across a range of other corporate social media, including Twitter (on solidarity accounts and through tags like #Rojava, #TwitterKurds, #Kobane, and #Raqqa), Instagram (#Rojava returned 70,043 posts as of 17 June 2017), and even Pinterest (a site better known for collecting material on craft, design, and recipes, which returns hundreds of results for searches like "Rojava Revolution" and "Kurdish Solidarity"). However, I have focussed here on Facebook and Libcom because they allow for longer-form discussion and contention, highlighting different understandings and practices of solidarity. Given the vast amount and variety of material available across Libcom and corporate social media, it is difficult to make definitive contrasts between how activists use these platforms for solidarity actions: this research points towards some trends and questions for further examination.

This chapter has important limitations. Firstly, my research only covers English-language content: given that a significant part of the Kurdish struggle has been the effort to preserve the Kurdish language, banned or severely restricted by the states overlapping with Kurdistan throughout the last century (Minorities at Risk Project 2004; Khalidi 2016; Sharifi 2014; Hakim 2014), research into Kurdish-language content would allow a deeper perspective of how those involved in the movement understand solidarity efforts, as would research carried out in Turkish, Arabic, and other regional languages. Secondly, more in-depth and wide-reaching research into collaboration with activists should follow from this.

Theorizing solidarity

As we attempt to develop "alternative economic, political, and social practices that oppose neoliberal capitalist globalization and other global injustices" (Ferguson 2009a: 185), theorizing solidarity is an urgent and necessary part of the practice of creating change. Solidarity must take into account power differences between movement participants, and the challenges of navigating other differences, such as language, geography, and culture. However, there are different perspectives on what constitutes meaningful solidarity, and on those who are deserving of solidarity efforts. Carol Gould, Ann Ferguson, and Chandra Talpade Mohanty are among those who explore visions of solidarity that cross borders and require those engaged in solidarity relations to consider their own positions and practices. Gould emphasises the role of empathy in building solidarity, arguing that while rational reflection has a role to play, "the features of empathy and imaginative reconstruction of the situation of others that characterize solidarity relations help to explain people's motivation to take norms of justice seriously" (Gould 2007: 162). Ferguson proposes a form of solidarity that draws on this emotional and imaginative connection, along with an awareness of the differences between people, and "involves a transformation among those who pledge it to work for a collective good, not merely for those in their own social location" (Ferguson 2009a: 192). Similarly, Mohanty argues that we need to account for power differences, which ultimately means activists and scholars must:

> identify and reenvision forms of collective resistance that women, especially, in their different communities enact in their everyday lives. It is their particular exploitation at this time, their potential epistemic privilege, as well as their particular forms of solidarity that can be the basis for reimagining a liberatory politics.
>
> *Mohanty (2003): 515–516*

These overlapping conceptions of solidarity are useful in understanding how we might respond to the possibilities embodied in the struggles for autonomy in Kurdish areas.

Those who are involved in the Kurdish struggle also frequently draw on a similar understanding of solidarity. Egret and Anderson:

> argue for a stance of critical solidarity, to maintain a critical, undogmatic perspective which sees the social movements in Bakur and Rojava for what they are. To criticize the problematic aspects but also to be in solidarity with the positive, liberatory movements taking place.
>
> *Egret & Anderson (2016): 38*

To facilitate this, most of the interviews in their collection ask the question, "what can those outside of Kurdistan do in solidarity?" Answers, of course, vary. Hilmi Aydoğdu and Hasan Hüseyin, representatives of the Democratic Society Congress, ask others to lobby their governments to remove the Kurdistan Workers' Party (PKK) from the list of terrorist organizations in Europe and the USA (Egret & Anderson 2016: 45); Zerdesht Kobanê calls for financial support for a children's hospital and other rebuilding efforts in Kobanê (Brighton Kurdish Solidarity 2016: 74); and Zuhal Tekiner, co-Mayor of Farqîn said:

> When you go home to the UK, please talk about every bullet that they fired, about every person who is dead, and make noise about this. Ask the state of Turkey to be accountable for every bullet they use. Remind Turkey of human rights.
>
> *Egret & Anderson (2016): 93*

Others, however, eschew or supplement these material, political, or rights-based understandings of solidarity with a vision that more radically transforms those engaged in solidarity efforts. After spending time in Rojava, Jo Magpie wrote, "the movement doesn't want you to help it, it wants you to join it" (Magpie 2016: 64). "To understand what's happening in Rojava, we also need a shift in consciousness, to understand the new paradigm that is emerging. And the first thing to do is to begin de-constructing our own understandings of reality" (Magpie 2016: 68). Dilar Dirik, a Kurdish activist and sociologist, argues that seeing solidarity as "one-directional, something one 'gives' and the other 'takes', is flawed from the start", challenging those who are critiquing the struggle for autonomy in Kurdish areas to "go make revolution in your own place!" (Dirik 2016). This suggests that many of those involved in the Kurdish struggle are seeking the kind of transformational and reflexive solidarity outlined above.

The Internet, and social media in particular, offers the potential to support both traditional and more radically transformational visions of solidarity. Social media "provide an opportunity to overcome geographic distance to demonstrate support for, and solidarity with, similarly minded groups in other cities, regions and countries" (Highfield 2016: 113). Social media can facilitate the deepening of the emotional connections, which Gould argues underlie effective solidarity, facilitate material aid (as in the 'Feed the Revolution' 2016 crowdfunding effort), mobilize political lobbying, and spread radical ideas and possibilities. However, the logic of corporate social media means these possibilities are incidental, and sometimes even actively discouraged. The focus on shaping relational activities (such as the ability to "like" and "favourite" others' content) is aimed at pleasing users and advertisers (van Dijck & Poell 2013: 5): affect is manipulated to meet companies' business models. Visibility for activist projects on social media is often in tension with state surveillance and censorship, and even when activists are able to gain attention, they may not be able to effectively shape the narrative and images shared (Neumayer, Rossi & Karlsson 2016). Even the apparently borderless and placeless nature of corporate social media is belied by the influence of Silicon Valley culture on their embedded values, and by censorship and surveillance by governments. Alternative, non-corporate social media platforms may, therefore, serve as a space where solidarity around anti-capitalist and autonomist movements can more meaningfully be negotiated and enacted.

Practicing solidarity online

It is challenging to characterize the forms of solidarity with the Kurdish movement practiced on Facebook: pages are set up by a range of different organizations and individuals, with different purposes, moderation practices, and users, although all of these efforts are subject to Facebook's algorithms. We looked at a range of public English-language pages, including "Kurdistan solidarity movement international" (752 likes); "Kurdistan solidarity campaign" (3,800 likes); "Kurdistan solidarity network" (216 likes); "Rojava Solidarity Worldwide" (3,200 likes); "Rojava Calling" (1,200 likes); "Anarchists in Support of Rojava-Kurdistan آنارشیستهای مدافع کوبان" (which has since been removed); "Save Kobane" (76,000 likes); "Assisting the Volunteers of Rojava" (4,200 likes); and "Support Rojava/Kurdistan" (7,200 likes). There are also local pages, such as "University of Glasgow Kurdish Solidarity Society" (101 likes) and "Rojava Solidarity NYC" (which has also since been removed). In addition to this, many pages aim to disseminate news about the Kurdish movement, or discuss particular aspects of it, such as "The Women's Revolution in Rojava" (53,000 likes) and "Kurdish Female Fighters/ YPJ" (50,000 likes), which while not explicitly aimed at building international support for the movement, implicitly support solidarity efforts by sharing positive news and analysis. More general political pages on Facebook, including "libcom.org" also share material related to the Kurdish movement.

Some of the links posted are to fundraisers and events providing material or political solidarity with the Kurdish movement, though these only make up a small proportion of the content on the pages we looked at. There were several links to the "Feed the Revolution" crowdfunding campaign and other fundraising efforts; invitations to a "Solidarity Hunger Strike" in the UK and to the Kurdish Solidarity event during London Pride; events like the "Rojava: Syria's radical alternative"; and a "free public meeting" in Melbourne, and "Readings from Rojava"; and the use of hashtags like #TurkeyHandsOffAfrin. One page includes a pinned document with details about how to travel to Kurdistan to volunteer. Many of the pages share content more directly from those in Kurdistan, including photos of those fighting (in particular, women holding weapons), subtitled video interviews with people in Kurdish areas, video footage of battles, memorials for those killed in action, and documentaries from visitors to the area. Some pages and groups also post memes, although these were rare in the examined content. Solidarity pages frequently posted news from commercial news media like ARA News, as well as from alternative news sources like KOM News. In-depth conversations, particularly conversations sustained over more than a day or two, were extremely rare on these pages. There are many indications that users consider Facebook to be an untrustworthy platform: the pinned tweet about volunteering in Kurdistan instructs people to contact the YPJ by email rather than through Facebook, the YPJ cover photo refers to their previous page being shut down, and several pages linked to an article about Facebook removing hashtags related to the Kurdish struggle (Kurdish Question 2017). While there is a wide range of material posted to Facebook, Facebook's algorithms and terms encourage users to privilege some practices (such as sharing images and video) over others, particularly sustained conversation and acts of solidarity that might be illegal in some countries.

While Libcom does not meet all of boyd and Ellison's (2007) criteria for a social networking site, it does run on user-generated content, allow users to create a profile page (including lists of organizations they belong to or have previously belonged to), track other users' contributions, and message other users. While the format differs from corporate social media, it is definitely *social* media. The site hosts material in a number of different formats, including blogs, news, history, discussion forums, and a library which often includes material sourced from elsewhere. In practice, these sections blur into each other, as blog posts, news stories, and other material frequently host long discussions in the comments, and discussion forums also refer back to content in other sections of the site. There is a range of material on Libcom that explicitly addresses solidarity efforts for the struggles for autonomy in Kurdistan. In 2015, one poster asked what proportion of anarchists support the Rojava revolution, writing, "I'm amazed it's not the main topic/concern of anarchists at the moment, and that there have been virtually no international volunteers" ('anagoldman' 2015), and another user replied, "Check out any number of threads on Rojava on this site and you'll see that's it's not a position of indifference. It's been one of the most debated issues on libcom recently, multiple threads with 100s of comments" ('Khawaga' 2015). Interest in the Kurdish struggle on the site has continued, with updates and discussions ongoing through to the time of writing. The question posed by anagoldman demonstrates an expectation from at least some users that Libcom is a site representing a broader community of unified interests and concerns.

This can also be seen in the tension between Libcom as a site for users to share their own content and analysis and the sense of a search for common ground. Libcom is a successful example of an autonomous digital infrastructure that hosts important resources and discussion, but it is less clear whether it has become a space where discussion shifts into meaningful action, at least when it comes to solidarity for the Kurdish movement. In one extended exchange on a post expressing critiques of the events in Rojava ('Peter Storm' 2015), one user, 'Connor Owens' (2015), criticizes Libcom for "putting out article after article expressing almost pathological opposition to the idea that anything positive could be going on in west Kurdistan". Subsequently, a member of the organizing collective replies:

> really, to have any kind of sensible dialogue, you need to get your head around the fact that Libcom is not some monolithic article-production machine. It's a website, administered by a handful of volunteers, who sometimes write and other times host articles written by people across the libertarian-left.
>
> *'Ed' (2015)*

Despite a general recognition that the organizing collective has a limited role in deciding which content and perspectives are shared on the site, numerous users on this thread place the debate within the context of a larger anarchist community. 'Chilli Sauce' (2015), for example, writes, "The PKK is not a libertarian organisation and, as such, doesn't warrant the support of anarchists", while 'Flint' (2015), disagrees with critics, asking, "Why must you continually argue that we shouldn't care? That we shouldn't be interested?" There is a clear expectation here that Libcom functions as at least one space where anarchists, as a community, debate appropriate practices of solidarity (in contrast with the supposedly value-neutral role of corporate platforms like Facebook and Twitter).

Libcom, in contrast with many other social media platforms, offers a space which can host in-depth discussion without word-length limitations or proprietary algorithmic interventions aimed at sustaining a corporate business model. Aspects of the Libcom site are, however, opaque to users. It is not clear, for example, how the featured articles and threads on the landing page are chosen. The "help out!" page ('Jef Costello' 2006) implies there is at least some scope for volunteers to shape content and organize material on particular topics. This is in contrast to Facebook's algorithms, which are invisible to most users and, even when they do become visible, privilege Facebook's commercial interests while offering little scope for users to understand or change them (Bucher 2017). Much of the Libcom discussion on the Kurdish struggle focusses on whether or not it should be considered a "real" revolution. For example, in 'Rojava Revolution and its backers', one user writes:

> [...] I would like to publish comments and thoughts somewhat critical on the revolutionary nature of the process that takes place in Rojava, as well as on solidarity campaigns that seem to me to be unconditional. [...] "The anarchists" always declared their hatred for the State and the Nation... And yet the Rojava has all of the features of a State, or at present of a "proto"-State.
>
> *'Richard 1917' (2016)*

Discussion on this thread includes comments defending or critiquing the struggle in Kurdistan (along with a few personal attacks), many of which reference other sources. Another discussion thread, in the comments of the reposting of a 2014 statement from the UK's Anarchist Federation, continues for ten pages, between December 2014 and October 2016. This depth and duration of discussion is difficult to find on most corporate social media, which discourage it by highlighting more recent and popular content, and the posts of page or group administrators.

Given the central role of women in the Kurdish struggle, and the focus on this in both mainstream and alternative coverage of the movement, it is unsurprising that many of the evaluations put forward on Libcom touch on whether it is "feminist enough". For example, a 2014 statement from the UK's Anarchist Federation reposted to Libcom expresses doubt as to the feminist character of the women's defence units.

> Whilst there are signs of feminist influences within them, it should be remembered that the women's fighting groups are segregated from male units, with no mixed fighting groups. Gaddafi and Saddam both had women's military brigades, but that did not mean that there was women's liberation in Libya and Iraq.
>
> *The Anarchist Federation (2014)*

Another post opens by repeating this scepticism about women's militant roles, and also asks, "how can lower class Kurdish women break from the PKK and truly liberate themselves? Is there any women's movement in Rojava that is genuinely independent of the largely middle class leadership of the PKK/PYD?" ('Anti War' 2015). There seems to be little reflection here on whether the commenters' own communities and affiliations are "feminist enough". It difficult to determine the gender of users, but the majority of usernames seem to indicate a demographic that skews heavily male (for example, 'Serge Forward', 'little_brother', 'JoeMaguire', and 'SpikeyMike' are on the first page of comments here, among other more ambiguous usernames). Other sections of Libcom might, similarly, invite questions as to whether they are "feminist enough". For example, threads on the forum soliciting reading suggestions focus heavily on male authors, with only one comment of 25 under a post about suggested reading (Libcom 2016) and three comments in the first 31 where a user asks what others are reading (Libcom 2010) suggesting texts by women. Libcom's suggested reading list on anarchism (Libcom 2012) includes only one female author (although they do have a separate section on 'Women and feminism'), something which none of those commenting on the list find noteworthy. As in many other activist networks, online and offline, "women and feminism" are spatially separated, and the question of women's participation is cordoned off rather than integral to the organization of the community.

Arguably, this suggests that although Libcom allows for and encourages deep and sustained discussion, this does not necessarily translate into a reflexive, transformational solidarity. Even forms of solidarity such as sending material contributions, travelling to the area, and lobbying states outside the area to put pressure on Turkey or other governments acting against the Kurdish struggle seem to be hindered by the desire to first evaluate the movement against a perfect revolutionary ideal (that it seems unlikely any of the users embody themselves). While there are times when Libcom users actively call for critical solidarity for the struggle (see, for example, 'Zaher Baher' 2016 and the comments), even here discussion focusses on evaluation, rather than deepening and enacting solidarity efforts.

This might also be related to the limitations of social media – corporate and independent – in building what Milan calls "new forms of transnational commonality" (Milan 2015: 6). Libcom is not shaped by the imperatives of corporate social media logic, but as an independent site it does not have the resources to easily reach a wide, transnational user-base; to provide translation to multiple languages; or to explore algorithms that might work to actively support organizing and resistance on the site. Participants in the Kurdish movement, and other anti-capitalist, feminist, and autonomist movements around the world can join the discussion on Libcom, but the distance – metaphorical and literal – between the sites and embodied experiences of their struggles and those of other Libcom users remain noticeable. While Milan argues that social media offer the possibility for sharing space in similar ways to Occupy camps (Milan 2015: 6–7), the necessity of negotiating commonality across difference is not noticeable in the same ways on Libcom, or on the Facebook groups we looked at, as it has been in many of the square's encampments.

Whereas people might legitimately raise questions about the possibility of Facebook or Twitter revolutions, no such possibility can reasonably be raised about Libcom. This is not to say, of course, that Libcom and other independent social media are unimportant. Attention to the Kurdish movement, as well as to many other related struggles around the world, is growing, and solidarity is often built diffusely across multiple spaces, online and offline. Information and discussion flows across multiple platforms, including between corporate news media, corporate social media, and independent social media. Libcom and other independent sites play a key role, and many of the connections that are created will have diffuse effects that aren't easily tracked.

Looking forward

Libcom, as an independent site, is not subject to the same social media logic that restricts the possibilities for effective solidarity offered by Facebook. However, Facebook's global reach makes it an obvious choice for activists engaged in solidarity efforts, as is clear from the wide range of content relevant to the Kurdish movement on the site. Libcom's focus on hosting a community with particular values and shared interests, and its affordances which encourage long and sustained discussion, offer possibilities for a deeply engaged and meaningful solidarity which, arguably, are far from being realized on the site. Often, there seems to be an assumption that a first step towards solidarity and mutual aid should be a careful evaluation of other struggles: whether these are revolutionary enough, feminist enough, anarchist enough. While the kind of reflexive, transformational solidarity outlined by feminist theorists and many participants in the Kurdish movement does exist, it is not as fully explored and enacted as we might hope. Meanwhile, the ability to easily share photos and video on Facebook may support the emotional connections that Gould and others argue underpin effective solidarity, but it is far from clear that this is taking place.

Social media may have the potential to nurture solidarity efforts, but barriers stubbornly remain. Content often flows between corporate and non-profit social media (including between Facebook and the Libcom site); people are capable of connecting across borders and, with the increased use of automatic translations, across languages; and there are new ways of organizing material aid. However, this preliminary research shows little evidence that either Facebook or Libcom are supporting significant solidarity efforts. Even though Facebook allows activists to create solidarity pages which have a wide reach, the organization of the site discourages transforming this into effective action – from the terms of use which discourage users from explicitly mentioning efforts to send material aid or engaging in other acts which may be illegal in their countries through, to the tendency to highlight "engaging" content. We might also ask what happens when solidarity pages disappear, as at least two of those we examined did. The reasons for this are unclear (they may have been removed by Facebook, shut down by users, or simply renamed), but whatever community and organizing energy formed around them would largely, and almost instantly, dissipate. Similarly, although Libcom is not bound by profit motives, it is shaped by the particular norms of the activist community which develops and inhabits it, and it does not have access to the same resources available to corporate social media. We might imagine very different social media materialities which better support solidarity efforts – algorithms that privilege discussions around organizing material aid, for example, or tools which more effectively and securely connect those wanting to visit Kurdish autonomous areas with those who might help them do so. Perhaps such imagined materialities offer ways not only of seeing the limitations of current social media more clearly, but also possibilities for activists to create new non-profit social media. Although, again, the stubborn issue of resources remains, especially as the development of effective social media infrastructure requires increasingly complex programming and increased computing power.

References

Ali, B. (2016). Eroding the State in Rojava. *Theory & Event*, 19(1).

'anagoldman' (2015, February 11). What proportion of anarchists support the Rojava revolution? Libcom. Retrieved from http://libcom.org/forums/middle-east/what-proportion-anarchists-support-rojava-revolution-11022015.

The Anarchist Federation (2014, December 1). Anarchist Federation statement on Rojava: December 2014. Libcom. Retrieved from http://libcom.org/news/anarchist-federation-statement-rojava-december-2014-02122014.

'Anti War' (2015, May 3). 'I have seen the future and it works.' – Critical questions for supporters of the Rojava revolution. Libcom. Retrieved from http://libcom.org/library/'i-have-seen-future-it-works'—-critical-questions-supporters-rojava-revolution.

boyd, D. M., & Ellison, N. B. (2007). Social Network Sites: Definition, History, and Scholarship. *Journal of Computer-Mediated Communication*, 13(1), pp. 210–230.

Brighton Kurdish Solidarity (2016). A meeting with Kobanê's Democratic Youth Union. In: E. Egret & T. Anderson (Eds.), *Struggles for Autonomy in Kurdistan* (pp. 72–74). London: Corporate Watch.

Bucher, T. (2017). The algorithmic imaginary: exploring the ordinary affects of Facebook algorithms. *Information, Communication & Society*, 20(1), pp. 30–44.

'Chilli Sauce' (2015, April 6). Dear cheerleaders, we need to have a chat about imperialism. Libcom. Retrieved from http://libcom.org/blog/dear-cheerleaders-we-need-have-chat-about-imperialism-04042015.

'Conner Owens' (2015, April 5). Dear cheerleaders, we need to have a chat about imperialism. Libcom. Retrieved from http://libcom.org/blog/dear-cheerleaders-we-need-have-chat-about-imperialism-04042015.

Croeser, S., & Highfield, T. (2015). Mapping Movements–Social Movement Research and Big Data: Critiques and Alternatives. In: G. Elmer, G. Langlois, & J. Redden (Eds.), *Compromised Data: From Social Media to Big Data* (pp. 173–201). New York: Bloomsbury Publishing USA.

van Dijck, J., & Poell, T. (2013). Understanding Social Media Logic. *Media and Communication*, 1(1), pp. 2–14.

Dirik, D. (2016, May 4). Challenging privilege: on solidarity and self-reflection. *ROAR Magazine*. Retrieved from https://roarmag.org/essays/privilege-revolution-rojava-solidarity.

'Ed' (2015, April 5). Dear cheerleaders, we need to have a chat about imperialism. Libcom. Retrieved from http://libcom.org/blog/dear-cheerleaders-we-need-have-chat-about-imperialism-04042015.

Egret, E., & Anderson, T. (Eds.) (2016). *Struggles for Autonomy in Kurdistan*. London: Corporate Watch.

Feed the Revolution (2016). Coop Funding. Retrieved from https://coopfunding.net/en/campaigns/feed-the-revolution.

Ferguson, A. (2009a). Iris Young, Global Responsibility, and Solidarity. In: A. Ferguson & M. Nagel (Eds.), *Dancing with Iris: The Philosophy of Iris Marion Young* (pp. 185–197). Oxford: Oxford University Press.

Ferguson, M. L. (2009b). Resonance and Dissonance: The Role of Personal Experience in Iris Marion Young's Feminist Phenomenology. In: A. Ferguson & M. Nagel (Eds.), *Dancing with Iris: The Philosophy of Iris Marion Young* (pp. 51–66). Oxford: Oxford University Press.

'Flint' (2015, April 6). Dear cheerleaders, we need to have a chat about imperialism. Libcom. Retrieved from http://libcom.org/blog/dear-cheerleaders-we-need-have-chat-about-imperialism-04042015.

Goldberg, M. (2015, November 25). American Leftists Need to Pay More Attention to Rojava. *Slate*. Retrieved from http://www.slate.com/blogs/xx_factor/2015/11/25/rojava_is_a_radical_experiment_in_democracy_in_northern_syria_american_leftists.html.

Gould, C. C. (2007). Transnational Solidarities. *Journal of Social Philosophy*, 38(1), pp. 148–164.

Hakim, H. (2014, February 2). Iraqi law recognizes Kurdish, other languages. *Al-Monitor*. Retrieved from http://www.al-monitor.com/pulse/politics/2014/02/iraq-kurds-minorities-language-rights.html.

Hamad, R. (2015, December 3). Feminism is still happening where you least expect it. *Daily Life*. Retrieved from http://www.dailylife.com.au/news-and-views/dl-opinion/feminism-is-still-happening-where-you-least-expect-it-20151202-gldzan.html.

Highfield, T. (2016). *Social media and everyday politics*. Cambridge: Polity Press.

'Jef Costello' (2006, September 2). help out! Libcom. Retrieved from http://libcom.org/notes/help-out.
Jineoloji. (2017, June 24). Looking Into History With Jineoloji. Retrieved from http://jineoloji.org/en/2017/06/24/looking-into-history-with-jineoloji.
Jinha News Agency (2015, September 28). French occupiers declare autonomy in solidarity with Kurdistan. Retrieved from http://jinha.com.tr/en/ALL-NEWS/content/view/32550.
Khalidi, A. (2016, December 31). Turkey shutters Kurdish language institute. Kurdistan24. Retrieved from http://www.kurdistan24.net/en/culture/74f1926e-6864-46c0-b2bf-c00d10f6a5f7/Turkey-shutters-Kurdish-language-institute.
'Khawaga' (2015, February 11). What proportion of anarchists support the Rojava revolution? Libcom. Retrieved from http://libcom.org/forums/middle-east/what-proportion-anarchists-support-rojava-revolution-11022015#comment-552694.
Knefel, J. (2016, June 7). A Hello to Arms: A New Generation of Steely-Gazed Anarcho-Communists Head Off to Syria. *Village Voice*. Retrieved from http://www.villagevoice.com/news/a-hello-to-arms-a-new-generation-of-steely-gazed-anarcho-communists-head-off-to-syria-8705087.
Kurdish Question (2017, June 28). Facebook removes tags relating to Rojava, YPG and Kurds. Retrieved from http://kurdishquestion.com/article/3943-facebook-removes-kurdish-tags-relating-to-rojava-ypg-and-kurds
Libcom (2007). Who are the libcom group? Retrieved from http://libcom.org/notes/about/who-are-libcom-group.
Libcom (2010). What Are You Reading? Retrieved from http://libcom.org/forums/history-culture/what-are-you-reading-24052010.
Libcom (2012). Anarchism: reading guide. Retrieved from http://libcom.org/library/anarchism-reading-guide.
Libcom (2016). Suggested Reading? Retrieved from http://libcom.org/forums/general/suggested-reading-30122016.
Libcom (2017). User account. Retrieved from http://libcom.org/user/register.
Magpie, J. (2016). A very serious women's revolution. In E. Egret & T. Anderson (Eds.), *Struggles for Autonomy in Kurdistan* (pp. 64–69). London: Corporate Watch.
Milan, S. (2015). When Algorithms Shape Collective Action: Social Media and the Dynamics of Cloud Protesting. *Social Media + Society*, 1(2).
Minorities at Risk Project (2004). Chronology for Kurds in Turkey. refworld. Retrieved from http://www.refworld.org/docid/469f38e91e.html.
Mohanty, C. T. (2003). "Under Western Eyes" Revisited: Feminist Solidarity through Anticapitalist Struggles. *Signs*, 28(2), pp. 499–535.
Neumayer, C., Rossi, L., & Karlsson, B. (2016). Contested Hashtags: Blockupy Frankfurt in Social Media. *International Journal of Communication*, 10, pp. 5558–5579.
Neumayer, C., & Svensson, J. (2016). Activism and radical politics in the digital age: Towards a typology. *Convergence*, 22(2), pp. 131–146.
Oakes, D., & Goswell, G. (2016, February 10). Australian who wanted to fight IS brands failed case against him "ridiculous, absurd". ABC. Retrieved from http://www.abc.net.au/news/2016-02-10/failed-case-against-jamie-williams-could-encourage-others/7155672.
Ocalan, A. (2011). Democratic Confederalism. International Initiative. Free Öcalan. Retrieved from http://www.freeocalan.org/wp-content/uploads/2012/09/Ocalan-Democratic-Confederalism.pdf.
'Peter Storm' (2015, April 4). Dear cheerleaders, we need to have a chat about imperialism. Libcom. Retrieved from http://libcom.org/blog/dear-cheerleaders-we-need-have-chat-about-imperialism-04042015.

'Richard 1917' (2016, March 8). Rojava Revolution and its backers. Libcom. Retrieved from http://libcom.org/forums/middle-east/rojava-revolution-its-backers-08032016.
Sharifi, A. (2014, May 22). Iran's Language War against the Kurdistan Region. RÛDAW. Retrieved from http://www.rudaw.net/english/opinion/220520141.
Treré, E., & Mattoni, A. (2015). Media ecologies and protest movements: main perspectives and key lessons. *Information, Communication & Society*, 19(3), pp. 290–306.
Yakinthou, C., & Croeser, S. (2016). Transforming Tunisia: Transitional Justice and Internet Governance in a Post-Revolutionary Society. *International Journal of Transitional Justice*, 10 (2), pp. 230–249.
'Zaher Baher' (2016, February 1). Our attitude towards Rojava must be critical solidarity. Libcom. Retrieved from http://libcom.org/library/our-attitude-towards-rojava-must-be-critical-solidarity.

3

NOMADS OF CYBER-URBAN SPACE

Media hybridity as resistance

Emiliano Treré

Introduction and outline

"Matter" matters in activism. Technological infrastructures represent the material substratum that sustains and facilitates the communicative activities of social movements and activist collectives. Laptops, hard drives, antennas, and cables allow protesters to organize, store content, network and transmit relevant information. Yet, the recognition of the significance of media materiality within digital activism has somehow fluctuated between accounts that either overemphasize its role in constraining activists' agency (Scholz 2010) or conceived it as the taken-for-granted background of digital protest (Tarrancón et al. 2011). The neglect of the material essence of media technologies has been paired by the tendency to analyze the spatiality of contemporary protest movements in terms of dichotomies, treating the physical and the digital as two separate territories, and generally disregarding the material multiplicity and spatial hybridity that characterize the practices of contemporary movements. Contrasting these fallacies, I will chart the material multiplicity of social movements as a complex phenomenon, conceiving the material and the social as co-constitutive, and examining the different *strata* that compose the material multiplicity of activist practices. Moreover, I will illustrate how activists perilously traverse the spatial hybridity constituted by the incessant interaction between online and offline relations.

In this chapter, I look at the Mexican Barrio Nómada activist collective from Ciudad Juárez. I explore its practices of "total communication" that entail the incessant combination of online environments and offline spaces, the merging of old and new media artifacts, the disruption of corporate social media, and the concomitant activation of autonomous platforms. By examining diverse manifestations of media materiality, the chapter contributes to the debate on the significance of media materiality within contemporary digitally networked activism. It demonstrates that total communication is not just a matter of communicative abundance, but that technological multiplicity and hybridity can represent forms of resistance *per se* because sustaining a varied technological ecology keeps the dissemination of critical content flowing under every adversity. It details the ways through which the Barrio is able to traverse the complexity of the modern cyber-urban environment, demonstrating that bodies still reside at the centre of collective action, but, in contrast to an image of counter-power as a smooth journey between "spaces of places" and "spaces of flows", it shows that Mexican activists' nomadic practices are plagued by insecurity and uncertainty.

Spatiality and materiality in digital activism: overcoming three fallacies

How do we investigate the multiplicity of media practices of a nomadic activist collective? How do we make sense of these practices, since the actors of the collective continuously merge different media artifacts and traverse several spaces? To answer these questions, it is necessary to move beyond three fallacies that have plagued the field of digital activism: the fallacy of *spatial dualism*; the fallacy of *technological presentism*; and the fallacy of *alternativeness*.

The fallacy of spatial dualism

At the beginning of the 2000s, some studies of social movements and online technologies emphasized the risks associated with the "virtualization" of movements. In an important edited collection on cyber-activism, McCaughey and Ayers (2003) wondered if there was still a role for the body in the new forms of online activism. This reflection was timely; enchanted by the innovative possibilities offered by online technologies, many researchers had proclaimed a new era of virtual revolts, and forgotten the key role that physical locations, local contexts, and embodied experiences play in protest and mobilization. The realm of the virtual was associated with an imaginary of seamlessness and horizontal communication, separated from the many constraints of the offline realm. This tendency to treat the digital/virtual/cyber and the offline/physical/real differently, which Merlyna Lim has called the "fallacy of spatial dualism" (Lim 2015: 118), has had profound consequences for how we understand digital activism. It has engendered a vision of digital protest as inherently emancipatory and separated from the materiality of physical spaces. New approaches are progressively abandoning initial concerns of the loss of physicality. Movements navigate what Castells (2007) calls the space of flows and the space of places, and what Lim denominates "cyber-urban space" (Lim 2015) and researchers have started to devote specific attention to the spatial dynamics of contention (Gerbaudo 2012), the imbrications between online and offline environments (Frenzel et al. 2014), and the role of the body in contemporary protests (Butler 2015).

Nonetheless, the imaginary of virtuality/immateriality associated with digital media within contentious activities still lurks within recent accounts. This may be partly explained by the fact that both science and technology studies (STS) and communication and media studies have an uneasy relationship with the materiality of media (Lievrouw 2014). A notable exception is Medium Theory, which has placed materiality of media systems and artifacts at the centre, but with a rather deterministic inclination. Precisely the protracted struggle against technological determinism has somehow had the unintended consequence of conflating determinism with the material (Leonardi & Barley 2008), depriving this aspect of the recognition it deserves.

For Leah Lievrouw, to restore the attention to materiality it is vital to focus on the mediation framework that accounts for the dynamic articulation of artifacts, practices and social arrangements. According to this scholar, artifacts can be *reconfigured* according to people's purposes and actions, but also devices and systems shape users' practices and expectations about what artifacts can and cannot do, and about what people are able to do with them (i.e. practices are *remediated*). Finally, social formations are open to *reformation*, insofar as they "respond and adapt to available systems and devices and to communication practices and norms" (Lievrouw 2014: pos. 1037). Lievrouw aligns her model with Hutchby's (2001) theory of affordances. In order to eschew the poles of technological and social determinism, this concept frames the interaction between the material and the social as a socio-material constellation, recognizing the two aspects as co-constituent parts of any potential action (Allen-Robertson 2017).

In this chapter, I follow Lim (2015) in conceptualizing contemporary movements as navigating "cyber-urban space", a socially constructed environment "produced in the interaction of, and within a continuum of, online and offline relations" (ibid: 118). My understanding of materiality draws on Lievrouw and Ian Hutchby's conceptual work in order to chart materiality as a complex, dynamic and multidimensional phenomenon, recognizing the social and the material as co-constitutive. Inspired by Bruno Latour, my conception of digital activism relies on the attribution of analytical symmetry to human and non-human actors, acknowledging the role of technological systems and material artifacts in constituting action (Johnson 1988). As Lievrouw (2011) herself has clarified, activist media are one of the most emblematic *loci* to observe the process of reconfiguring technological artifacts. For decades, these aspects have been at the centre of alternative/community/citizen media explorations, and recently of social movement studies interested in the movement-media dynamic (Mattoni & Treré 2014).

The fallacy of technological presentism

Many accounts of digital protests are affected by a pronounced technological presentism. Elsewhere, Alice Mattoni and I have defined this fallacy as the "technological-fascination bias", referring to "the tendency of treating the latest technological platform as a fetish when considering social movements" (Mattoni

& Treré 2014: 255). The need to overcome a reductionist approach biased towards technological newness has infused recent years' various strands of research at the intersection between media and political participation. A multi-faceted field of "hybrid research" has emerged (Iannelli 2016: 36): from Andrew Chadwick's "hybrid media systems" (Chadwick 2013) to research that relies on the ecological trope to make sense of the dynamic between media and social movements (Mercea et al. 2016; Treré 2012). In this chapter, I share the key assumptions of these conceptualizations in order to eschew the technological fascination with the new and investigate the communicative complexity, multiplicity, and hybridity of the Barrio collective.

The fallacy of alternativeness

Accounts of digital protest have tended to remain uncritical regarding the corporate nature of digital platforms, overlooking the contradictions of social media power, and their implications for activist practices. Hence, the problematic equation "social media as alternative media" still resonates within the field. In order to overcome this fallacy, studies in digital activism (Dencik & Leistert 2015; Fuchs 2014; Galis & Neumayer 2016; Poell & van Dijck 2016) and alternative media (Rodríguez et al. 2014; Hemer & Tufte 2016) have converged over the recognition of the increasing relevance of the political economy of digital platforms when investigating activist practices and their material artifacts, echoing the current attempt to reconcile infrastructure studies (from STS) and platform studies (from media studies) (Plantin et al. 2018).

This aspect is also largely absent in STS approaches, in the conceptual frameworks of Lievrouw and Hutchby, and in other recent conceptualizations such as W. Lance Bennett and Alexandra Segerberg's "connective action" (Bennett and Segerberg 2013). Nevertheless, it is key to understand "the tensions arising when media environments increasingly essential to our daily lives (infrastructures) are dominated by corporate entities (platforms)" (Plantin et al. 2018: 3). Indeed, contemporary activism is characterized by "a complicated marriage" with social media platforms (Galis & Neumayer 2016: 2), whose materiality needs to be critically unveiled in order to appreciate them "as active agents shaping the symbolic and organizational processes of social actors" (Milan 2015: 897). Following these approaches, my understanding of "the material" is informed by a "socio-material sensitivity" (Carlile et al. 2013) that investigates the consequences of materiality in the context of the increasing corporatization of digital environments, and the resulting negotiations and tactics of activists in their everyday struggle against digital capitalism (Barassi 2015).

Overall, my case study – the Mexican Barrio Nómada activist collective from Ciudad Juárez – aims to overcome these three fallacies. To go beyond the fallacy of spatial dualism, I look at how the Barrio navigates "cyber-urban space". I chart materiality as a complex, dynamic and multidimensional phenomenon, assuming the social and the material as co-constitutive. To correct the fallacy of presentism, I investigate the communicative complexity, multiplicity, and hybridity of the

Mexican collective. And finally, to expose the alternativeness fallacy, I adopt a "socio-material sensitivity" grounded in political economy in order to scrutinize the consequences of materiality when activist practices are increasingly carried out within corporate environments.

Mexican violence, Ciudad Juárez and the emergence of the Barrio Nómada

Adopting a decolonial, feminist approach to the outburst of violence in Mexico and in the Global South, activist-philosopher Sayak Valencia (2010) argues that violence itself has become a product within hyper-consumerist neoliberal capitalism. Tortured and dismembered bodies have become commodities to be traded and used for profit in an age of widespread impunity and governmental austerity. According to Valencia, contemporary Mexico, and especially its border spaces, is experiencing *Gore capitalism*, i.e. a new, extreme manifestation of neoliberal capitalism, where death has become the most profitable business, human rights have deteriorated, and civil society is almost helpless. Ciudad Juárez represents the epitome of Gore capitalism, and it has also morphed into a prophetic exercise of science of the present: to become "Juaritos" (Mexican slang for Juárez) is the fate that could touch the Mexican state as a whole, if there is no reversal of trend in the spiral of ferocity that has shacked the foundations of the country.

Ciudad Juárez has always been a territory of transit, of migrants and commercial flows. The 1990s were determinant to forge the scene of violence that characterizes the Juárez of the present, and the 1994 Free Trade Agreement with the USA marked the beginning of a new era of violence. At present, the rivalry between cartel groups has generated a climate of macabre violence that includes beheadings, public mutilations, summary executions, disappearances, and kidnappings.

Within this situation, many niches of resistance have emerged, and both individuals and organized groups have found an antidote against barbarism in art, culture, and education. In 2010, the Zyrko Nómada de Combate (Nomadic Fighting Circus) group was formed by several artists from Juárez who decided to rebel together against an omnipresent "culture of death". Zyrko Nómada was a group of jugglers, poets, hip-hop musicians, street theatre artists, independent journalists and digital activists who carried out their activities in parks, abandoned houses, communal spaces, bars, museums, theatres, and universities. They tried to involve the citizenry also through workshops that covered a wide range of artistic practices including graffiti, video installations, street theatre performances, analogue and digital photography, digital audio recording techniques, the realization of short films, and the resistance in digital environments.

After a year of activity, a branch of the Zyrko Nómada was transformed into the Barrio. The idea was that if activists needed to continue to denounce the situation of Juarez, it was necessary to spread the word in all Mexican cities and beyond. The Zyrko decided that, although a part of the collective would have necessarily remained in Juárez to continue fighting *in loco*, another part had to start the denunciation outside the city according to the motto of the collective: "Juaritos is the future" (Blissett 2012), that is to say, Juárez is a vision of what Mexico could be like within a few years, representing the most brutal expression of the results of a mixture of uncontrolled crime, militarization, and impunity for criminals.

Methodologies

To study the practices of the nomadic activists, I have combined different methodologies. In September 2011, I built a Wiki platform where I started to ask questions and suggest reflections about the communicative dynamics of the collective. It is well known that, unlike a blog, where comments do not have the same "importance" as posts, the Wiki platform allows all registered users to make modifications and collaborate on an equal basis in the development of the document. The Wiki page allowed me to track the collective's practices and trajectories during the period of investigation.

In addition, 11 individual interviews and a group interview with Barrio activists (for a total of more than 20 hours of digital recording) were carried out to deepen the reflection on the most important aspects emerging from the Wiki. In three cases, the interviews were conducted through Skype, due to the difficulty of physically gathering some of the activists. The research involved the use of the "active interviewing" technique developed by Holstein and Gubrium (1995) that provides agency to the research participants through broad questions, conceiving the interviewees not as mere containers of answers, but as active subjects and constructors of knowledge.

A qualitative analysis of the content of nearly 200 messages from Facebook, Twitter, the blog and the mailing list of the group was also carried out. The content analysis was based on Ryan and Bernard's (2003) model with themes to be analyzed built from the topics that are most frequently repeated in the interviews and on the Wiki and which appear as the most important for the actors of the collective. Research is complemented by the data gathered during the participation of Barrio activists in meetings, workshops, seminars and exhibitions organized in Querétaro, Mexico City, and Puebla. Additional insights were derived from the cyber-activism workshop that I co-organized with the Barrio at the Autonomous University of Querétaro (Mexico). The research on which this chapter is based was intended to be a piece of "engaged research" (Milan 2010); it seeks to make a difference to the communities that are investigated. In this case, the key aim was to critically reflect on the challenges and opportunities of the communicative practices of the Barrio collective.

Practicing total communication

In times of technological plenitude, activist groups can blend multiple artifacts, technologies and platforms to create and spread their content. We are thus faced with a complex ecology of media technologies, whose adoption is a source of continuous negotiations, adaptations, and adjustments (Barassi 2015; Treré 2012). Never was this so palpable as with the exploration of contemporary's activist practices. The internet does not represent a merely technological layer that is added to a plethora of pre-existing technological choices, but it exemplifies instead a broad ecosystem of technological possibilities, hybrid interconnections and reconfigurations. It is a platform where all media, like the radio, the television, and the newspaper are undergoing a process of remediation (Bolter & Grusin 2000). The Barrio is exploiting this communicative exuberance to its fullest. The collective has one main blog and various peripheral ones, two accounts on Facebook, three accounts on Twitter, several accounts on YouTube, one mailing list, plus assorted accounts for autonomous television transmission on live-streaming platforms, and radio broadcast on online servers. The Barrio blog brings together in a single macro-platform a series of micro-platforms that offer the most disparate services: the *Rizoma Radio* online broadcaster; the *Ollin TV* platform; the *Offline Publisher*, which is the online page of the publisher of the Barrio that prints his publications in both paper and digital format (its name is particularly evocative, especially to communication scholars); the literary project *El libro portátil* (The Portable Book); the newspaper *Juaritos Times*, and the contemporary art project *Hilo Rojo* (Red Wire). Hence, literary texts, alternative television, radio programmes, videos and the traditional posts of the blog coexist in a single technological platform that represents the digital headquarter of the collective, and yet it only accounts for a fraction of their communicative essence. Although digital resistance tactics today constitute a considerable part of the Barrio's activities, the creation of posters, graffiti, stickers, theatre, music and circus performances still lies firmly at the heart of the collective. With the words "what is not printed does not exist", an activist of the Barrio caught my attention during a conversation. Even if this statement may sound strange in the mouth of a heavily mediatized activist, it made me reflect on the ephemeral nature of online environments and about the need to multiply content visibility through the incessant production of books, flyers, stickers, and graffiti, which is key to Barrio's confrontational tactics. As one Barrio activist perfectly articulates it:

> We have an idea that we want people to listen to, so we have to use every possible means, offline and online. We disseminate our messages with dance, music, poetry, theatre, literature, free software, stamps on t-shirts, magazines, and walls. And then the blog, Twitter, Facebook, etc. The world is complex, there are people who are totally "cybernetic", but there are many people who do not have access to digital technologies. Our aim is to communicate with all the people and thus we combine media: it is the idea of total communication.

The idea of "total communication" pervades the communicative practices of the Barrio. The pressing need to reach a broad universe of both digitally connected and disconnected people is the *raison d'être* of their incessant navigation of the different layers of media hybridity that are in a state of permanent tension. These tensions go beyond the three fallacies analyzed in the conceptual section of this chapter, as it is shown in Table 3.1. Thus, the findings sections will be organized around these three hybrid communicative tensions.

TABLE 3.1 Relation between fallacies and the hybrid communicative tensions of "total communication"

Fallacies	*Barrio Total Communication – Hybrid tensions*
Spatial dualism	Cyber-urban space: Online and offline interweaving
Technological presentism	Digital nomadism between new and old media: cyber-nomadism kit, mobile "Alejandrías" and back-up practices
Alternativeness	Liquid activism: the disruptive use of social media

First hybrid communicative tension: online and offline interweaving

Barrio activists consider physical relationships as key: the building of networks through informal talks, hugging, the handing of leaflets, workshops, performances, jam sessions, etc. All these practices represent the engine of the collective since interpersonal relationships provide an irreplaceable plus. In the words of a Barrio activist:

> We travel a lot and we move to go where the people are, to spread our messages and ideas on how to change things in Juárez and Mexico, and denounce barbarism and war. We do it both online and offline, but the contacts, the possibility of seeing us, touching us, hugging us, laughing together... All these things, and more, we just need to do them and we will never stop doing them. It is also part of our idea of total communication, but it goes beyond this, it is something fundamental and irreplaceable.

For Barrio activists, the online and the offline are just two interrelated and inseparable faces of the total communication coin, integrated realms that are never opposed, but instead incessantly feeding each other. While digital networks are necessary to continue the spreading of critical contents, they are at the same time key to organize the whole range of physical activities carried out in different parts of the country, contacting other groups and promoting events in museums, universities and community spaces. The natural combination of digital artifacts and physical encounters that characterize the practices of total communication radically opposes the vision of a separate and somehow evanescent virtual sphere. On the contrary, it reveals the plasticity of Barrio activists relentlessly crossing and integrating environments: their dusty backpacks full of cables, memory cards, and antennas; their blog announcing the umpteenth gig; their radio playing in the background a freshly recorded track on the move. This plasticity is particularly striking because the bodies of the activists are at the centre of the action. Their physical relations and multiple encounters give us a picture of a vibrant, passionately lived cyber-urban space, where the intensity of the online and the offline intertwine and mutually reinforce each other.

Second hybrid communicative tension: digital nomadism between new and old media

Digital nomads of the present[1]

When a part of the Zyrko Nómada was transformed into the Barrio Nómada there was a strong intensification of digital activism, but the building of physical ties increased as well. Barrio activists began to use digital technologies to communicate with the part of the collective that continued working in Juárez, while concurrently organizing their nomadism by networking with communities and groups throughout the country, as well as with global activist networks at the European, North-American and Latin American level. One of the most remarkable parts of the cyber-activism seminar that I organized together with Barrio activists was when one of them unveiled the significance of his "cyber-nomadism kit", i.e. a medium-sized backpack that contains all the tools for articulating dissidence about *Juaritos* on the move. The kit is composed of a powerful 11-inch laptop with the Ubuntu free software operating system; an external 500-gigabyte hard drive; a 16-gigabyte SD card; a repeater to power (and hack) wireless networks; a smartphone with an 8-gigabyte micro SD memory; a professional portable microphone; a high-resolution webcam; a high-resolution digital camera; rechargeable micro-speakers; phone cards for different Mexican states; a USB key for broadband connections; and a box with all the stickers and the leaflets regarding the activities of the Barrio. These varied artifacts enable the activists of the collective to carry out a multitude of practices on the move, including recording and transmitting radio and television programs; taking pictures and recording videos; creating and broadcasting bases for improvised live performances; and hacking wireless networks to send emails, update the blog, curate social media platforms, chat, and edit photos, videos and sound files.

But one might be tempted to imagine the digital nomadism of the Barrio as a fluid, smooth ride across multiple spaces and media materialities. Despite the wide array of technological possibilities at their disposal, their savviness in appropriating them and their ability in navigating them, Barrio activists' spatial journey is plagued by the many contradictions of the violent and profoundly unstable context of contemporary Mexico, with the constant threat of being assaulted, robbed, and killed either by the Narcos or by the corrupt police.

Bridging materialities: "mobile Alejandrías" and back-up practices

One of the most fascinating practices of Barrio activists is their use of what they define as "mobile Alejandrías". With this term, they poetically evoke the image of the library of Alexandria with reference to hard drives on which blog back-ups, social media contacts and relevant files of the Barrio are first stored, and then tactically concealed in strategic places inside Mexico and abroad. These hidden artifacts are activated in case of technical issues and other complications with corporate platforms (see below), so that Barrio activists can use the saved databases of contacts and digital material to restore and upload another version of the blog, and create other accounts on social media platforms. While activists predispose other social media accounts, their Riseup.net mailing list temporarily intensifies its activities until the new accounts are operational.

This represents an interesting case of crossover between the materiality of hard drives and the cyber-materiality of digital data and social networks. In addition, some members of the collective use the ordinary mail to send materials related to the Barrio such as books, CDs, DVDs, stickers and magazines, with the aim of providing people with "not only bits but also something to touch and pass from hand to hand", as one Barrio activist remarks. Sometimes this material includes USB sticks filled with Barrio's data that are materially sent through the ordinary mail to the most remote and disconnected areas of the country. The recipients of this material are citizens that have expressed their will to remain informed about the activities of the Barrio, but can only sporadically plug into a reliable internet connection, often through low-bandwidth networks that do not allow them to stream videos and open large files.

In sum, the media hybridity of the Barrio comprises intricate layers of new and old media that activists incessantly, and perilously navigate. These media serve various purposes, display different levels of visibility, and are activated/deactivated/replaced at different times. Furthermore, we have appreciated how the political economy of their communication matters, since older media formats are preferred in order to reach more technologically isolated publics.

Third hybrid communicative tension: liquid activism and the disruptive use of social media

Recent years have witnessed the powerful comeback of critical theory in the field of media and communication, especially through the political economy of communication, and the analysis of social media platforms (Fuchs 2017). This area of research has exhibited the exploitative nature of Web 2.0 and of social media platforms, such as Facebook, YouTube and Twitter, and their embeddedness in the dynamics of neoliberal capitalism and its logic of always-on consumption. As these studies have shown, social media function as enclosures that mine our personal data for marketing purposes, reinvigorating the exploitative mechanisms of more traditional media, but at an unprecedented scale. Barrio activists are well aware of the corporate nature of social media technologies. Yet, they try to show that if these platforms take advantage of their contents in the logic of capitalist exploitation, they also exploit the possibilities offered by Facebook, Twitter, and YouTube to increase their visibility. As one activist explains:

> We know the risks, we know who is behind these platforms, how they use our data and our networks to profit. But we use them as they use us; it is as if we were a Trojan horse, infiltrating in their mechanisms, taking advantage of the possibilities to have more visibility in the networks.

Using 2.0 environments has become a necessity for this collective, whose goal is to reach the highest number of followers, particularly people who do not normally read content on online radical platforms or fanzines, and can only be found on Facebook and other popular social media. Like many contemporary movements, Barrio actors "colonize" and appropriate these platforms developing resistance practices in a constant dialectic amid the will to maximize their visibility, and the precaution related to the dangers that these networks suppose (Dencik & Leistert 2015).

These dangers also include the surveillance of police and other authorities. In recent years, several Twitter users were imprisoned in Mexico for sending "false" messages related to narco-trafficking activities, and penalties were created or aggravated in different states of the country in relation to "disruptive" uses of social networks. Aware that the situation in Mexico is becoming increasingly problematic also in relation to social media, Barrio activists take precautions in writing messages, check the sources and the origin of the information they spread, and relentlessly expand their media ecology. In the case of a sudden shutdown of their social media accounts, other already arranged platforms can be used to replace them (the mailing list and the blog). At the same time, new social accounts are created by deploying back-up data from hard drives located in strategic locations (as we noted in the previous section). The Barrio mailing list is hosted on Riseup.net, which provides online communication tools for people and groups working on emancipatory social change, and guarantees that the data transmitted will not be delivered to public authorities or private companies. The evolving assortment of the platforms and networks used, in conjunction with their continuous nomadism, make the people of the collective difficult to trace by the authorities. As an activist tells me, "horizontality is a weapon. We are gelatinous, difficult to individuate, we constantly move and we are nomads, diffuse: our nature is liquid".

The rejection of leadership and the liquidity of their communicative practices are forms of struggle that the Barrio puts in place to challenge the control and the surveillance of 2.0 environments. There is nothing inherently emancipatory in social media: these platforms epitomize the contradictions of contemporary capitalism; their role is ambivalent and elusive, and the possibilities they provide for practicing activism have to be constantly negotiated, as the daily practices of the Barrio clearly elucidate.

Final remarks: material multiplicity, resistance and the perilous journey through cyber-urban space

This chapter has sought to explore the communicative practices developed by the Barrio Nómada collective to rebel against the culture of death and the extreme violence that characterizes the Mexican city of Ciudad Juárez. In particular, I have focussed on how Barrio activists navigate and reconfigure the materiality of artifacts and the cyber-materiality of online platforms. Throughout the chapter, we have observed how the idea of "total communication" that orients the practices of the collective is fulfilled in the incessant interplay, merging and navigation of three layers of media hybridity:

1. physical/digital space;
2. new/old media;
3. alternative/mainstream platforms.

The exploration of the Barrio's activist practices and their three layers of hybrid communicative tension provide an empirical contribution able to overcome the three main fallacies in the study on digital activism. The chapter contributes to the debate on media materiality by illustrating empirically how and why activists appropriate, combine and assemble a plethora of technological artifacts. By adopting a critical perspective that recognizes the contradictions of social media power. The chapter demonstrates that, although total communication thrives on the technological exuberance of the digital age, it is not just a matter of communicative abundance, but also a tactic of resistance *in itself*. First, at a more manifest level, the burgeoning of the communicative manifestations of the collective means that there are fewer possibilities that all critical content can be erased or lost at the same time. Second, at a more subterranean level, back-up hard drives and other hidden artifacts allow the recovery of data at any time, while other internal media channels provisionally compensate the loss of communicative effectiveness. Thus, the technological multiplicity, hybridity and deep media stratification of the Barrio represent an effective form of struggle and resistance *per se*: sustaining a wide and varied technological ecology is therefore fundamental to keeping the dissemination of critical content flowing under every possible condition.

Moreover, the chapter contributes to the debate on spatiality of social movements and activist collectives. It details how and in which ways the Barrio is able to appropriate and traverse the complexity of modern cyber-urban space. It demonstrates that bodies still firmly reside at the centre of collective action (Butler 2015): errant, nomadic, constantly under threat. The activists' journey is precarious, perilous, and hazardous. The reality of counter-power in Mexico could not be further away from the seemingly frictionless interplay between the spaces of flows and the spaces of places theorized by Castells (2007). Instead, it is an incessant quest, a dangerous leap into uncharted territories, a continuous hunt for new ways of surviving both offline and online, and to maintain the resistance flowing by any media necessary. Within contemporary Mexico, spatial hybridity and material multiplicity embody a painful necessity, the scream of a generation of activist-artists that are exploiting every possible communicative resource at their disposal in a desperate attempt to stem the fall of the Mexican state into the mouth of Gore capitalism.

Note

1 The title of this section, and of the whole chapter, is intended as a tribute to Alberto Melucci's masterpiece *Nomads of the present: Social movements and individual needs in contemporary society*, published in 1989.

References

Allen-Robertson, J. (2017). The materiality of digital media: The hard disk drive, phonograph, magnetic tape and optical media in technical close-up. *New Media & Society*, 19(3), pp. 455–470.

Barassi, V. (2015). *Activism on the web: Everyday struggles against digital capitalism*. London: Routledge.

Bennett, W. L., & Segerberg, A. (2013). *The logic of connective action: Digital media and the personalization of contentious politics*. Cambridge: Cambridge University Press.

Bolter, J. D., & Grusin, R. (2000). *Remediation: Understanding new media*. Cambridge, MA: MIT Press.

Blissett, A. (2012). Ciudad Juárez es el futuro. Suplemento Panóptico 34, Tribuna de Querétaro.

Butler, J. (2015). *Notes toward a performative theory of assembly*. Cambridge, MA: Harvard University Press.

Carlile, P. R., Nicolini, D., LangleyA., & Tsoukas, H. (2013). How matter matters: objects, artifacts, and materiality in organization studies. Introducing the Third Volume of "Perspectives on Organization Studies". In: P. R. Carlile, D. Nicolini, A. Langley and H. Tsoukas (Eds.). *How Matter Matters: Objects, Artifacts, and Materiality in Organization Studies* (pp. 1–15). Oxford: Oxford University Press.

Castells, M. (2007). Communication, power and counter-power in the network society. *International Journal of Communication*, 1(1), pp. 238–266.

Chadwick, A. (2013). *The hybrid media system: Politics and power*. Oxford: Oxford University Press.

Dencik, L., & Leistert, O. (Eds.) (2015). *Critical perspectives on social media and protest: Between control and emancipation*. Lanham, MD: Rowman & Littlefield International.

Frenzel, F., Feigenbaum, A., & McCurdy, P. (2014). Protest camps: An emerging field of social movement research. *The Sociological Review*, 62(3), pp. 457–474.

Fuchs, C. (2014). *OccupyMedia! The Occupy Movement and Social Media in Crisis Capitalism*. Winchester: Zero Books.

Fuchs, C. (2017). *Social media: A critical introduction*. London: Sage.

Galis, V., & Neumayer, C. (2016). Laying claim to social media by activists: a cyber-material détournement. *Social media+ society*, 2(3).

Gerbaudo, P. (2012). *Tweets and the Street: Social media and contemporary activism*. London: Pluto Press.

González Rodríguez, S. (2002). *Huesos en el desierto*. Barcelona: Anagrama.

Hemer, O., & Tufte, T. (Eds.) (2016). *Voice & Matter: Communication, Development and the Cultural Return*. Gothenburg: Nordicom.

Holstein, J., & Gubrium, J. (1995). *The active interview*. London: Sage.

Hutchby, I. (2001). Technologies, texts and affordances. *Sociology: The Journal of the British Sociological Association*, 35(2), pp. 441–456.

Iannelli, L. (2016). *Hybrid Politics: Media and Participation*. London: Sage.

Johnson, J. (1988). Mixing humans and nonhumans together: The sociology of a door-closer. *Social problems*, 35(3), pp. 298–310.

Leonardi, P. M., & Barley, S. R. (2008). Materiality and change: Challenges to building better theory about technology and organizing. *Information and Organization*, 18(3), pp. 159–176.

Lievrouw, L. (2011). *Alternative and activist new media*. Cambridge: Polity Press.

Lievrouw, L. (2014). Materiality and media in communication and technology studies: an unfinished project. In: T. Gillespie, P. J. Boczkowski & K. A. Foot (Eds.) *Media*

Technologies: Essays on Communication, Materiality, and Society (pp. 21–52). Cambridge, MA: The MIT Press.

Lim, M. (2015). A CyberUrban Space Odyssey: The spatiality of contemporary social movements. *New Geographies*, 7, pp. 117–123.

Mattoni, A., & Treré, E. (2014). Media practices, mediation processes, and mediatization in the study of social movements. *Communication Theory*, 24(3), pp. 252–271.

McCaughey, M., & Ayers, M. (2003). *Cyberactivism: Online activism in theory and practice.* New York: Routledge.

Mercea, D., Iannelli, L., & Loader, B. D. (2016). Special Issue on Protest Communication Ecologies. *Information, Communication and Society*, 19(3).

Milan, S. (2010). Toward an epistemology of engaged research. *International Journal of Communication*, 4, pp. 856–858.

Milan, S. (2015). When algorithms shape collective action: Social media and the dynamics of cloud protesting. *Social Media+Society*, 1(2).

Plantin, J. C., Lagoze, C., Edwards, P. N., & Sandvig, C. (2018). Infrastructure studies meet platform studies in the age of Google and Facebook. *New Media & Society*, 20(1), pp. 293–310.

Poell, T., & Dijck, J. (2016). Constructing public space: global perspectives on social media and popular contestation. *International Journal of Communication*, 10, pp. 226–234.

Raley, R. (2009). *Tactical media.* Minneapolis, MN: University Of Minnesota Press.

Rodríguez, C., Ferron, B., & Shamas, K. (2014). Four challenges in the field of alternative, radical and citizens' media research. *Media, Culture & Society*, 36(2), pp. 150–166.

Ryan, G. W., & Bernard, H. R. (2003). Techniques to Identify themes. *FieldMethods*, 15(1), pp. 85–109.

Scholz, T. (2010). Infrastructure: Its transformations and effect on digital activism. In: M. C. Joyce (Ed.), *Digital activism decoded: The new mechanics of change* (pp. 17–31). New York: IDEA.

TarrancónA., Borge-HolthoeferJ., & MorenoY. (2011). Estudio Sobre el 15M en las Redes Sociales. University of Zaragoza, Institute for Biocomputation and Physics of Complex Systems (BIFI) and CIERZO Development. Retrieved from https://www.enriquedans.com/2011/06/estudio-sobre-el-15m-en-redes-sociales.html.

Treré, E. (2012). Social Movements as Information Ecologies: Exploring the Coevolution of Multiple Internet Technologies for Activism. *International Journal of Communication*, 6, pp. 2359–2377.

Valencia, S. (2010). *Capitalismo Gore.* Madrid: Editorial Melusina.

PART II

Temporality

4

(SOCIAL) MEDIA TIME, CONNECTIVE MEMORY AND ACTIVIST TELEVISION HISTORIES

The case of *TV Stop* (1987–2005)

Tina Askanius

Introduction

> Do you remember TV Stop? When the naked guy strolled through the supermarket? When the recordings of the May 18th riots forced police to produce a new white paper? When prisoners were filmed breaking out? You now have the possibility to re-watch some of our most reckless, flippant and thought-provoking transmissions online.

With these opening lines, a press release distributed on 6 April 2012 announced the online relaunch of the Copenhagen-based activist TV channel *TV Stop* (1987–2005). *TV Stop* was formed by people involved in the Freetown Christiania as well as the squatter movement and operated out of the 3rd floor of the 1970s squat, "Folkets Hus" (The People's House). During its heyday between 1990 and 1995, when broadcasts were aired every night between 11pm and midnight, the channel gained popular attention, not least for its street-level reporting from within demonstrations and direct actions in Denmark and the neighbouring countries Germany and Sweden. The recordings from the anti-Maastricht demonstrations on 18 May 1993, documenting police shootings of civilians during the massive EU protests in Copenhagen, make for an illustrative case of how they sought to take on the role of media-as-watch-dog from the perspective of those in the streets when mainstream media failed to do so (Mathiasen et al. 1998). With its experimental left-wing advocacy reporting, *TV Stop* thus worked for a short period of time in the mid 1990s as the voice of a generation of activists and autonomous anarchists in the country but is considered to have had significant impact on media policies and the style of reporting in Danish TV journalism (Gansing 2013). When they shut down in 2005, they had been trying to keep afloat for quite some time and mainly had been airing reruns while struggling internally with how to position themselves in a changing media landscape. As the group reappeared in 2012, they had digitized considerable parts of the old VHS cassettes, opened up a YouTube channel to store and distribute their old broadcasts and a Facebook page to promote their online presence and potentially draw new audiences to the material.

The case of *TV Stop* and its efforts to revive itself online provide a rich opportunity for delving into questions of social media materialities from a temporal and historical perspective. I ask how social media are used as (historical) archives in ways that seek to facilitate connective memory between past, present and future political struggles in the specific context of activist video and television practices. The case of *TV Stop* is used to examine how they understand their own trajectory as activist media in relation to continuities and changes in the materialities and temporalities of the television medium with the advent of, first the internet, and later social media. How do they appropriate social media as digital archives to store and disseminate analogue material today? How do they understand the potential and limitations of social media in connecting historical and contemporary activism across generations and political struggles?

This contribution to critical debates on social media materialities and protest thus focusses specifically on the theories and practices of what we may loosely refer to as video activism. Today, digital media technologies and logics shape how activist videos are produced, distributed and experienced, and they are, for the most part, deeply enmeshed in the power dynamics and techno-commercial materialities of social media. Yet these practices have roots in previous forms of analogue, non-commercial television cultures and underground video collectives that run as far back as to the so-called "Portapak revolution" and guerrilla television movement of the 1960s and 1970s (see e.g. Boyle 1997). In this sense, the case study inscribes itself into an ongoing effort to pin down and understand what video activism means in a digital age as these practices are increasingly situated within the mechanisms of mobile technologies, digital networking and corporate control (see e.g. Askanius 2013; 2014). I am thus not only interested in probing the implications of digital proliferation, new forms of immediacy and the growing ubiquity of cameras to the specific practices of activist video and television production, but also in how we might understand these digital modes of activism as part of a broader historical trajectory. In this manner, I follow a shift in the cultural form that the channel uses to express itself – from analogue to digital – and in doing so, point to some of the possibilities but also problems in "going digital". I trace not merely the history of this specific channel, but also a general shift from analogue to digital video materiality, which essentially involves different forms of temporality, storage, memory.

I take as a starting point that important insights emerge if we rewind the tape to examine groups and networks involved in the historical forms of activist video and television practices. These practices precede contemporary activism characterized by online connective action based on the sharing of personalized content and personal action frames (Bennett & Segerberg 2012), and not least video campaigning and advocacy and experimentation with television as a protest form and activist medium. When I single out and focus on the processes of temporality and memory involved in the specificity of *TV Stop*'s social media relaunch, I seek to extrapolate from this case insights into how the material characteristics of social networking sites shape temporalities and alter the performative nature of memory more generally.

Connective memory, temporality and archive activism

To help me understand the lived experience of these continuities and changes, I turn to critical perspectives within the media/time/memory nexus drawing primarily on notions related to *time* and *temporal regimes* (Kaun 2015, 2017; Kaun & Stiernstedt 2012, 2014) as well as memory – connective memory (Hoskins 2011) and inter-generational memory (Ruiz 2014; Mitchell & Elwood 2013). The notion of connective memory is used to describe how memories are increasingly connected with and distributed across complex networks of digital media and technologies in a new media ecology (cf. also Garde-Hansen et al. 2009). To Hoskins, it is precisely these "digitally-enhanced paradoxes of flux and permanence, and immediacy (of access) and volume", that scale today's memory and he urges scholars to interrogate the prospects for the "sharedness, stability and continuity" of memory in a context where actors such as Google, YouTube and Facebook dictate the online spaces in which memory is held and passed on (Hoskins 2011: 22–23). I thus use the work of Hoskins to explore connective memories as performed on *TV Stop*'s social media; i.e. how YouTube is appropriated as an archive/database and Facebook as a noticeboard pushing traffic to "old news" from the archives anew.

This mix of concepts offers a framework through which we can think about the case of *TV Stop* in relation to media materialities. I am concerned with materiality in the specific context of television production and the pre-digital properties of the media landscape in which the channel operated. The majority of the broadcasts are on VHS, a largely obsolete medium, and all are in the process of decomposing. As the physical format of VHS is relatively bulky, *TV Stop*'s tape archive takes up physical space in boxes, on shelves, etc. This begs an understanding of materiality which emphasizes media as physical substance – as factual artifacts – that consist, in this case, of magnetic tape, head drums, plastic spools, casing and sleeves, etc. These material properties stand in contrast to the more intangible *social* media materialities, which in this context are understood not only in terms of the hard disks and servers now housing the digitized material but also as the algorithms and business models, which regulate and privilege certain modes of engagement with the content once uploaded onto social media. These materialities are examined in relation to how they produce time regimes of "speed, presentness and immediacy" (Kaun 2017: 473), which tend to annihilate both past and future. To be sure, social media are primarily built for present movements (Milan 2015) as they privilege cultures of "constant flow, speed and immediacy" (Kaun 2015: 222) and, through algorithms that compute popularity and interactions, produce regimes of "real-timeness" (Milan 2015: 890). At the same time, I consider how the reverse process – of trying to freeze and recover times past – is at play when social media are appropriated as archives to store and host data and recirculate collective memory in ways that open up possibilities for "connective memory" (Hoskins 2011) and for "archive activism" (Juhasz 2006). From the perspective of archive activism, we may understand social media, when put to work as digital archives, as mnemonic resources for remembering and reinvigorating debates, issues and struggles lived by past generations of activists. In this sense, social media are changing the ways in which activist histories are written and how memories are performed.

Methods

I use the case of *TV Stop* to reflect upon connective memory, archival activism and media time/temporalities in relation to social media materialities. These perspectives and concepts give me an analytical purchase on some of the key themes emerging from the mining of the empirical data. The case study draws on a combination of in-depth interviews and a thematic analysis of the digitized videos and the commemorative and performative practices of those engaging on the group's Facebook page, YouTube channel and webpage. The primary material consists of data from interviews conducted with five former activists, each lasting two–three hours. Two additional background interviews were conducted with people who were also involved in the activist media scene in Denmark at the time of *TV Stop* and who took over their broadcasting licence to initiate new alternative television projects (*TVTV*, 2005–2009 and *Kaos TV*, 2007–2014).

The secondary data set contains a mix of Facebook posts and comments (April 2012–May 2017), documents such as press releases, news articles on the relaunch and the 156 videos in the YouTube archive, all of which was subject to a thematic analysis and brought into dialogue with the main themes identified in the interview data. After having mined this rich data set, I identified three key themes related to the notion of time, memory and social media. These are, first, the idea of social media archives as a means of *storing and fixating time*. Second, I unpack social media temporalities in relation to a sense of wanting to *keep up with time* while feeling as if they are *running out of time*. Finally, I identify and analyze the idea of social media as nostalgic practices, and as part of a broader experience of *longing for lost times*.

Storing time: social media as archive and vehicles for connective memory

Even though news reporting on various confrontations between police and protesters, as well as reports from within demonstrations, is perhaps what the channel is best remembered for today, *TV Stop*'s range of programmes was made up of a mix of different forms of content: news reports, talk shows, mock-commercials, satiric sketches, concert recordings from the underground music scene in Copenhagen, and much more. This diversity is reflected in the body of 156 videos the group has chosen for online circulation. Despite being digitized, the grained and pixelated quality of the videos bears unmistakable traces of the material conditions of their production and distribution. The videos posted onto Facebook generate responses from mainly two groups of people: former loyal viewers or former *TV Stop* activists – so-called "Stoppers" as they refer to themselves. Only occasionally do young (new) audiences leave a comment. In this sense, social media seem to work less as a space to attract traffic from new audiences and more as an internal noticeboard and place of remembrance in which old activists and viewers keep informed and reconnect with each other. In the immediate aftermath of the relaunch, while the group was still in the process of digitizing, Facebook was used mainly to keep people updated about newly digitized video uploaded onto YouTube and the website. With time, the platform is rather used to sustain engagement around the content by sending out reminders of certain popular transmissions' anniversaries, pointing out how they mark important dates and historical political events with reminiscence to current events. For example, a post from Facebook with the headline "Today 20 years ago, anti-fascists and local citizens of Roskilde chased neo-Nazis out of the city as Jonni Hansen (DNSB[1]) attempted to organise an international Rudolf Hess march" (Facebook post 19 August 2015).

Often, as demonstrated above, a post presenting a broadcast from the archive will link to a topical newspaper article on the subject matter. By using the digital archive to "re-temporize events through their interactive assembling and mapping of disparate simultaneities" (Hoskins 2011: 281) and pointing to changes and continuities over time, these clips are reinstalled into public debate and consciousness. By publishing the old transmissions of anti-fascist protests strategically on certain red-letter-days, *TV Stop* thus seeks to tap into current debates in a context where neo-fascism and extreme-right activism is on the rise in Scandinavia.

According to the team behind the relaunch:

> It is about making sure that people who haven't seen this before get access to it. Especially the reports we did about the fight against neo-Nazism and fascism in the 1990s have been really important for me to get out there and made accessible.
>
> *(Interviewee 2)*

Respondents express an urge to pass on the histories of and lessons from significant events and struggles to new generations:

> We have a dream about this being passed on to kids in school. This is what the political landscape of the 1990s looked like on the radical left, and the far-right for that matter, and this is what the media landscape was like. I need to believe that we made a difference. I would love if my children in school could be presented with this material.
>
> *(Interviewee 1)*

Here we see reflected the affordances of social media as vehicles for what Ruiz (2014) has called "intergenerational memory" in social movements. She argues that, in a time where history, theory and context often get lost in the "nowness" of protests, media technologies can potentially span the ruptures and discontinuities between generations of activists and fill gaps in "our knowledge of how we got to where we are today" by "creating a mechanism through which the past is accumulated in the present" (Ruiz 2014: unpaginated). Archives – as sites of memory – have always been entangled with media technologies in some shape or form, but today social media have come to play an increasingly important role as memory archives and as a place of remembrance (Kaun & Stiernstedt 2012). The move to digital archiving in corporate social media however is changing how protest memory is held in profound ways that are subject to debate and in-group negotiations among activists.

Negotiations over the materialities of the digital archive

TV Stop's YouTube channel has first and foremost been appropriated as a database – a storage room. It has, if not replaced, then complemented the group's extensive raw film and VHS archive, which before the digitizing process began, was scattered across different physical storage sites. Boxes of unfiled VHS tapes with little or no signposting on the cassettes had up until then been spread around basements and storage warehouses in different parts of Copenhagen. As all other material objects, film is subjected to time and decay. The urge to digitize in this sense grew out of a very concrete *race against time* as they realized the impending risk of losing the raw material altogether because of the effect of time on the magnetic tapes which are, as all VHS from the 1980s and 1990s, currently in the process of rapid deterioration. In the transition from analogue to digital, the materiality of the videos moves from physical matter (substance stored in boxes and on shelves catalogued and organized manually) to materialities understood in terms of digital content enmeshed in algorithmic infrastructures for digital storage. Importantly, rather than an archive (striving for systematic organization and narrative), social media are best understood as an *arbitrary* data database, i.e. a loose collection of information items without beginning or end (Kaun & Stiernstedt 2014). On some levels, this conflicts with the group's intentions of creating historically contextualized narratives informed/induced by, if not chronology, then at least historical connectivity. One interviewee describes how "by mistake we lost the registration of the cassette bands at some point when we moved. So, the whole process of digitizing has been like looking for a needle in a haystack". The videos available online are thus a product of part coincidence and part what has been deemed worthy of remediation by a small circle of people and, in this sense, reflect the power relations that undergird archival efforts and historical narratives (Ankerson 2011). One of those in charge contemplates how:

> It's a very kind of violent kill-your-darlings project. It may well be that I think this or that tape is really important, but just because I attended that demonstration doesn't necessarily make it relevant to an online audience today [...] so I've played hardball dictator when digitizing.
>
> *(Interviewee 2)*

Those within the group who took on the time-consuming job of digitizing the tapes were also those who got to tell the story of the channel. Some respondents express discontent that the uploaded content only represents a limited period in the channel's history. Further, several comments are left by viewers asking the administrators for specific clips they feel have been left out of the storying of the channel and the canonizing of its transmissions.

The decision to go for social media for the relaunch was made by a small group of former activists. "It didn't take us long to decide to use YouTube because it was easy and we would save money on servers and host" (Interviewee 1). They explain their motivations as a matter of convenience because of the ease with which YouTube can be used to store and redistribute video and Facebook put to work to promote the videos hosted on YouTube. Social media's proficiencies as major time- and resource savers outweighs concern for how their techno-material characteristics might be irreconcilable with radical politics and media practices. Activists today operate in an ambiguous space. They are well aware of how, in a context where the internet is increasingly centralized into gated communities like Facebook, potential visibility and "free" storage come with a price: corporate control, monitoring and monetizing of content. The group behind the relaunch, however, argues that social media are a means to achieve a bigger, more important goal:

> I say fuck the means. If you only knew how much money we've gotten from the EU to make anti-EU campaigns. We were always pragmatic like that. It is a new version of an old discussion. Should we be cuddling up in our own little corner of the internet? I mean the German activists in the 90s wanted to make their own internet, free from US military and all that. That was back when these ideas of a free net were still alive. [...] If we place ourselves outside the system, we'll be standing there with our 30 best friends and the question is whether such a thing as outside the system even exists.
>
> *(Interviewee 5)*

Chanan points out that there is a paradox in the way that contemporary activists are "using the products of consumerism to try and combat the power of the same global corporate capitalism that sells them these very tools and instruments of free counter-cultural production to begin with" (Chanan 2012: 54). The reflections of these former activists remind us, however, that this paradox has a history that runs back before the time of social media:

> It can be compared to what we faced back then where we were on a channel that had anything from commercial to Christian television and porn movies. This was all part of the patchwork we had to be part of if we wanted the airtime and to get our messages across. Today, if you want to disseminate your messages as widely as possible you will also have to compromise and use the distributor with the largest potential audience, right?
>
> *(Interviewee 5)*

In this manner, visibility and possibilities of reaching new audiences with historical material are seen to outweigh the material constraints imposed by social media that operate within a broader system of "communicative capitalism" (Dean 2008). Despite knowing how social media operate through murky terms of use, in which content ownership is put in the hands of corporate actors and rights to privacy are signed off, they see no alternative if they are to keep up with the times.

Keeping up with/running out of time: social media temporalities

> Back in 1987, Sven started building a sound mixer. We wanted it to be better and different from anything you could get on the market. He's still working on it...
>
> *(Interviewee 3)*

Even if the statement above is tongue-in-cheek, it still epitomizes the sense of struggling to keep up with the times that, according to the respondents, has saturated the last few years of working on the channel. The second analytical theme thus delves into notions of time and temporalities with a point of departure in a sense of running out of time and essentially becoming obsolete as this is expressed by former Stoppers:

> If we had continued, I'm pretty sure time would have caught up with us. I mean we would still be sitting here today discussing whether or not to get a Facebook page while everyone else would have already had it for years.
>
> *(Interviewee 1)*

One former activist describes how the horizontal structure and democratic organization system meant that vast amounts of time was spent on decision-making processes:

> The big difference between then and now is that we don't have hour-long assemblies where we would discuss a subject such as whether or not to use YouTube. We discussed forever whether to use that thing called "the internet" or buy a dishwasher.
>
> *(Interviewee 2)*

In her work on three historical movements in the USA, Kaun (2017) discusses the contradiction between long-term organizing for social change and the time regimes of the media used for these purposes. She traces the increasing social acceleration related to media technologies employed by activists in relation to their political work and identifies a desynchronization between what she calls social media time, on the one hand, and political time, on the other. This desynchronization essentially disrupts activists' possibilities of connecting past and present struggles in meaningful ways and of building viable political projects. We might extend her ideas here also to encompass a certain inter-generational disconnect across the media-political time nexus to help understand how these "veteran video activists" articulate a sense of having run out of time, falling behind, or being outpaced by time and the cultures of immediacy in digital media:

> For us, it was this technological shift in the media landscape that shut us down. It was a combination of a decreasing influx of people, the new 0% unemployment policies and the democratization of video. The whole television process changed.
>
> *(Interviewee 4)*

Back in the late 1990s, the introduction of the internet with its privileging of speed and immediacy thus created tensions related to temporal regimes by clashing with the slow internal temporalities and long-held production traditions of the channel. The internet required technological skills the group did not possess and was heralded by a younger generation of activists whose motivations for engaging they did not necessarily understand or support. Respondents speak of the introduction of the internet as coinciding with the arrival of a new and, to them, somewhat dubious generation of activists unwilling to invest *time* in the collective:

> I remember there was a shift in how new people came into the group from being like "I don't know when or if I'll ever stop" to being a generation of people who came for a limited period of time until they could move on to something new, into film school for example. It felt a bit like CV hunters.
>
> *(Interviewee 1)*

Reflecting back on these societal changes in labour market policies and neoliberalization of society more generally, one respondent contemplates:

> There was this third generation just before we stopped. [...] We had always had CV hunters but before we could just filter them out because there were so many of us.
>
> *(Interviewee 2)*

This experience of a generational shift and new political winds blowing over the country feeds into a subtle articulation of nostalgia and sense of longing for lost times surrounding the relaunch.

Longing for lost times: social media as nostalgia

> I've had so many crises about more or less letting go of activism and about not being part of the scene anymore. So, when I first started this project, just getting the chance to open up that Pandora's box of everything that I'd missed so much was motivation enough for the many hours of work I put into digitizing. So, for me there is some nostalgia in it too.
>
> *(Interviewee 1)*

In a recent study of the reorientation of left-libertarian activists in Sweden after the Gothenburg riots of 2001, which marked the end of a cycle of contestation in the country, Jacobsson and Sörbom (2015) found that activists engage in different coping strategies to reconstruct community in the immediate and long-term aftermath of a movement coming to an end. In a similar manner, we may fruitfully think of *TV Stop*'s efforts to revive themselves online as part of project of "preserving some of the movement infrastructure" (Jacobsson and Sörbom 2015: 716) and recreating a sense of collective identity and agency that many of them long for in their everyday life with kids, jobs and mortgages:

> I guess life happens. Here we are with our kids and our full-time jobs in our – well, if not single-family house in the suburbs, then freehold flats. Sometimes when I get sad my brother promises me that we'll be politically active again when we retire. And that sort of comforts me. It's unbearable not to be doing anything.
>
> *(Interviewee 2)*

A similar nostalgic sensibility characterizes the ways in which former viewers engage with and respond to revisiting the archived material on Facebook: "the most important youth TV of my era" (Facebook post 28 March 2012) or "Hell yeah - the young years revisited!" (Facebook post 25 January 2013). Another post accompanied by the caption "And then suddenly 23 years went by…" (18 May 2016) epitomizes articulations of time having passed with the blink of an eye. Time and the transitoriness of time is thus a recurring theme in both administrators' posts and comments from viewers. Juhasz (2006) sees in archive video, revamped for a present-day context, an inherent form of nostalgia, as video *per se* is an "attempt to hold on to time given its inevitable loss" (Juhasz 2006: 321). Yet, this is not necessarily a passive, unproductive melancholia. Rather, nostalgia as produced and experienced in relation to video allows for a "refiguring of time" and in doing so is potentially "productive of new feelings and knowledge that might lead to action" (Juhasz 2006: 322). To Juhasz, the act of "relodging those frozen moments in contemporary contexts" in the hope that they be reanimated is a form of "archive activism" (Juhasz (2006: 320). If we accept her assertion that "one generation's yearning could fuel another's learning", we might come to understand the sentiments expressed by respondents and viewers as a communal, and potentially action-oriented, rather than private nostalgia.

"It's a bit of a Fight Club thing"

The loss of time connects to the experience of a loss of community. To the respondents, the closing-down of the channel marked the end of an era and a shift in their life trajectories. They express losing the community, which inherently came with "being a Stopper" and a personal sadness associated with this. One respondent describes this community, which to him is partly revived and relived by watching the tapes, as based on shared moral and professional ethics rather than ideology:

> Our strength was that we had a shared moral compass because we were such a closely-knit network. We were all different and probably voted differently but we had very strong and similar ideas of the ethics of what to film and what not to film.
>
> *(Interviewee 5)*

Paying testimony to the "common public time" traditionally produced by television (Scannell 2014), former viewers describe how watching the late-night transmission was often the last thing they did before going to bed alone while knowing friends were watching as well. This common time in turn becomes an important part of how collective memories of these years are formed. Despite years having passed, a sense of belonging to a community, often described in terms of a secret club in which membership never expires, remains intact to some degree. One respondent even described this as similar to being part of *Fight Club:*[2]

> I remember one night when I was really sad about how it was all ending and how we were passing on the broadcasting license, my brother said to me: "Don't forget that there are 400 of us out there now". 400 people spread out across the Danish media industries, infiltrating the system. It's a bit of a *Fight Club* thing: we don't talk about it but we all know we're out there somewhere and we'll detect each other there in a lunch room somewhere occasionally.
>
> *(Interviewee 2)*

In fact, many of the people who started as activists in *TV Stop* in the late 1980s and early 1990s today work in the Danish media industry: "You can go into any production company or television station in the country and point out a dozen people who have been a Stopper" (Interviewee 3). In this sense, their stories and memories of the closing down of the channel and the end of an era in activist history in the country is also a story about how the so called Portapak movement came to an end as people gradually left for the industry much like it happened in other parts of the Western world (see e.g. Boyle 1997).

Concluding remarks

In order to properly understand the relation between activism, protest and social media materialities today, we need to pay analytical attention to the relatively recent past of activist media practices, and the voices and historical accounts of those who lived through continuities and ruptures in the development of activist media. Their narratives of past failures and successes offer valuable lessons for activists today. The case of *TV Stop* provides insights into how, today, a television collective of the past seeks to appropriate digital media in an aspiration to connect issues and struggles across time and generations. In a sense, social media gave new life to *TV Stop*, which with the recirculation of digitized material sought to attract audiences not only to commemorate the channel as a historically important cultural institution, but also to reinstall long-standing debates and concerns at the heart of the activist scene in the country. By republishing and recontextualizing broadcasts of historical events with connection or relevance to current news and protest events, these practices thus become a way of trying to disrupt a culture of nowness and newness in social media, which tends to shun history and its lessons. Social media as digital archives thus hold the promise of "potential future re-initiations or re-connections between individuals and groups that would have once been very difficult to find prior to the connective turn" (Hoskins 2011:26). But the analysis also raises critical questions as to the constraints of materiality and struggles around the choice to go online, first with the arrival of the internet, and later with the advent of social media. Not least, the analysis is suggestive of how struggles to reconcile temporalities and techno-social materialities in contemporary media landscapes are strongly reminiscent of the dilemmas and concerns faced by those involved in pre-digital forms of activism.

Memories of *TV Stop*, as performed by former Stoppers and their viewers, represent a specific kind of *media* memory, which Kaun and Stiernstedt (2012: 339) understand to be "people's memories of media texts, media experiences and practices related to a specific medium". When projecting these distinct media memories onto social media, shaped by the twin temporal regimes of "the immediate" (constant flow and circulation) and "the archival" (memory and storage of data) (Kaun 2017: 472), connective memories between and across generations of activists are potentially forged. Yet the temporality and materiality of social media also entail a potential loss of chronology and historical decontextualization. So, there is a duality at play in how social media time regimes, when put to work for real-time protesting and organizing, are biased towards constant flow and newness and thereby fail to connect struggles across time. But when appropriated for archival purposes they may also create connections between different periods of contestation. We may consider the relaunch of *TV Stop* as driven by three interlaced incentives to *store and preserve time*, to *catch up with time* and essentially a techno-material development they themselves are sceptical of – but also as impelled by the urge to *remember times passed* and reminding people of the value of remembering and making connections between past and present struggles.

Notes

1 The Danish National Socialist Movement (DNSB) is a neo-Nazi party founded in 1991. The party considers itself the inheritor of the National Socialist Workers' Party of Denmark (DNSAP), the largest Nazi party in Denmark before and during the Second World War.

2 *Fight Club* (1999) is an American film directed by David Fincher depicting a secret, anti-consumerist underground network of members who fight recreationally to ultimately bring down corporate America.

References

Ankerson, M. S. (2011). Writing web histories with an eye on the analog past. *New Media & Society*, 14(3), pp. 384–400.

Askanius, T. (2013). Online video activism and political mash-up genres. *JOMEC Journal Journalism Media and Cultural Studies*, 4. Retrieved from https://publications.cardiffuniversitypress.org/index.php/JOMEC/article/view/339 [Accessed 18 September 2017].

Askanius, T. (2014). Video for change. In: K. Gwinn Wilkins, T. Tufte and R. Obregon (Eds.) *Handbook on Development Communication and Social Change* (pp. 453–470). Malden, MA: Wiley Blackwell.

Bennett, W. L. & Segerberg, A. (2012). The logic of connective action: Digital media and the personalization of contentious politics. *Information, Communication & Society*, 15(5), pp. 739–768.

Boyle, D. (1997). *Subject to change. Guerrilla television revisited.* New York: Oxford University Press.

Chanan, M. (2012). Protest and video activism. *Journal of European Popular Culture*, 3(1), pp. 51–60.

Dean, J. (2008). Communicative capitalism: circulation and the foreclosure of politics. In: M. Boler (Ed.) *Digital Media and Democracy* (pp. 101–121). London: The MIT Press.

Gansing, K. (2013). *Transversal media practices: Media archaeology, art and technological development.* Doctoral Thesis. Malmö Högskola.

Garde-Hansen, J., Hoskins, A., & Reading, A., (Eds.) (2009). *Save As…Digital Memories.* Basingstoke: Palgrave Macmillan.

Gregory, S. (2010). Cameras everywhere: Ubiquitous video documentation of human rights, new forms of video activism, and consideration of safety, security, dignity and consent. *Journal of Human Rights Practice*, 2(2), pp. 191–207.

Hoskins, A. (2011). Media, memory, metaphor: Remembering and the connective Turn. *Parallax*, 17(4), pp. 19–31.

Jacobsson, K. & Sörbom, A. (2015). After a cycle of contention: Post-Gothenburg strategies of left-Libertarian activists in Sweden. *Social Movement Studies*, 14(6), pp. 713–732.

Juhasz, A. (2006). Video remains. Nostalgia, technology and queer archive activism. *The GLQ Archive*, 12(2), pp. 319–328.

Kaun, A. (2015). Regimes of time: Media practices of the dispossessed. *Time & Society*, 24(2), pp. 221–243.

Kaun, A. (2017). 'Our time to act has come': desynchronization, social media time and protest movements. *Media, Culture & Society*, 39(4), pp. 469–486.

Kaun, A. & Stiernstedt, F. (2012). Media memories: The case of youth radio DT64. *Participations. Journal of Audience and Reception Studies*, 9(2), pp. 337–359.

Kaun, A. & Stiernstedt, F. (2014). Facebook time: Technological and institutional affordances for media memories. *New Media & Society*, 16(7), pp. 1154–1168.

Mathiasen, A.-P., Nordkap, C., Rugaard, L. & Valeur, E. (1998). *Nørrebro – Sten for sten. En hvidbog om Nørrebrosagen.* Copenhagen: DR Multimedie.

Milan, S. (2015). From social movements to cloud protesting: the evolution of collective identity. *Information, Communication & Society*, 18(8), pp. 887–900.

Mitchell, K. & Elwood, S. (2013). Intergenerational mapping and the cultural politics of memory. *Space and Polity*, 17(1), pp. 33–52.

Ruiz, P. (2014). Technology, activism and the dynamics of intergenerational memory. Conference paper presented in Moving Memories Remembering and Reviving Conflict, Protest and Social Unrest in Connected Times, University of London, 27 November.

Scannell, P. (2014). The historicality of central broadcasting institutions. In: M. Djerf-Pierre &M. Ekström M. (Eds) *A History of Swedish Broadcasting. Communicative Ethos, Genres and Institutional Change* (pp. 355–366). Gothenburg: Nordicom.

5

FACEBOOK'S COMMUNICATION PROTOCOLS, ALGORITHMIC FILTERS, AND PROTEST

A critical socio-technical perspective

Lorenzo Coretti and Daniele Pica

Introduction

The past decade has seen the rise of what prominent academics refer to as spontaneous and horizontal forms of protest, which have seemingly superseded established formal organizations at the forefront of contention. Milan (2015: 1) defines these as "leaderless, molecular organizing mechanisms that rely on social media to personalize action frames". The causes of this shift can be found in rapid technological development, a widespread cynicism towards the official politics of representative democracy, and a progressive disengagement from conventional forms of political participation (Della Porta & Tarrow 2005; Clement 2011). These forms of protest have been interpreted as "connective action" (Bennett & Segerberg 2012, 2013), "networked collective action" (Rainie and Wellman, 2014), or "networked movements" (Juris 2004, 2008). These terms, though not conceptually equivalent, share a common view of technology as an organizing principle. As Bennett and Segerberg (2012: 742) state, these new forms of protest have seen "technology platforms and applications taking the role of established political organizations", in the form of political parties, workers' unions, and non-governmental organizations.

This chapter argues that an understanding of these new forms of protest can be gained through a critical socio-technical approach and a longitudinal study grounded in theories of materiality. Communication protocols and algorithmic filters that govern the architecture of social media form the technical focus of this study. Lifecycle theory, on the other hand, with its emphasis on organizational transformations, forms the sociological focus. The chapter provides an analysis of how the materiality of Facebook affects social movements in terms of organization, collective identity formation, and mobilization power, sparking "depressive cycles" along their lifespan. It explores this phenomenon by drawing on a longitudinal study of the Purple Movement (Popolo Viola), an Italian activist network that coordinated a series of protest activities between 2009 and 2012 (for an exhaustive background see Coretti 2014; Coretti & Pica 2015a, 2015b). Rather than pointing out the mere intrinsic functional identity of Facebook technology, in the form of its algorithmic filters and communication protocols, the chapter aims to explore the consequences they help materialize. Protocols and algorithms act as "psychological tools" (Vygotsky 1978), i.e. generative resources that, intentionally or unintentionally, enable complex organizational functions, but also continually produce identities and culture (Kallinikos, Leonardi & Nardi 2012). Ultimately, what matters is not only the material nature of these technological artifacts, but also the "reality" they are changing. Hence, instead of seeking a cause-effect relationship between technology and society, this chapter asks whether and how the corporate interests embedded within the communication protocols and the algorithmic filters of Facebook, influence social movements that adopt this platform as their main tool for communication in the long term. This includes analysing how users/activists interpret these restrictions, embracing and/or resisting them, and how the organization of these movements can be reshaped or disappear.

Communication protocols and algorithmic filters

Following Schmidt and Simone (1996), communication protocols are intended as formalized rules embedded in technological artifacts. A protocol reduces the complexity of user-to-user cooperation by providing a pre-computation of organizational structures that decrease possibilities of action for users. According to Suchman (1987), a protocol can be designed as a map or a checklist, either by offering a general heuristic framework for distributed decision-making within a relatively open environment, or by providing a script whereby options are narrow. The effectiveness of Facebook's protocols depends on how much their design encourages real-time communication. Protocols thus represent the laws that govern the communication and organization of a platform, influencing group formation and interaction.

Algorithmic filters are tools designed to lower complexity brought about by information and interaction overload in social media in a way which is supposedly beneficial to both platforms and users. Social media steer users' attention based on the realization that if it takes too long to locate something they will disengage because of limited cognitive abilities. Hence, algorithmic filters allow for a social media user to easily navigate in an ocean of information, giving priority, in the case of Facebook, to three factors: affinity, weight, and time decay (Bucher 2012). Affinity pertains to the closeness among users; weight depends on how popular a post is; and time decay gives primacy to most recent publications. Generally, algorithmic filters make use of quantitative data built around the digital footprints of users (Fuchs 2017; Höök, Benyon & Munro 2003; Ljungberg & Sørensen 2000). Algorithms thus represent the laws that govern how attention is gained in social media and what information is prioritized. The relationship between communication protocols and algorithmic filters is a reciprocally positive one, as both limit the horizon of possibilities for users by applying either universal rules, as in the case of protocols, or personalized rules, as in the case of filters, to improve interaction and reduce information and interaction overload (Mathiassen & Sørensen 2008).

Facebook's communication protocols and algorithmic filters are considered here as socio-technical processes, whereby human, social, and technical factors coexist. Following Svensson (2017) and Klinger and Svensson (2017), this chapter considers the design of Facebook as the expression of a programming input based on problems that need to be solved, leading to a formulation of sets of calculations in a big-data context, and, eventually, a final output. This process is defined by van Dijck and Poell (2013) as programmability. It indicates "the ability of a social media platform to trigger and steer users' creative or communicative contributions" (ibid: 5). As Kavada (2009: 822) states, "(t)hese settings are not considered simply as containers of the interaction, but as spaces that shape and influence it". Crucially, the final output entails a complex set of outcomes which differ considerably for the actors involved in the network. The main focus of this study is to understand how coordination protocols and algorithmic filters influence the lifecycle of social movements. The next section presents in more details the socio-technical theoretical backdrop informing this study.

Critical theory and social media

Theorists such as Fuchs (2011), van Dijck and Poell (2013), as well as Kaun and Stiernstedt (2014), strongly inspire the theoretical framework of this analysis. According to these authors, the relationship between users and technology can be assessed by considering the commercial interests that shape the design and functionalities of technological tools as well as how users interpret and act upon these functionalities throughout time.

This approach does not consider technology in a vacuum but, rather, as a socio-technical process where tensions arise between its implicit form, as designed by engineers, and its explicit form, as the way users engage with the platform (van Dijck & Poell 2013). In fact, distinctive affordances and patterns of communication emerge according to the particular nature of the platforms which are being analysed. A medium such as Diaspora rests upon the same principles of sharing, participation and collaboration which characterize a platform like Facebook. However, the profit-driven interests which govern the algorithms and protocols of Facebook translate into a radically different idea of sharing. This ideological difference can be illustrated using van Dijck's (2013) concepts of *connectedness* and *connectivity*. As van Dijck points out, social media aim to promote the sharing of information among its users. Non-profit social media focus on the promotion of *connectedness*, i.e. they manage pre-existing relationships and the creation of new ones, foster the creation of new groups and networks, and facilitate the dissemination of information. Profit-driven social media, such as Facebook, still aim to generate connectedness. However, for these platforms, connectedness is a means rather than a goal in itself. The final objective is, rather, *connectivity*, by which any act of sharing relates to the final aim of providing user-data to third party marketers and advertisers (ibid). In order to maximize connectivity and increase value for marketers, Facebook seeks to accelerate information sharing. These dynamics could entail negative consequences for social movements. The algorithmic acceleration of Facebook's data streams, enhancing the news-oriented nature of activist communication, hinders processes of collective identity building (van Dijck & Poell 2013) in favour of ephemeral immediacy as opposed to continuity (Kaun & Stiernstedt 2014). As Poell and van Dijck (2015: 534) state, "media power has neither been transferred to the public, nor to activists for that matter; instead, power has partly shifted to the technological mechanisms and algorithmic selections operated by large social media corporations". Based on these considerations, this study argues that the adoption of Facebook provides movements with efficient means for short-term mobilization and circulation of information. However, on a long-term basis, it destabilizes collective identity building processes, in turn defusing potentials for mobilization, and ultimately accelerating group decline.

Lifecycle theory

According to lifecycle theory (Dawson & Gettys 1929; Blumer 1969; Della Porta & Diani, 2006), the formation of social movements habitually follows a period of social unrest, characterised by grievances such as social injustice, disruptive social changes, and the inability to deal with new social situations. This state of increasing polarization and discontent can last for many years, sometimes entire generations. Social unrest is typically followed by a brief stage of excitement (otherwise called emergence, or social ferment), whereby agitation, despite being mostly uncoordinated and inconclusive, fosters bonds of solidarity among citizens and strengthens individual motivations to overcome barriers to participation. In the subsequent stage of formalization (or coalescence), movements start organizing in order not to disperse the human capital that supported the initial agitation. Here, provisional decision-making centres emerge alongside embryonic forms of internal democracy. This stage ends when the movement finds its definite form and nature, and a well-established ideology. This stage is termed institutionalization (or bureaucratization). Formal bureaucratic centres materialize, wherein decision-making and leadership converge. At the end of this stage, which is normally the longest one, movements decline for two obvious reasons: success or breakdown (Blumer 1969; Miller 1999). Breakdown may take place through organizational failure, repression by the authorities, and co-optation, when leaders are "bought" by the institutions that are the target of the movements' campaigns, with the often-false premise of changing things from the inside (Miller 1999). Alternatively, the mainstream might adopt the movements' goals and objectives, giving them no longer a reason to exist (Macionis 2001). Finally, movements may "escape" into a state of encapsulation, turning into a "more or less self-contained subculture" (Castells, quoted in Boggs 1986: 75).

These frameworks strongly emphasize organizational development, especially in the stages of formalization and institutionalization. In order to explore such development, it is useful to distinguish the movement as a whole from the organizational and decisional centre(s) that emerge throughout their lifecycle. In the former instance, the term "social movements" is employed, whereas in the latter, the term "social movement organization (SMO)" is adopted (Zald & McCarthy 1980). Leadership is predictably located in the latter. These two collective actors differ greatly. Following Gerlach and Hine's (1970) SPIN model, social movements can be described as being segmented, polycentric, and integrated constellations of various constituents. They are segmented, as they entail the sum of different units with different interests and flexible margins. Moreover, they are polycentric, as they consist of multiple coordination and decision-making centres. Finally, they are also integrated with interpersonal relationships, common interests and beliefs that provide the glue connecting different instances within the movement, thus creating a sense of collective identity (Gerlach 2001). Conversely, the structure of an SMO depends on contingencies that are related to the social and cultural environment in which the aggregation processes take place, and are influenced by the architecture of the environment in which decisions are taken, be such environment physical or technological. In general terms, whereas movements tend to be inclusive in order to attract the highest number of followers, SMOs might assume different configurations, from inclusive to exclusive (Zald & Ash 1966; McCarthy & Zald 1977). Moreover, while social movements value horizontalism and lack of (or flexible) leadership (Juris 2004, 2008; Fenton 2008), some SMOs might tend to be more hierarchical and centralized in order to streamline decision-making processes (McCarthy & Zald 1977). Similar configurations have been noted by Gerbaudo (2012), who introduces the concept of choreography of protest, and by Poell et al. (2016), who define leadership as connective.

The lifecycle of Popolo Viola

It can be argued that the unrest stage of Popolo Viola dates back from 1993, the year Italian tycoon Silvio Berlusconi announced his debut in the political arena, immediately sparking a wave of discussion regarding a manifest conflict between his entrepreneurial, media-related, and political interests. Berlusconi's conflict of interest, together with rising unemployment levels, and widespread corruption in the Italian political system, concurred to form the opportunity structures for Popolo Viola (Coretti 2014).

By 2008, the political panorama in Italy is characterized by Berlusconi's strong leadership as the head of government in combination with weak opposition in parliament. His leadership is strengthened by unsustainable levels of concentration of ownership in the media and very little space for dissent. In fact, as Prime Minister, Berlusconi has control of over 90% of Italian television, and, thus, undisputed power in the realm of mass media. In this context, the rising social media sphere provides an alternative channel for personal expression. It is here that unrest turns into excitement. The unvoiced frustration of millions of citizens seems to have finally found a soapbox for people to speak openly and without restrictions. It seems almost natural that, in a few months, hundreds of groups and pages spring up to express dissent with the politics of Berlusconi's government.

Among these activists/bloggers, a group from Catania, Sicily, headed by the anonymous figure of San Precario (the name comes from the nature of temporary work, it being precarious and uncertain), proposes, alongside other activists, the idea of a national demonstration to ask for Berlusconi's resignation in the name of democracy and freedom of expression. In October 2009, the group launches the Facebook Page "Una Manifestazione Nazionale per Chiedere le Dimissioni di Berlusconi" ("A National Demonstration to Ask for Berlusconi's Resignation"), announcing a rally to take place in Rome on 5 December 2009. The page quickly reaches an unexpected consensus. After only a few weeks, more than 300,000 users join the page and announce via Facebook their presence at the event, which would later be called "No Berlusconi Day". At the same time, hundreds of local groups form and join the initiative, both inside and outside Italy.

The success of the demonstration is unexpected and unprecedented in its spontaneity. Afterwards, the protest continues, both on- and offline, coordinated and publicized by the organizers on a new Facebook page, called "Il Popolo Viola" ("The Purple People"). The new page soon gathers more than 450,000 subscribers. Despite its increasing popularity, the movement soon becomes plagued by internal struggles and factionalism, with two major splits taking place. The first one follows the formalization of the movement, in January 2010, leading to the birth of "Resistenza Viola" ("Purple Resistance"); the second follows the institutionalization of the movement, in the summer of 2010, with followers of Resistenza Viola converging with a new wave of "exiles" into a new subject, "Rete Viola" ("Purple Network"). After these two splits, the influence of the movement declines significantly.

Facebook's communication protocols and organizational settings

Both splits in Popolo Viola are directly affected by the movement's use of Facebook and the power that Facebook provides to its leadership. When the movement enters its formalization stage, a group of followers points out that no democratic process can take place without a discussion of the page's management. As one activist reports, at the first national meeting, where the provisional coordinating group is elected:

> [...] the main issues raised by the audience regarded, in the first place, who was supposed to manage the national page; secondly, who was supposed to decide what content has to be distributed.
>
> *Interviewee no.3, in Coretti (2014): 189*

As far as these two points are concerned, the meeting does not seem to offer any space for discussion. San Precario, present as a member of the group from Catania, intends to maintain control over the page. After all, he has contributed to the birth of the movement and has created both pages. Moreover, he has allowed the use of the "trademark" Popolo Viola providing material to whomever had shown a genuine interest in creating sub-groups and sub-pages. Finally, sharing management with anybody else would allegedly open the door to the risk of defacement by infiltrators, or to other thoughtless acts. These justifications are not convincing enough for some local groups, who threaten to leave the movement if shared management of the page is not implemented.

The schism that takes place at movement-level reflects onto these groups, creating a chain-reaction of many micro-schisms. Hundreds of "official" groups and pages are now mirrored by an equal number of counter-groups and counter-pages which, in spite of being inspired by the same values, become more occupied with protesting against the "official" Popolo Viola than against Berlusconi's government. In March 2010, a press release, signed by nine activists, announces the birth of the new sub-movement. According to the "rebels":

> Resistenza Viola is an answer to the despotic behaviour adopted by the leaders of Popolo Viola. The horizontal structure is only the façade of the movement. Behind this disguise, there is a highly centralised organisation where decisions are taken from above, with no possibility of discussion for the local groups and the single activists.
>
> *cited in Coretti (2014): 191*

A similar process occurs after the institutionalization of the movement. The creation of an official non-profit organization is meant to guarantee independence from other institutions which previously helped the movement organize street demonstrations but also attempted to appropriate them. However, a new group of rebel activists considers the new entity to be an "empty box", and begins a discussion that relates to the whole nature of Popolo Viola, from its identity to internal democracy. Instead of promoting a productive debate, the conversation soon becomes an argument which contributes to a new spiral of fragmentation. The split with Rete Viola replicates the dynamics that were in place during the first schism: firstly, division at a macro-level, and then, consequently, a series of micro-splits within local groups. The ecosystem of Popolo Viola on Facebook seems to disintegrate into countless small flyweight groups and pages.

The main difference between Popolo Viola and Rete Viola lies in their different organizational processes and structures, rather than in the different backgrounds or different principles of their affiliates. Popolo Viola labels itself as a "fluid and molecular" movement, where everybody is free to contribute to the anti-Berlusconi cause. On the other hand, Rete Viola is based around a constituency of local assemblies, a shared manifesto, and elected representatives. This partly explains the socio-technical approach of this chapter. In the first split, there is the incompatibility between the proprietary nature of Facebook pages and the horizontal and participatory values of Popolo Viola; in the second split, there is the manifest inability of the movement's cadre to adopt an agreed set of internal regulations.

The splits discussed above suggest that the enabling potential of the code of Facebook pages is restricted to movement elites while excluding vast majorities of users/activists. Through time, the materiality of Facebook pages comes into being as users conform or resist to code. First of all, the study of Popolo Viola shows that official SMOs in networked movements might not be actual decision-making centres, unless they coincide with the official communication platform's management. If we consider a movement as a network, the institutionalized node might not be necessarily the one holding control over the movement. The communication protocols of Facebook's pages enable large flows of information exchange and mobilizing potential, but Facebook's administration rules uphold proprietary, centralized and hierarchical management that also make it easy for whoever has founded the pages to retain control and avoid democratic management. In other words, Facebook's design provides technical leaders with both communicative power and the opportunity to retain such power. Page protocols assign unobstructed control to their founder/admin profiles, providing them with de facto ownership over the movement's intellectual property. Typically, this power retention is favoured by the fact that movement pages have the potential to attract considerable numbers of followers only during the excitement stage of the life-cycle, a potential that is hardly replicable during following stages (Coretti 2014).

Facebook pages have been programmed with a specific desired outcome in mind, i.e. to provide companies with a broadcasting medium for marketing. In order to satisfy this objective, page ownership has always been centralized and hierarchical.[1] While this process benefits brands, with the potential to broadcast information to millions of users at once, it clashes with the values of distributed control and deliberation that characterize, ideally, the governance of networked movements that are by nature segmented and polycentric. Such configuration therefore deprives constituents of influence and the movement as a whole of spaces of deliberation. If Facebook's own desired outcome is achieved thanks to widespread adoption of pages by corporate brands, movements which adopt this communication tool might attain unintended consequences, namely schismogenesis and oligarchization.

Whereas, according to Zald and Ash (1966), oligarchization is the process which leads power to concentrate in few hands, schismogenesis can be described as "a process of differentiation in the norms of individual behaviour resulting from cumulative interaction between individuals" (Bateson 1936: 175). It occurs when one or more factions abandon a movement (Zald & Ash 1966: 337). As the minor constituents' voices in a movement fail to reach resonance, these voices are likely to seek other ways to protest, thus creating antagonistic sub-movements which weaken the overall impact of contention. Hence, oligarchization, promoting power conflicts, turns polycentrism into factionalism, segmentation into fragmentation, and integration into disintegration.

The fragmentation of movements such as Popolo Viola is not a direct cause-effect relationship that depends merely on Facebook's communication protocols. Rather, they depend on the movement's inability to rely on a set of shared rules. In Popolo Viola, the adoption of a statute or a manifesto becomes urgent only after oligarchization is acknowledged to be hampering the mobilizing power of the movement. Networked movements may disregard the presence of a statute in order to promote inclusivity. Many movements in the past have suffered internal divisions over such issues. Kavada (2013) reports on polarization inside the European Social Forum (ESF) between the "verticals", i.e. the activists promoting centralization, hierarchy, and top-down communication, and the "horizontals", who instead supported a decentralized distribution of power. Like the ESF, Popolo Viola has gone through an internal discussion on whether or not to adopt a set of rules to regulate decision-making processes and leadership. Rather than technology alone, it is the failure of this democratic process which determined, as further explored in the following section, the deterioration of the movement's collective identity, leading to its ultimate decline.

Facebook's algorithmic filters and collective identity

This section aims to discuss how patterns of interaction and discussion on Facebook influence processes of social movements' collective identity building throughout time. Taylor and Whittier define collective identity as "the shared definition of a group that derives from members' common interests, experiences, and solidarity" (Taylor & Whittier 1999: 170). Following Melucci's concept of "identization" (Melucci 1995: 43–44), collective identity can be assessed temporally, as a continuous process of collective identification made of reciprocal and repeated interaction and negotiation among actors. This process not only affects the outcome of collective action but also becomes an objective in itself (Gamson 1992).

Facebook algorithms affect information flows in the movement in two ways. Firstly, they verticalize communication and limit personal frames, by exposing users mainly to popular content and promoting interaction via Newsfeed rather than through visits to the actual pages (Coretti 2014; Coretti & Pica 2015b). Whereas these patterns multiply opportunities for a multi-step flow of communication, they also discourage users from seeking specific movement-related information, and promote access to selected content only. Secondly, the programmability of Facebook pages progressively marginalize the visibility of user-generated content, promoting the circulation of information or content uploaded by administrators only. The reasons behind this process are clear if one looks at the political economy of Facebook. With brands being their main customer segment, Facebook intends to reassure these lucrative clients that information flows (and consequently, brand reputation) are steadily in their hands rather than at the mercy of possibly angry customers. Whereas these changes are favourable to marketers, they are detrimental to social movements that benefit from horizontal communication in fostering collective identity. The consequence of this phenomenon is that individual users might be discouraged from creatively expressing themselves on pages, a phenomenon exacerbated by the erasure of the "discussions" tab in October 2011, and by Facebook's choice of limiting page reach since 2013. With this latter decision, Facebook decided to increase profitability by selling fans to brands, with the result that only well-funded pages could reach the majority of their own followers through sponsored content, complicating the operations of modestly funded activist pages.

A further major issue regards the cognitive aspects of collective identity. Firstly, interaction on Facebook pages is dominated by effortless forms of information exchange (Coretti 2014; Coretti & Pica 2015b). The aim of this form of communication is to establish a social presence rather than to create the basis for the informed discussion that is necessary for a shared definition of the aims and means of a social movement. Secondly, interaction on Facebook pages consists mainly of users commenting admins' status updates rather than other users' comments, hindering the potential for the establishment of strong ties among users (Coretti 2014; Coretti & Pica 2015b), and reinforcing mere affiliative ties (Flanagin et al. 2006), where the only link between participants in discussions is the common connection to the movement's cause. This process might be further accelerated by what Kaun (2015; 2016) defines as desynchronization, a disjunction between real-time speed of interaction and the slower community building processes.

The cycle of depression

This section shows the interdependence between the organizational issues of networked movements and collective identity formation. The emphasis on communication protocols and algorithmic filters sheds light on the tensions created by conflicting interests and the negative consequences these can have on mobilization. The potential for mobilization displayed by Facebook pages such as Popolo Viola is effective only as far as these dimensions are aligned. The patterns illustrated in the previous sections show that a cycle of depression is in place, with large scale mobilization efforts under threat on a medium- and long-term basis. Whereas the network effects afforded by the digital platform speed up the excitement stage, the cycle of depression leads to an acceleration of the decline stage of the lifecycle. When organizational processes concentrate power in oligarchies, the risk of schismogenesis increases, affecting negatively collective identity, and ultimately the mobilizing power of a movement is hindered.

The discussion following this longitudinal analysis shows that, in the long run, incompatibility exists between, on the one hand, the programmability of Facebook, implemented by its communication protocols and algorithmic filters, and, on the other hand, the participatory values of networked movements. This incongruity speeds up their lifecycle, problematizing formalization and institutionalization processes, and causing online forms of protest to wax and wane quickly. However, the cycle of depression cannot merely be ascribed to the platform's design. It rather mirrors the principles of the agents involved. Movement leaders may benefit from the proprietary logics of Facebook, but such benefit is short-sighted and is most likely brief. This internet-centrist logic might be guided by a misbelief that social media act as autonomous agents that, at best, shorten the lifespan of collective action, and, at worst, could "facilitate and eventually legitimize centralized and authoritarian practices" (Treré & Barassi 2015: 299).

Conclusion

This chapter provides an in-depth analysis of how Facebook's architecture affects social movements in terms of organization, collective identity formation, and, in turn, mobilization power. Firstly, the use of commercial social media, Facebook pages in particular, exacerbates the contradiction between the values of horizontalism, inclusivity, and leaderlessness of networked movements, and, on the other hand, the often hierarchical and centralized nature of social movement organizations. Secondly, the desired outcomes of Facebook's programmability promote a shift of power from officially elected SMOs to technical leaders, in other words, those activists in control of the platform of communication. Furthermore, the opaque nature of this shift encourages oligarchization and retention of control by these de facto leaders, at the expenses of collegiality, transparency, and accountability.

The use of Facebook pages is likely to affect movements' lifecycle considerably by hindering the processes of formalization and institutionalization. By reinforcing hierarchical stratification and reshaping organizational processes, Facebook pages undermine collective identity, accelerating or even bringing into being oligarchization, fragmentation, and schismogenesis. Paradoxically, whereas mobilization processes are sped up by algorithmic distribution of information, the search for a cohesive collective and organizational identity is slowed down. Hence, the cycle of depression is not merely an outcome but also a fundamental condition of misalignment between organization, collective identity, and mobilization. The analysis also points to the central role played by the materiality of technology which requires novel analytical tools to overcome the limitations of the existing lifecycle frameworks. Traditional frameworks cannot adequately comprehend and explain the interdependence between leadership issues and collective identity formation in networked movements. Finally, research will need to test the cycle of depression on different case studies and further understand the contradictions between marketing-oriented design and grassroots efforts towards social change.

Note

1 With the exclusion of the period between June 2010 and February 2011, during which owners could be removed from administrating pages between.

References

Bateson, G. (1936). *Naven 1936*. Reprint.London: Facsimile Publisher.

Bennett, W. L., and Segerberg, A. (2012). The Logic of Connective Action. *Information, Communication, and Society*, 15(5), pp. 739–768.

Bennett, W. L., and Segerberg, A. (2013). *The Logic of Connective Action: Digital Media and the Personalization of Contentious Politics*. Cambridge: Cambridge University Press.

Blumer, H. (1969). Collective behavior. In: A. M. Lee (Ed.) *Principles of sociology* (3rd Ed.). New York: Barnes and Noble Books.

Boggs, C. (1986). *Social Movements and Political Power: Emerging Forms of Radicalism in the West*. Philadelphia, PA: Temple University Press.
Boyd, D. (2010). Social Network Sites as Networked Publics: Affordances, Dynamics, and Implications. In: Z. Papacharissi (Ed.) *Networked Self: Identity, Community, and Culture on Social Network Sites* (pp. 39–58). London: Routledge.
Bucher, T. (2012). Want to be on the top? Algorithmic power and the threat of invisibility on Facebook. *New Media & Society*, 14(7), pp. 1164–1180.
Clement, M. T. (2011). 'Let Them Build Sea Walls': Ecological Crisis, Economic Crisis and the Political Economic Opportunity Structure. *Critical Sociology*, 37(4), pp. 447–463.
Coretti, L. (2014). *The Purple Movement: Social Media and Activism in Berlusconi's Italy*. PhD Thesis University of Westminster UK.
Coretti, L. (2017). Dead movement walking (and biting): The strategic use of old Facebook pages for new campaigns – The case of the Italian referenda in 2011 and 2016. Paper presented at the Workshop Protest Media Ecologies: Communicative Affordances for Social Change in the Digital Era, Scuola Normale Superiore, Florence, April 2017.
Coretti, L., & Pica, D. (2015a). The Purple Movement: How Facebook's design undermined the Anti-Berlusconi protest in Italy. *Journal of Italian Cinema & Media Studies*, 3(3), pp. 305–318.
Coretti, L., & Pica, D. (2015b). The rise and fall of collective identity in networked movements: communication protocols, Facebook, and the anti-Berlusconi protest. *Information, Communication and Society*, 18(8), pp. 951–967.
Davenport, T. H., & Beck, J. C. (2001). *The Attention Economy: Understanding the New Currency of Business*. Boston, MA: Harvard Business School Press.
Dawson, C. A., & Gettys, W. E. (1929). *An Introduction to Sociology*. New York: Ronald Press.
Della Porta, D., & Diani, M. (2006). *Social Movements: An Introduction* (2nd Ed.). London: Wiley.
Della Porta, D., & Tarrow, S. G. (2005). *Transnational protest and global activism*. Oxford: Rowman and Littlefield.
van Dijck, J. (2013). *The Culture of Connectivity*. Oxford: Oxford University Press.
van Dijck, J., & Poell, T. (2013). Understanding Social Media Logic. *Media and Communication*, 1(1), pp. 2–14.
Fenton, N. (2008). Mediating Solidarity. *Global Media and Communication*, 4(1), pp. 37–57.
Flanagin, A. J., Stohl, C., & Bimber, B. (2006). Modelling the Structure of Collective Action. *Communication Monographs*, 73(1), pp. 29–54.
Fuchs, C. (2011). *Foundations of Critical Media and Information Studies*. New York: Routledge.
Fuchs, C. (2017). From digital positivism and administrative big data analytics towards critical digital and social media research!, *European Journal of Communication*, 32(1), 37–49.
Gamson, W. A. (1992). *Talking Politics*. Cambridge: Cambridge University Press.
Gerbaudo, P. (2012). *Tweets and the Street: Social media and contemporary activism*. London: Pluto Press.
Gerlach, L. (2001). The structure of social movements: Environmental activism and its opponents. In: J. Arquilla, & D. Ronfeldt (Eds.) *Networks and Netwars: The Future of Terror, Crime, and Militancy* (pp. 289–310). Santa Monica, CA: Rand.
Gerlach, L., & Hine, V. (1970). *People, Power and Chance*. Indianapolis, IN: Bobbs-Merrill.
Höök, K., D. Benyon, & A. J. Munro, (Eds). (2003). *Designing Information Spaces: The Social Navigation Approach. Computer Supported Cooperative Work*. London: Springer-Verlag.
Juris, J. S. (2004). Networked social movements. In: M. Castells (Ed.) *The Network Society* (pp. 341–362). London: Edward Elgar.
Juris, J. S. (2008). *Networking futures: the movements against corporate globalization*. Durham, NC: Duke University Press.

Kallinikos, J., Leonardi, P. M., & Nardi, B. A. (2012). The Challenge of Materiality: Origins, Scope, and Prospects. In: P. M. Leonardi, B. A. Nardi, & J. Kallinikos (Eds.) *Materiality and Organizing* (pp. 3–22). Oxford: Oxford University Press.

Kaun, A., & Stiernstedt, F. (2014). Facebook Time: Technological and institutional affordances for media memories. *New Media & Society*, 15(17), pp. 1154–1168.

Kaun, A. (2015). Regimes of time: Media practices of the dispossessed. *Time & Society*, 24(2), pp. 221–243.

Kaun, A. (2016). 'Our time to act has come': desynchronization, social media time and protest movements. *Media, Culture & Society*, 39(4), pp. 469–486.

Kavada, A. (2009). Email lists and the construction of an open and multifaceted identity: The case of the London 2004 European Social Forum. *Information, Communication and Society*, 12(6), pp. 817–839.

Kavada, A. (2013). Internet cultures and protest movements: The cultural links between strategy, organizing and online communication. In: B. Cammaerts et al. (Eds.) *Mediation and Protest Movements* (pp. 77–94). Bristol: intellect Books.

Klinger, U., & Svensson, J. (2017). *The End of Media Logics? On Algorithms and Agency*. Manuscript submitted for publication.

Ljungberg, F., & Sørensen, C. (2000). Overload: From transaction to interaction. In: K. Braa, C. Sørensen, & B. Dahlbom (Eds.) *Planet Internet* (pp. 113–136). Lund: Studentlitteratur.

Mathiassen, L., & Sørensen, C. (2008). Towards A Theory of Organizational Information Services. *Journal of Information Technology*, 23(4), pp. 313–329.

Macionis, J. J. (2001). *Sociology* (8th ed). Upper Saddle River, NJ: Prentice Hall.

Melucci, A. (1995). The Process of Collective Identity. In: H. Johnston & B. Klandermans (Eds.) *Social Movements and Culture* (pp. 41–63). Minneapolis, MN: University of Minnesota Press.

McCarthy, J. D., & Zald, M. (1977). Resource Mobilization and Social Movements: A Partial Theory. *The American Journal of Sociology*, 82(6), pp. 1212–1241.

Milan, S. (2015). When Algorithms Shape Collective Action: Social Media and the Dynamics of Cloud Protesting. *Social Media + Society*, 1(2), pp. 1–10.

Miller, F. D. (1999) The end of SDS and the emergence of weatherman: Demise through success. In: J. Freeman & V. Johnson (Eds.) *Waves of protest: Social Movements since the Sixties* (pp. 303–324). Lanham, MD: Rowman & Littlefield.

Morris, A. D., & Staggenborg, S. (2004). Leadership in Social Movements. In: D. Snow, S. A. Soule, & H. Kriesi (Eds.) *The Blackwell Companion to Social Movements* (pp. 171–196). Oxford: Blackwell Publishing.

Poell, T., Abdulla, R., Rieder, B., Woltering, R., & Liesbeth, Z. (2016). Protest leadership in the age of social media. *Information, Communication & Society*, 19(7), pp. 994–1014.

Poell, T., & van Dijck, J. (2015). Social Media and activist communication. In: C. Atton (Ed.) *The Routledge companion to alternative and community media* (pp. 527–537). London: Routledge.

RainieL., & WellmanB. (2014). *Networked: The new social operating system*. Cambridge, MA: MIT Press.

Schmidt, K., & Simone, C. (1996). Coordination mechanisms: Towards a conceptual foundation of CSCW systems design. *Computer Supported Cooperative Work: The Journal of Collaborative Computing (CSCW)*, 5(2–3), pp. 155–200.

Suchman, L. (1987). *Plans and situated action. The problem of human-machine communication*. Cambridge: Cambridge University Press.

Svensson, J. (2017). Social Media and Protest in Algorithmic Society. Paper presented at the Workshop Protest Media Ecologies: Communicative Affordances for Social Change in the Digital Era, Scuola Normale Superiore, Florence, April 2017.

Treré, E., & Barassi, V. (2015). Net-authoritarianism? How web ideologies reinforce political hierarchies in the Italian 5 Star Movement. *Journal of Italian Cinema & Media Studies*, 3 (3), pp. 287–304.

Vygotsky, L. (1978). *Mind in Society*. Cambridge, MA: Harvard University Press.

Zald, M. N., & Ash, R. (1966). Social movement organizations: Growth, decay and change. *Social Forces*, 44(3), pp. 327–341.

Zald, M. N. & McCarthy, J. D. (1980). Social movement industries: competition and cooperation among movement organizations. In: L. Kriesberg (Ed.) *Research in Social Movements, Conflicts and Change* (pp. 1–20). Greenwich, CT: JAI Press.

6

SOCIAL MEDIA AS ACTIVIST ARCHIVES

Christina Neumayer and David M. Struthers

Introduction

During the protests against the G20 summit in Hamburg, Germany in July 2017 a man walked into a group of masked individuals and took a selfie in front of a fire burning in the street. Another photographer captured this moment. The resulting photograph was reproduced as the Riot Hipster meme multiple times on the same day, sometimes combined with Godzilla in the background, a scene from the movie Independence Day, or with the Hindenburg disaster (http://knowyourmeme.com/photos/1273595-riot-hipster). The German newspaper *Der Spiegel* reported that this was only one out of a large number of selfies taken during the protests in Hamburg. The man in the picture did not start the fires himself (Löwe 2017), yet through his presence he participated, spectating and photographing. *Der Spiegel* shared the original unaltered photograph on Twitter followed by @JimmyRushmore, accompanied by the tweet "That feeling when you're overthrowing capitalism but just can't resist taking a selfie on your iPhone 7." His tweet had received 40,694 Retweets, 73,632 Likes, and 1,800 comments by the time of writing.

This episode exemplifies changing processes in activists' loss of control in the struggle over visibility in the contested and complex flow of images, representations and data in social media. This struggle is not new. Gamson and Wolfsfeld (1993) describe social movements and media as interacting systems engaged in a struggle over meaning of protest events. They stress a power imbalance and dependency that favours the media at the expense of social movements, given that gaining voice depended entirely on representation by journalists. Whereas established organizations receive automatic standing in their representations, movements must struggle if mass media are to convey their message – rather than distort, mistranslate, or ignore it entirely (Gamson & Wolfsfeld 1993: 117). In parallel, certain ideas, values, and languages are welcomed while others are less popular or rendered invisible by media norms and practices. These meanings, Gamson & Wolfsfeld (1993) argue, often push activists into adapting to the language of the mass media and the mainstream. In light of struggle over control of representation in mass media, social media introduce a new round of struggle over control and visibility.

Today, citizen reporting and eye witnessing through smartphones may have changed the dynamics of how protest events are witnessed. "Connective witnessing" (Mortensen 2015) of protest events in social media environments blurs the boundaries between mobilization, participation, and documentation. Bennett and Segerberg (2012) describe this form of contentious action based on sharing personalized and individual content in social media networks as "connective action". Rather than developing a collective identity, they argue, individuals now share their personal stories and grievances as inclusive slogans such as "I am the 99%" in the Occupy protests. Individuals contribute to a cause by sharing, linking, and other forms of expressing solidarity through social media, but by doing so, they also adhere to the social media logic and give up control over their data in their struggle over visibility (Poell & van Dijck 2015).

The power of representation in the era of mass media came through mass visibility determined by human actors, often in newsrooms. Determinations over-represented in contemporary social media include an actor even less visible to users than in prior years. Representational power in social media also lies in the "pictures of our actions made of bits, stored in databases, available to algorithms," and "we need to begin to theorize both actors and images that circulate invisibility" (Turner 2014: 254). These invisible algorithmic actors, the techno-commercial materiality of social media, further accelerated mediation, which changed the temporality of protest itself, and increased the visibility and traceability of personalized activist communication (see Kaun 2015; Kaun & Stiernstedt 2014; Poell & van Dijck 2015). Moreover, social movements often attempt to evade mechanisms of control that can put individual participants and their political work at risk by employing self-censorship practices as part of their struggle for visibility and recognition (Uldam 2017). Social media materialities and participant practices shape activist imagery (such as images of violent performance or personalized expressions) in social media.

In this chapter, we critically unpack the idea of social media as an archive of protest communication in relation to its techno-commercial materiality. We do so by reviewing conceptual and empirical work that critically engages with social media and protest and link this body of literature to the idea of the archive. We examine the process of data creation through its storage in social media archives and how algorithmic determinations of representation in social media produce archives that are incomplete. In the course of this argument, we contrast mediated protest in the early 20th century with contemporary protests from the perspective of the historian writing a history from below. We outline how the processes of acceleration and personalization increase the visibility of particular forms of communication; discuss the practices of avoidance and silencing in social movements' communication due to techno-commercial social media materialities and the resulting incomplete archives; and unpack how the process of over- and under-representation of certain forms of activist communication take shape, as users generally have limited access to the databases of commercial social media platforms. We argue that through building non-commercial alternatives in the form of activist archives created in collaboration with social movements, we can uncover imbalances of power and tell a more inclusive story about contemporary social movements operating within social media materialities.

Personalization, acceleration, and over-representation

The Riot Hipster is an illustration of how social media selfie culture intersects with activists' (self-)representation. Activists covering their faces to avoid identification are joined by the bearded hipster taking a selfie. The holding up of the mobile phone gives him an almost iconic appearance; his pose facing the mobile phone gives the impression that he is looking into a mirror. The expression of the self through social media by taking a selfie becomes part of being in the event. The photographer taking a picture of the young man taking a selfie then puts this act of self-representation into the broader context that would have otherwise been filtered out by the narrow field of view of a front facing camera. The subsequent rebroadcast of this scene as the Riot Hipster meme happens almost instantaneously thereafter. Taking a selfie as a way of saying "I am here" and "I am part of this event" is transformed into an impersonalized meme. Instead of showing the self, the selfie becomes *the* representation of hipsters and selfies in spectacular protest events. Acceleration and personalization both increase in this process. The activists in the image trying to protect their anonymity by concealing their faces as well as the man in the image who later becomes the Riot Hipster are not in control of the accelerated dissemination of the image.

Forms of personalization and personal expression based on personal action frames shared in social media as a productive form of political action have been discussed as "connective action" (Bennett & Segerberg 2012), but also as sub-activism (Bakardjieva 2009) and more widely as a personalization of politics (Bennett 2012). In recent protests, there are many examples of mobilizing selfies in social media into connective action, such as the "We are the 99%" selfies of the Occupy Wall Street movement and the "We are all Khaled Said" selfies promoting the Egyptian revolution in 2011 (Alaimo 2015). These personalized forms of sharing mobilized a "we" to express political resistance are, however, based on ephemeral and instable forms of collectivity built on filtering processes such as hashtags or trending topics (see Poell & van Dijck 2015). In the example of the Riot Hipster, a selfie taken to potentially show presence and solidarity in a protest event is turned into a new ephemeral collective built around the Riot Hipster meme (and hashtag) – detached from the political protest event.

The techno-commercial infrastructure of social media based on personalization and filtering processes may privilege certain visual content and genres over others and potentially decontextualize by taking the attention away from the political (see Bayerl & Stoynov 2016). The embodied material travels and "connects knowledge productions to global flows that are always already there" (Blaagaard 2013: 371). In these flows, the "[c]ontextual knowledge about the source and the motif is often not preserved or accessible when these visuals drift in more-or-less predictable online patterns" (Blaagaard, Mortensen & Neumayer 2017: 1117). The selfie then can be considered a commodity itself (Iqani & Schroeder 2016), a visual form that the individual seems to be in control of, but the selfie's aesthetics are being mediated and shaped by the techno-commercial infrastructure of social media platforms. Social media's "technological features, such as 'retweeting', liking, following, and 'friending', as well as algorithmic selection mechanisms [...] privilege particular types of content" (Poell & van Dijck 2015: 528) such as spectacular images over content that illuminates larger political issues (Poell & Borra 2012). For the Riot Hipster, the seeming self-control of the selfie by choice of situation, frames, and filters (shaped by the material characteristics of social media platforms) is taken away by another party taking the photograph. The act of taking a selfie is turned into a different, unintended visual genre – a meme – of the subject. Social media logic co-opted the protest scene emerging from activist grievances for individual mediated self-expression and its memefication detached the image from the political context. The recirculation of the images in new genres and forms seem to help maintain power and dependency imbalances between social movements and social media (as observed by Gamson and Wolfsfeld 1993, in mass media), leaving limited room for voicing political critique.

The unprecedented speed of this process through acceleration in a social media logic can have advantages for mobilization but can also undermine the sustainability of social movements (Bennett & Segerberg 2012; Gerbaudo 2017; Poell & van Dijck 2015; Tilly 2004). Kaun (2015) argued that social movements adjust their practices under the regimes of time that social media impose on them. What Fuchs (2014a) called the capitalist regime of time is based on the future oriented logics of acceleration of consumption and accumulation of data for surplus value production, and social media themselves impose the time structure of capitalism in our everyday lives and of political protest. In an attempt to understand the temporalizing practices of social media, Barassi (2015) argued that the immediacy of social media demands instantaneous and continuous communication by activists to compete with the constant noise or (as the example of the Riot Hipster shows) their political messages being co-opted. While social media time renders data and archives ephemeral and only temporarily visible to the individual, this goes hand in hand with the storing and archiving of data for producing surplus value (Kaun & Stiernstedt 2014) and speculative future capital (Fuchs 2014a). These data archives of the social are compromised by techno-commercial profit-making infrastructures (Langlois, Redden & Elmer 2015). While social media archives are built upon user-generated content, Gehl (2011) argues, they are inherently undemocratic as only social media corporations have access to the affective and personalized data stored about users. Combined, acceleration and personalization over-represent certain forms, genres, and actions. Simultaneously, social movements have developed tactics of avoidance and invisibility to try and escape the immediate traceability, capitalist co-optation and (despite the ephemeral public visibility) the permanence of social media data which can put them at risk.

Avoidance, silencing, and under-representation

In parallel to activists increasing their visibility and self-representation, social movements often have tactical motivations to remain invisible, intentionally obscuring their organizing from those in power. Being visible while avoiding becoming part of the media's spectacle has always been a complicated endeavour for movements (Lester & Hutchins 2009; Melucci 1996; Rucht 2004). Many scholars have critically engaged with the notion of resistance in the digital age and stressed the dangers of surveillance and control by authorities as well as the corporate sector that controls social web platforms (see Cammaerts 2008; Fuchs 2014b; Sandoval 2014). Activists navigating today's corporate social media, need to find ways to avoid being seen while simultaneously trying to produce visibility for their political agenda. Social movements avoid mechanisms of control over their mediated communication and other personal (meta-)data that can put them and their political work at risk and find it vital to utilize secure communication along with their use of traceable social media platforms. The risk of exposure can result in self-censorship practices as part of struggles for visibility and recognition (Brighenti 2007; Neumayer, Rossi & Karlsson 2016; Uldam 2017). Avoidance can also be a consequence of the techno-commercial social media infrastructure which might contradict value systems of activists engaging in struggles against the current economic system (Galis & Neumayer 2016).

This leads to activists producing visibility and publicity jointly with deploying strategies of concealment and secrecy (Neumayer & Stald 2014). When exposed to a high level of insecurity, particularly in relation to utilizing tactics like property damage, it is a common practice to avoid all public and mobile communication that could potentially be traced back to an individual. Some of these tactics include using pre-paid SIM cards that cannot be linked to a personal identity, not taking photos or videos of demonstrations (despite this being a means of making police violence visible) due to the risk of identification, or using a collective Twitter and Facebook account instead of publicly posting on their personal accounts (see Askanius & Gustafsson 2010; Leistert 2012; Neumayer & Stald 2014; Uldam 2017). Activists can tamper with social media to achieve various goals, from reduced visibility (within censored or highly surveyed platforms) to selective visibility to specific groups of users. Brunton and Nissenbaum (2015: 1) refer to this process as "obfuscation", a "deliberate addition of ambiguous, confusing, or misleading information to interfere with surveillance and data collection". Jessie Daniels (2009: 661) conceptualizes cloaked websites as "published by individuals or groups that conceal authorship or feign legitimacy in order to deliberately disguise a hidden political agenda". Such techniques are essential for social movements, particularly in social media where connecting data points for profiling of individuals exposes activists to a high level of risk.

Whether these techniques of obfuscation and concealment are tolerated on social media platforms is eventually a decision made by social media corporations. One social media tactic for anonymizing identities is using a pseudonym. Activists, Tufekci (2017:142) argued (based on the LGBT movement), "were pushed off Facebook by vengeful people who reported them for not using their real names". Activists trying to hide from authorities face the realities of social media materialities. Each platform's policies determine what remains visible and what is removed or censored, while algorithms structure what is seen or hidden, and what has the right to be permanently forgotten. Youmans and York (2012) draw on different case studies to show how user policies of social media platforms can lead to the removal of activist content, anonymous profiles, as well as the handing over of sensitive user data to governments. Social media corporations will determine whether the tactics employed to be forgotten or to remain invisible in the first place remain. This has led to clear choices on what to include (in print and) in public communication on corporate social media platforms, and what to leave to a most ephemeral form of communication, the human voice.

While tactics and strategies of obfuscation, disguise, avoidance, and rendering content and authorship invisible have long been employed by social movements, they challenge assumptions concerning social media as archival repositories. Contemporary social media materialities complicate practices of obfuscation and give way to new forms of control. Avoidance then leads to invisibility in social media, resulting in social media databases (or archives) that are not only heavily biased but also obfuscated. With this line of argument, Poell (2015: 199) suggested that techniques of disguise such as using symbolic language, misspellings and pseudonyms may obfuscate activists' traces, but they provide an "unjustified sense of security" and steer activists away "from directly expressing political critique". While we might see an over-representation of personalized forms of connective action and the spectacle of property destruction or violence, expressions of political critique might be inherently under-represented in social media archives as a result of these invisibilities.

Invisibilities and incomplete archives

Anarchists in the early 20th century aimed for maximum publicity for their ideals and to create the broadest possible movement. However, they exercised caution in their public utterances in often fruitless attempts to avoid prosecution during a period in which technology limited the speed and increased the cost of communication compared to today (Struthers forthcoming). These factors contributed to uneven documentary records of the movement in this period. One of the primary motivations of social historians and certainly those writing "history from below" has been to uncover these and other "silenced" voices by creatively re-examining known sources and discovering new ones (Trouillot 1995). Activist practices of avoidance increase the difficulty for historians attempting to document their clandestine activities.

Today, social media data have served as an invaluable resource for recent studies of social movements (see Neumayer & Rossi 2016, for an overview). While social media data can enable a comprehensive overview of activists' social media communication, demonstrate patterns of activity, and shed light on online social networks, there is much that remains invisible (Croeser & Highfield 2015). For historians, source creation is followed by archiving, retrieval, and interpretation (Trouillot 1995). Due to the interplay between anarchists' attempting to avoid arrest or repression and their desire to grow a movement, historical research on anarchism often relies on their extensive movement-created print media and state policing records. But still, much remains opaque and only knowable through later personal remembrances. This is the case with the world's first "car" bombing. An anarchist named Mario Buda filled a wagon with dynamite and exploded it on Wall Street in 1919. He escaped to his home country of Italy and was never caught. We only know about him through interviews with his acquaintances decades later (Avrich 2005[1995]).

Despite the idea that in contemporary social media all movements and interactions are stored as data points that can be connected to tell stories and even predict action, telling a history from below requires careful deliberation. When every political act can potentially be traced, personalized, rebroadcast and shared in social media, the right to remain invisible might become even more important for clandestine social movements. Research about media and social movements has often dealt with the question of visibility (see Lester & Hutchins 2009; Neumayer & Rossi 2018; Rucht 2004; Uldam 2017). One of the primary concerns of media studies is the broadcasting and dissemination of ideas, making voices heard in the sense of people wanting to share their ideas. Yet, there is a tension between activists wanting to grow their movement through broadcasting their views and their desire to avoid repression. Similar to the recent creation of a "right to be forgotten", what about social movements that actively and intentionally seek to obscure, disrupt, and eliminate their own legibility? What happens when people intentionally want to obscure their actions, to silence their voices from the public and historical record to further their own goals? And what consequences do the silencing of their voices have on social media as archives about political protest?

Following Foucault (2003[1969]) in *The Archaeology of Knowledge*, archives consist not only of shelves and artifacts that the historian can investigate, but include the larger apparatus and set of rules and power relationships that allow archives to exist, including the institution and even the building in which it is located. Similarly, data from social media are stored and archived within its own materialities. While content supported by the processes of acceleration and personalization is contained in these archives, much remains invisible through activist practices of avoidance or is only visible to social media corporations. The techno-commercial infrastructure organized by algorithmic classification sorts based on likes, hashtags, mentions, comments, and favours. In his exploration into the materialities of information, Paul Dourish (2017) argued that materiality is not only the archive itself but also the technologies we can use to produce the material that can be archived. How we create data in an interactive process with media technologies is an essential part of the materialities of information, which is concerned with the material forms of representation of digital data leading to particular interpretations and actions (Dourish & Mazmanian 2013).

The epistemology underlying social media data archives is based on an idea of data points. Latour and Woolgar (1986), in their observations in scientific laboratories, argued that audiences accept facts as reality because of the mystifying manner in which they are constructed. Along similar lines, social media data, accessed through an application programming interfaces (APIs) provided by large corporations, have been used as a basis for statements of fact, despite these data being likely filtered and incomplete because they are structured through algorithms that remain invisible (Neumayer & Rossi 2016). The immediacy of these data archives produced by APIs follows the techno-commercial temporal regime of social media. The information that social movements share through their social media communication can immediately be turned into data-points as raw materials of pre-emption for different purposes (see Fuchs 2014a; Elmer & Opel 2008). Once communication is mediated by a technology it becomes traceable and storable and can be used as a data point. While scholars have considered technology avoidance or individuals choosing to not use certain technologies (Baumer et al. 2015), communication avoidance also impacts our ability to study under-represented groups and individuals. If we want to understand how activists navigate social media environments, we need to take into account the silences and the ephemerality of social movements' communication imposed by social media.

Activist social media archives

Research based on big social media data archives underlying the processes of acceleration and personalization often focusses on what is visible and over-emphasized (see Croeser & Highfield 2015; Neumayer & Rossi 2016). Returning to our example of the Riot Hipster, social media foster activist communication that represents an "intensely insular, 'me-centric' and distorted view of the world – always outward from the 'I'" (Elmer 2015: 152). While these personalized and accelerated forms of communication lead the way to "connective action" (as in Bennett & Segerberg 2012), there is a lack of recognition for "collectivity" in these processes (Gerbaudo & Treré 2015; Treré & Mattoni 2016). Social media data might be collectively produced in an Instagram/Twitter hashtag, a Facebook page, and a YouTube channel. However, "activists have control over neither the social media architectures through which they communicate nor the data they collectively produce through Twitter hashtags, and Facebook pages and groups" (Poell 2015: 199). What happens with the data they produce on these platforms is not known to the activists and only visible to the social media corporations. This results in archives that are not produced in solidarity with activists – neither respecting their right to be forgotten nor focussing on their collective grievances (see Croeser & Highfield 2015). How then, can we turn personalized stories and the images of the self into a collective and collaborative project to counteract processes of over- and under-representation in techno-commercial social media?

A first step, we argue, is the opening of the black box of the materiality of social media "as active agents shaping the symbolic and organizational processes of social actors" (Milan, 2015: 897). By doing so, we can counteract the individualization and personalization fostered in social media materialities by trying to circumvent or co-opt social media (see Galis & Neumayer 2016; Poell 2015) to develop collaborative archives of social movements. By unpacking what is over-represented and visible in social media, we also understand why activists intentionally decide not to share. Historians writing a history from below are motivated to recover obscured voices. The focus on uncovering lead Michel-Rolph Trouillot to evocatively note how power worked to "silence the past" of historical actors during their lives and after death in archives (Trouillot 1995). Broadening our scope requires a break with both the acceleration and the personalization of social media. We need to retrospectively connect data points, but instead of aiming at personalization through profiling based on data points, we understand this as a collective project to reveal how power of social media platforms can lead to silences and invisibilities.

Giving activists control over their data and acknowledging their right to be forgotten tells a story that cannot be told within social media materialities. Many pictures taken and stories told during protest events remain invisible and are never shared (Elmer 2015: 145). Greg Elmer and Andy Opel produced the documentary entitled *Pre-empting Dissent* (2015) in an attempt to tell a participatory story about protest events that is not being told by the immediate and personalized visibility created in social media. Documentary film maker Ross Domoney (2014: 574) described his projects as a "collective effort in which everyone participating adds a key facet to the story". As historians uncover documents to tell a history from below, these documentaries are a collaborative project with social movements where activists lay claim to control their own data. By doing so, we can uncover the invisible actors of power underlying social media.

Moving from the documentary to a larger collaborative project of archiving protest material must happen within an infrastructure that respects the norms and ethics of social movements and media activists. As Elmer (2015: 158) pointedly argued, we must develop an infrastructure that "challenges the first person, selfie-obsessed interface and images, that narrow and internalize our fields of vision, imaginaries and potential sites of political engagement and struggles for social justice". Images that become visible in social media as testimony from protest events do not necessarily represent an individual perspective that is representative of a collective. Moving from these connective personalized statements into a collective project also means a close collaboration with activists in a partisan project (Galis & Hansson 2012), giving social movements control over the content and data points they produce. A collaborative project of building an archive for historians and media activists means moving beyond social media materialities through a collaborative effort to connect data points in a non-commercial project. Writing a history from below by building these archives might then uncover the power that obscures voices in social media.

Conclusion

Understanding social media as an archive of social movement communication emphasizes how these repositories are shaped by social media materialities. Social media corporations turn the flood of images and personalized stories from protest events into data, but their archives over-represent certain genres, visual forms, and protest slogans. The processes of acceleration and personalization in social media overemphasize images and forms of protest that adhere to its material logic and over-represent personalized stories. They can also put clandestine social movements at risk, as the data shared in social media is not controlled by movements, which leads to techniques of obfuscation and a deradicalization of political critique.

Following the path of the critical historian writing a history from below, making visible control and oppression becomes increasingly challenging in social media archives. Telling an inclusive story about social movements and connecting data points that are rendered invisible by power that silences voices in social media, requires uncovering the actors taking part in the politics of visibility imposed by the materialities of social media. Media activists and historians must strive to tell inclusive stories of social movements through archives produced in a collaborative effort. This has long been a challenging task due to the vulnerability and ephemerality of mediated activist communication. The notion of silencing utilized by historians helps our understanding of how gaps are created in our data and the role of power, silencing and loss of control over data in this process. Scholars must understand and respect the invisibilities and silences intentionally created by social movements, and the effect that internal decisions within social media corporations have over the data they collect and store. Telling inclusive stories of social movements and writing a history from below must look beyond limited social media archives to data generated through collaboration with movements that can help to understand the power that silences voices in social media communication. Departing from the techno-commercial materialities and creating more inclusive spaces where activists reclaim control over their data can be a way to dismantle invisible agents of power in social media.

References

Alaimo, K. (2015). How the Facebook Arabic page "We are all Khaled Said" helped promote the Egyptian revolution. *Social Media and Society*, 1(2).

Askanius, T., & Gustafsson, N. (2010). Mainstreaming the alternative: The changing media practices of protest movements. *Interface*, 2(2), pp. 23–41.

Avrich, P. (2005[1995]). *Anarchist Voices: An Oral History of Anarchism in America*. Chico, CA: AK Press.

Bakardjieva, M. (2009). Subactivism: Lifeworld and Politics in the Age of the Internet. *The Information Society*, 25(2), pp. 91–104.

Barassi, V. (2015). Social Media, Immediacy and the Time for Democracy: Critical Reflections on Social Media as 'Temporalizing Practices'. In: L. Dencik, & O. Leistert (Eds). *Critical Perspectives on Social Media and Protest: Between Control and Emancipation* (pp.73–88). London, New York: Rowman & Littlefield.

Baumer, E. P., Ames, M. G., Burrell, J., Brubaker, J. R., & Dourish, P. (2015). Why study technology non-use? *First Monday*, 20(11).

Bayerl, P. S., & Stoynov, L. (2016). Revenge by photoshop: Memefying police acts in the public dialogue about injustice. *New Media & Society*, 18(6), pp. 1006–1026.

Bennett, W. L. (2012). The personalization of politics: Political identity, social media, and changing patterns of participation. *The ANNALS of the American Academy of Political and Social Science*, 644(1), pp. 20–39.

Bennett, W. L., & Segerberg, A. (2012). The logic of connective action: Digital media and the personalization of contentious politics. *Information, Communication & Society*, 15(5), pp. 739–768.

Blaagaard, B. (2013). Post-human viewing: a discussion of the ethics of mobile phone imagery. *Visual Communication*, 12(3), pp. 359–374.

Blaagaard, B., Mortensen, M., & Neumayer, C. (2017). Digital images and globalized conflict. *Media, Culture & Society*, 39(8), pp. 1111–1121.

Brighenti, A. (2007). Visibility: A category for the social sciences. *Current sociology*, 55(3), pp. 323–342.

Brunton, F., & Nissenbaum, H. (2015). *Obfuscation: A user's guide for privacy and protest*. Cambridge, MA: MIT Press.

Cammaerts, B. (2008). Critiques on the participatory potentials of Web 2.0. *Communication, Culture and Critique*, 1(4), pp. 358–377.

Croeser, S., & Highfield, T. (2015). Mapping Movements – Social Movement Research and Big Data: Critiques and Alternatives. In: G. Langlois, J. Redden, & G. Elmer (Eds.). *Compromised Data: From Social Media to Big Data* (pp.173–201). New York, London: Bloomsbury.

Daniels, J. (2009). Cloaked websites: propaganda, cyber-racism and epistemology in the digital era. *New Media & Society*, 11(5), pp. 659–683.

Domoney, R., & Triantafyllou, G. (2014). Ross Domoney and Giorgos Triantafyllou: An interview. *City*, 18(4–5), pp. 574–576.

Dourish, P. (2017). *The Stuff of Bits: An Essay on the Materialities of Information*. Cambridge, MA: MIT Press.

Dourish, P., & Mazmanian, M. (2013). Media as Material: Information Representation as Material Foundations of Organizational Practice. In: P. R. Carlile, D. Nicolini, A. Langley, & H. Tsoukas (Eds). *How Matter Matters: Objects, Artifacts, and Materiality in Organization Studies* (pp. 92–118). Oxford: Oxford University Press.

Elmer, G. (2015). Preempting Dissent: From Participatory Policing to Collaborative Filmmaking. In: L. Dencik, & O. Leistert (Eds). *Critical Perspectives on Social Media and Protest: Between Control and Emancipation* (pp.145–160). London, New York: Rowman & Littlefield.

Elmer, G., & Opel, A. (2008). *Preempting dissent: The politics of an inevitable future*. Winnipeg: Arbeiter Ring.

Foucault, M. (2003[1969]). *The Archaeology of Knowledge*. New York: Routledge.

Fuchs, C. (2014a). Digital prosumption labour on social media in the context of the capitalist regime of time. *Time & Society*, 23(1), pp. 97–123.

Fuchs, C. (2014b). *OccupyMedia!: The occupy movement and social media in crisis capitalism*. Alresford: John Hunt Publishing.

Galis, V., & Hansson, A. (2012). Partisan scholarship in technoscientific controversies: Reflections on research experience. *Science as Culture*, 21(3), pp. 335–364.

Galis, V., & Neumayer, C. (2016). Laying claim to social media by activists: a cyber-material détournement. *Social Media + Society*, 2(3).

Gamson, W. A., & Wolfsfeld, G. (1993). Movements and media as interacting systems. *The Annals of the American Academy of Political and Social Science*, 528(1), pp. 114–125.

Gehl, R. W. (2011). The archive and the processor: The internal logic of Web 2.0. *New Media & Society*, 13(8), pp. 1228–1244.

Gerbaudo, P. (2017). From Cyber-Autonomism to Cyber-Populism: An Ideological Analysis of the Evolution of Digital Activism. *tripleC: Communication, Capitalism & Critique*, 15 (2), pp. 477–489.

Gerbaudo, P., & Treré, E. (2015). In search of the 'we' of social media activism: Introduction to the special issue on social media and protest identities. *Information, Communication & Society*, 18(8), pp. 865–871.

Iqani, M., & Schroeder, J. E. (2016). #selfie: digital self-portraits as commodity form and consumption practice. *Consumption Markets & Culture*, 19(5), pp. 405–415.

Kaun, A. (2015). Regimes of time: Media practices of the dispossessed. *Time & Society*, 24(2), pp. 221–243.

Kaun, A., & Stiernstedt, F. (2014). Facebook time: Technological and institutional affordances for media memories. *New Media & Society*, 16(7), pp. 1154–1168.

Langlois, G., Redden, J., & Elmer, G. (Eds.) (2015). *Compromised Data: From Social Media to Big Data*. New York, London: Bloomsbury.

Latour, B., & Woolgar, S. (1986). *Laboratory life: The construction of scientific facts*. Princeton, NJ: Princeton University Press.

Leistert, O. (2012). Resistance against cyber-surveillance within social movements and how surveillance adapts. *Surveillance & Society*, 9(4), pp. 441–456.

Lester, L., & Hutchins, B. (2009). Power games: environmental protest, news media and the internet. *Media, Culture & Society*, 31(4), pp. 579–595.

Löwe, P. (2017, 8 July). Selfie vor Krawallkulisse. *Der Spiegel*. Retrieved from http://www.spiegel.de/panorama/gesellschaft/g20-krawalle-selfie-bei-randale-im-schanzenviertel-a-1156799.html.

Melucci, A. (1996). *Challenging codes: Collective action in the information age*. Cambridge: Cambridge University Press.

Milan, S. (2015). From social movements to cloud protesting: the evolution of collective identity. *Information, Communication & Society*, 18(8), pp. 887–900.

Mortensen, M. (2015). Connective witnessing: Reconfiguring the relationship between the individual and the collective. *Information, Communication & Society*, 18(11), pp. 1393–1406.

Neumayer, C., & Rossi, L. (2016). 15 Years of Protest and Media Technologies Scholarship: A Sociotechnical Timeline. *Social Media + Society*, 2(3).

Neumayer, C., & Rossi, L. (2018). Images of protest in social media: Struggle over visibility and visual narratives. *New Media & Society*, online before print, DOI: doi:1461444818770602.

Neumayer, C., Rossi, L., & KarlssonB. (2016). Contested Hashtags: Blockupy Frankfurt in Social Media. *International Journal of Communication*, 10(22), pp. 5558–5579.

Neumayer, C., & Stald, G. (2014). The mobile phone in street protest: Texting, tweeting, tracking, and tracing. *Mobile Media & Communication*, 2(2), pp. 117–133.

Poell, T. (2015). Social Media Activism and State Censorship. In: D. Trottier, and C. Fuchs (Eds). *Social Media, Politics and the State: Protests, Revolutions, Riots, Crime and Policing in the Age of Facebook, Twitter and YouTube* (pp.189–206). London: Routledge.

Poell, T., & Borra, E. (2012). Twitter, YouTube, and Flickr as platforms of alternative journalism: The social media account of the 2010 Toronto G20 protests. *Journalism*, 13(6), pp. 695–713.

Poell, T. & van Dijck, J. (2015). Social Media and Activist Communication. In C. Atton (Ed.) *The Routledge Companion to Alternative and Community Media* (pp. 527–537). London: Routledge.

Rucht, D. (2004). The quadruple "A." Media strategies of protest movements since the 1960s. In: W. B. van de Donk, B. D. Loader, P. G. Nixon, and D. Rucht (Eds). *Cyberprotest: New Media, Citizens and Social Movements* (pp. 25–48). London: Routledge.

Sandoval, M. (2014). *From corporate to social media: Critical perspectives on corporate social responsibility in media and communication industries*. London, New York: Routledge.

Struthers, D. M. (forthcoming). *The World in a City: Multiethnic Radicalism in Early Twentieth Century Los Angeles*. Champaign, IL: University of Illinois Press.

Tilly, C. (2004). *Social movements, 1768–2004*. Boulder, CO: Paradigm Publishers

Treré, E., & Mattoni, A. (2016). Media ecologies and protest movements: main perspectives and key lessons. *Information, Communication & Society*, 19(3), pp. 290–306.

Trouillot, M. (1995). *Silencing the Past: Power and the Production of History*. Boston, MA: Beacon Press.

Tufekci, Z. (2017). *Twitter and tear gas: The power and fragility of networked protest*. New Haven, CT: Yale University Press.

Turner, F. (2014). The World Outside and the Pictures in Our Networks. In: T. Gillespie, P. J. Boczkowski, & K. A. Foot (Eds). *Media Technologies: Essays on Communication, Materiality, and Society* (pp.251–260). Cambridge, MA: MIT Press.

Uldam, J. (2017, 21 April). Social media visibility: challenges to activism. *Media, Culture & Society*, online before print, DOI: doi:10.1177/0163443717704997.

Youmans, W. L., & York, J. C. (2012). Social media and the activist toolkit: User agreements, corporate interests, and the information infrastructure of modern social movements. *Journal of Communication*, 62(2), pp. 315–329.

PART III

Platformization

7

THEORIZING CIVIC ENGAGEMENT AND SOCIAL MEDIA

The case of the "refugee crisis" and volunteer organizing in Sweden

Julie Uldam and Anne Kaun

Introduction

Social media have been vested with hopes that they can help reinvigorate civic engagement by providing new possibilities for bottom-up, self-organizing engagement (Castells 2012; Van Laer & Van Aelst 2010). The advent and increasing popularization of social media has been noted as an important vehicle for these possibilities (Dobusch & Schoeneborn 2015). Civic engagement here is understood as paying attention to political and social issues, an attention expressed in a variety of ways that often go beyond parliamentarian politics (Uldam & Vestergaard 2015). Following Dahlgren (2009), we understand civic engagement as subjective states that are the prerequisite for participation. This includes community-driven initiatives such as print shop collectives, community radio, protest camps such as Occupy, but also non-governmental organization (NGO) campaigning and direct action (Baines 2015; Cammaerts 2009; Feigenbaum et al. 2013). Celebratory accounts of the Arab Spring uprisings, and the Occupy and Indignados movements often focus on technological affordances of social media such as instantaneous, dialogical communication (DeLuca et al. 2012). While these affordances are important to the emancipatory potential of social media, they are merely one part of a much bigger picture. We need to look beyond affordances and also consider user practices, discourses and media power. When we do so, we can move beyond the celebratory focus on technological affordances and better understand both the possibilities for and limits to civic engagement. We suggest an analytical framework for examining the role of social media platforms' commercial interests in relation to civic engagement, paying particular attention to the materiality of social media platforms.

To illustrate our framework, we draw on examples from volunteering initiatives to assist migrants arriving in Sweden. The role of social media platforms in volunteering has been shown to facilitate volunteers' engagement with NGOs, albeit in fickle ways (Uldam 2010), especially, in relation to collective identity formation, but also for organizing events including information dissemination and preparation of activities (Uldam 2010; Lovejoy & Saxton 2012). Zooming in on volunteering and migration as forms of civic engagement, social media platforms have also been considered essential in organizing both migrants and volunteers in the context of the so-called refugee crisis peaking in summer 2015. Gillespie et al. (2016), for example, reviewed the role of different applications for information dissemination among refugees on their way to Europe. They conclude that the access to information via digital media was essential in helping refugees navigate their changing physical surroundings. Chouliaraki and Georgiou (2017) show how major NGOs in Chios use social media, especially the chat application WhatsApp on their mobile devices, to constantly update each other about offline developments such as the nocturnal arrival of dinghies. Smaller NGOs were found to be excluded from the major NGOs' communication on WhatsApp and instead used Twitter. NGO communication with migrants was found limited to pre-digital modes such as leaflets and posters, even though an estimated 80 per cent of migrants owned smartphones. Contributing to these important insights, we focus on the role of social media for volunteers in Sweden to illustrate the application of our analytical framework.

An illustrative case study: The migration crisis in Sweden

In 2015, the UNHCR reported approximately 60 million refugees worldwide, and 163,000 refugees were registered as asylum seekers in Sweden (Forsberg 2015). Sweden's status as a transit country contributed to the importance of volunteer initiatives meeting the urgent needs of arriving refugees. The groups explored in this chapter all started on Facebook. To draw on these groups to illustrate our framework, we have combined an analysis of the Facebook pages and groups with in-depth interviews with central organizers of volunteer initiatives in Sweden. We included organizations that featured prominently in mainstream news reporting. The Facebook pages and groups were monitored in terms of the main activities of members and moderators as well as the structure of conversations. For each group, we interviewed the person who set up the Facebook presence and maintained it throughout the most intense periods. The interviews were conducted late summer and autumn 2016. Combining online observations with interviews has enabled us to go beyond a focus on platforms and illustrate all dimensions of our framework.

Four groups were dominant in organizing urgent relief for migrants and refugees arriving in Sweden. The group *Al Tadamon* (meaning solidarity in Arabic) was set up in May 2015 to provide urgent help for one of the biggest shelters in Sweden. The group mainly coordinated the collection and distribution of clothes and necessities for the shelter. The group collaborated with the Swedish Migration Agency and partly took responsibility for supplying newly arrived asylum seekers with necessities, which normally falls within the responsibility of the agency. The group "We who welcome refugees at Stockholm's central station" (*Vi som tar emot flyktingar på Stockholms central*) started their Facebook group in September 2015 with the aim of coordinating urgent relief for arriving and transiting migrants in

Stockholm's central station. The group grew rapidly in the first few days, reaching more than 15,000 members and coordinated the collection and distribution of food, clothes, tickets for onward travel, transport to transit shelters and legal support. The group "Refugees Welcome Stockholm" (RWS) was an offshoot from this group. RWS took over the coordination of relief work at the central station. Volunteers set up a transit shelter for refugees who needed to rest during their journey through the country while not wanting to officially register in Sweden. RWS continues to support protests against the new and stricter migration law that was introduced in summer 2016. "We do what we can" (*Vi gör vad vi kan*) was co-founded by playwriter and director Paula Stenström Öhman and PR strategist Petra Kauraisa. Initially they aimed to collect 500,000 SEK to travel with necessities to Lesvos in Greece to provide urgent relief. The initial goal was quickly reached and in total the initiative collected almost 11 million SEK and 250 tonnes of clothes and other non-food items.

Analytics of civic engagement and social media

To develop a better understanding of the possibilities and challenges that social media can offer civic engagement (including volunteering) we suggest analytics of social media that goes beyond affordances. Our framework considers the materiality of platforms in relation to issues such as everyday organizing, struggles to mobilize for systemic change, and authority impediments to visibility among wider publics. Our aim is to avoid techno-determinism and media-centric focal points. Instead, the approach we suggest considers the context of civic engagement in social media, paying attention to (i) affordances, (ii) power relations, (iii) practices and (iv) discourses. In doing so, we draw on Couldry's (2012) model of a socially oriented media theory. Like Couldry's model, the analytics of social media that we suggest could be applicable to analysing civic engagement beyond social media platforms, since it is non-media centric. In outlining his model, Couldry proposes a pyramid with four apexes that each represents a focal point in media research:

> We can turn the pyramid four ways up, with the type of research we want to prioritize at the top, while others form the pyramid base. No way of turning the pyramid is 'right', or 'better', since the apexes name different priorities for research: media *texts*; the *political economy* of media production, distribution and reception; the *technical properties* of each medium; and the *social uses* to which media technologies and media contents are put.
>
> *Couldry, 2012: 6 (emphasis in original)*

Paying equal attention to all four focal points is often not feasible. It is, nonetheless, important to consider their role, even if just one apex is in focus. We find this approach to studying media highly useful, because it acknowledges the interrelations between the four aspects of the role of the media while also allowing for pragmatic choices regarding delimitations. We therefore adopt this approach while fine-tuning it for studying civic engagement in social media. In the following, we outline our four-dimensional framework for studying civic engagement in social media and discuss the interrelated roles of each dimension. We find the following graphic (Figure 7.1) useful, because its circular connectors illustrate the four dimensions' continuous interrelations.

Power relations

Couldry (2012) labels one dimension "Political economy" in order to address, critique and ultimately supplement the political economy research tradition and its focus on media production, often presupposing economic determinations. We find this errand an extremely important contribution to media studies. However, focussing on civic engagement and social media, we propose a dimension labelled "Power relations". We do so to capture wider power relations beyond production and accumulation, and to include questions of visibility and agency. While social media can potentially help civil society actors access and circulate information in unprecedented ways, these technologies are embedded in unequal power relations that privilege government and corporate elites (Curran et al. 2012; Dahlgren 2009).

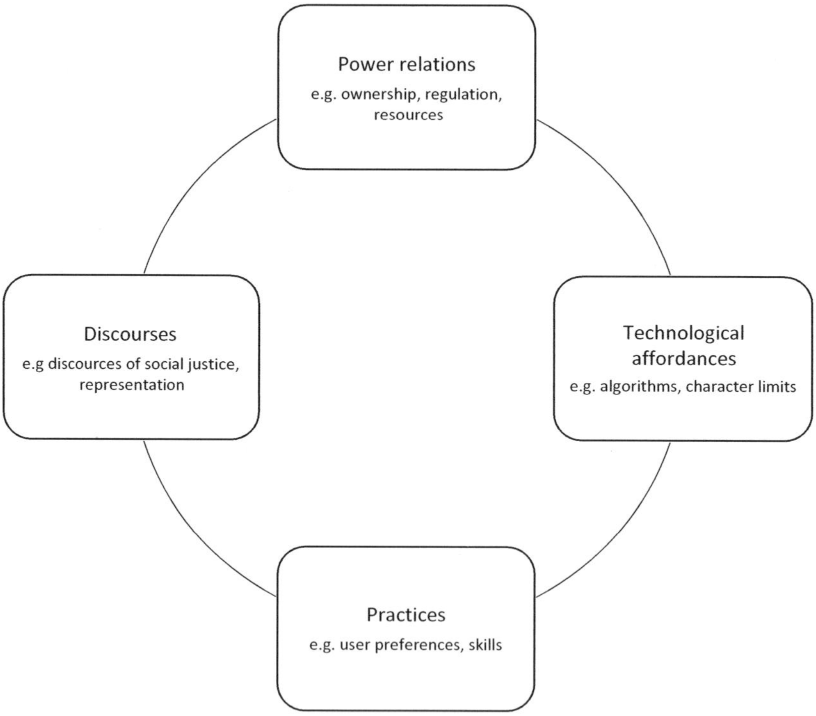

FIGURE 7.1 An analytical model of civic engagement and social media.

Our dimension of power relations includes issues of ownership and production, ethical implications for producers as well as produsers (commercial, state, and civic) and implications for visibility. Social media platforms are characterized by increasing ownership concentration, with multinational media corporations such as Google and Facebook dominating the majority of social media platforms (Fuchs 2015; van Dijck 2013). Particularly government policies and regulations as well as platforms' terms of service (ToS) are important in this respect. Examples of Facebook deleting left-wing political group pages show that the platform is all but neutral (Gillespie 2010). This is propelled by the commercial logic that underpins major social media platforms such as Facebook and YouTube (Papacharissi & Fernback 2005; Uldam & Askanius 2013).

Youmans and York (2012) show how policies and user agreements of commercial social media platforms inhibit some forms of political participation by preventing anonymity and prohibiting certain content, such as Facebook banning the page "We Are All Khaled Said" which was used to mobilize protesters during the Egyptian uprising. The influence of policies and user agreements of commercial social media platforms has also been shown to curb civic engagement, e.g. when the blog hosting site Wordpress.com referred to their policy of no anonymity and removed a website that criticized the oil company BP following a request from that company (Uldam 2016). The commercial logic of popular social media platforms means that companies such as Facebook must cater for broad segments of users and advertisers (Youmans & York 2012). This often entails ToS that impede anonymity and privileges copyright over creative subvertising, in some cases enabling corporations to censor antagonistic political participation (Uldam 2018; Youmans & York 2012). Access to the data gathered as well as tools for analysis are limited to the major commercial players contributing another layer of unequal power relations (Dahlberg 2015). Interests and conditions of unequal power relations further asymmetrical visibilities, because the specifics of their collection and price are not made transparent. This obscures exactly what is being observed and on what basis and logics, enabling governments and corporations to monitor citizens' activities without being seen themselves and instilling uncertainty in those being watched (Brighenti 2010). In this way, social media augment visibility asymmetries by rendering them less transparent and accountable (Brighenti 2010; Flyverbom 2016). To the extent that civic users are aware of these asymmetries of visibility, they risk impeding participation in radical politics by instilling self-censorship (Uldam 2016).

With social media information flows have become more complex changing from a privileged position of broadcast media and mainstream press towards networked digital media, while other aspects of power relations are maintained or even reinforced. Investigating the Twitter news flows during the Tunisian and Egyptian uprisings, Lotan (2011) find that news is increasingly co-constructed by bloggers, activists and journalists. The embeddedness of social media platforms in existing power relations also presents constraints to civic engagement and volunteering, for example when it comes to the visibility of corporate elites versus grass-root activism.

Another aspect of changing power relations is the centrality that social media platforms achieve. Our research on volunteers' uses of social media platforms to help migrants arriving in Sweden demonstrates the monopoly position of Facebook among Swedish volunteer groups. All the groups we studied chose Facebook as their main, and often only, platform for connecting with volunteers, migrants and wider publics. This turn to Facebook as a coordination platform is emblematic for this kind of initiative and the choice has mainly been unquestioned by coordinators and administrators. Power relations play out not only in terms of choosing – or feeling the pressure to choose – a platform. The Facebook platform itself is structured through and reinforces specific power relations. There are, for example, clear hierarchies between administrators of groups and pages in relation to group members and followers. Administrators and moderators steer the forms of engagement, while posts by members often remain invisible due to the set-up of a Facebook group or page. The founder of *Al Tadamon* argues that donating time to volunteer activities makes volunteers reason more efficiently, and Facebook reinforces this division between people who envision and curate the exchanges and those who are at the receiving end.

Technological affordances

While we argue for the importance of looking beyond technological affordances, we still want to stress the importance of paying attention to them. Affordances are central to the materiality of media, encompassing their technological infrastructures, and the possibilities for action that they afford users (Gibson 2015[1979]). Media technologies, including social media platforms, are constructed following a certain set of ideas (Kaun & Stiernstedt 2014). Viewing the technological infrastructures of social media platforms as both conditioned by ideas and conditioning action potential enables us to consider the ways in which they are embedded in wider power structures and commercial interests. We approach affordances as technical features that enable and constrain possibilities for action (Bucher & Helmond 2017). While we agree that imagined and perceived aspects of affordances are important, indeed key (e.g. Bucher & Helmond 2017; McVeigh-Schultz & Baym 2015), our focus remains on technical features as a starting point in order to pay attention to the minutiae of their workings. However, we do not suggest backgrounding imagined and perceived aspects. In our framework, the interplay between affordances as technical features and the dimension of practices captures social, imagined and perceived aspects of affordances. Moreover, the interplay with power relations helps capture social and societal aspects such as skills, regulatory and commercial interests.

Flyverbom and Murray (forthcoming) propose the notion of data-structures to capture the invisible workings and consequences of the strategic uses to influence public opinion and regulatory interests, and *vice versa*. They stress the importance of paying attention to inside processes of data organization and structuring. Rieder et al. (2015) illustrate the technicity of Facebook's specific feature sets, database architectures, and interfaces with their standardized information fields; and the ways in which they filter and organize the data that can be retrieved from Facebook's application programming interface (API) (e.g. using Netvizz), as well as their implications for the visibility of posts. These challenges are grounded in the market-driven logics of commercial social media platforms (Fuchs 2017). Van Dijck and Poell (2013) discuss the commercial interests that influence platforms in terms of techno-commercial materiality. Facebook and the possibilities for reach enabled by its news feed algorithm aptly illustrates the importance of commercial interests to technological affordances.

As a commercial platform, Facebook follows a business model that is largely based on the near impossibility of organic reach (Collister 2015). This business model is structured around technological affordances. The algorithm that determines the visibility of posts and tweets in social media platforms impedes organic reach to motivate users to pay for boosted reach (Dahlberg 2015). It does so through a combination of metrics and machine learning, which structure the visibility of content in users' news feeds and are kept undisclosed and constantly moderated to ensure that they stay undisclosed (Rieder et al. 2015). In addition to revenues from advertising, commercial social media have developed business models based on the collection of data that are reanalyzed and sold to third parties (Andrejevic 2013). As a consequence, organizations and social actors with resources (either capital to pay for reach or people with skills to circumvent the algorithm) are privileged in struggles for visibility in Facebook. This illustrates the interplay between affordances (the algorithm), power relations (the business model), and practices (skills).

In our study of volunteer groups, we found that the structure of pages privileges the visibility of posts of administrators over posts by members and followers. For the volunteer groups, this asymmetrical visibility established another layer of power relations within the platform giving voice to group members organizing relief while marginalizing the voice of the receivers (the refugees). Another consequence of Facebook's algorithm is that much of the information we receive via social media platforms presents one aspect of an issue, bits of information or factoids that often connect like-minded users rather than challenging our presumptions or offering new perspectives.

Technological affordances also have organizational implications. Scholars have shown how social media affordances enable decentralized, networked forms of organizing and fluid organization (Bennett & Segerberg 2012; Dobusch & Schoeneborn 2015; Kavada 2015; den Hond et al. 2015). These possibilities are also evident in our study of volunteers in Sweden. In this specific context, particularly fluid organizing emerged as prevalent. In addition to this, the technological affordances of Facebook provided certain constraints to organizing, as the fluid volunteer organizations evolved over time, professionalized and changed their focus. The structure of Facebook, however, does not allow for adaptions to organizational evolution. This is captured by the founder and administrator of *Al Tadamon*:

> The only thing that I experienced as a constraint was that we started as group and then we had so many members and we realized that it would have been better to have page instead. [...] We didn't know that we would become an organization with a budget and everything.
>
> *(Interview from 26 August 2016)*

Another aspect of the ways in which the Facebook algorithm steers visibility in users' news feeds relates to temporality. The algorithm privileges interaction over recency, which means that posts that trigger new replies gain more visibility despite their datedness. This has implications for the possibility of coordinating people and help efforts. Carefully curated threads and posts might be messed up through comments on older posts that give the impression that these are the most recent and most urgent requests (see Rieder et al. 2015). In our study on volunteers, the curated thread structure was particularly important for the group "We who welcome refugees at Stockholm's central station", since this was the only way to distinguish between different needs and areas of works. As the initiator explains:

> So, the whole Facebook structure is rather strict. [...] So if you go for the thread structure, you have to stick with it. [...] It really is not meant to be used in that way. [...] We tried to limit the number of threads, but anyway in between it was like that people started writing in one thread, for example the mosque thread, and then all of a sudden everything became much more general and didn't have anything to do with the mosque anymore.
>
> *(Interview from 16 September 2016)*

Practices

The notion of media practices refers to what we do with media (Couldry 2004). What we do when we use media is not necessarily what we were intended to do. Just think of text messaging on mobile phones which was intended as an emergency communication tool and not the popular everyday communication channel that it is today. Couldry (2012) develops the notion of media practices as an "open set of practices relating to, or oriented around, media" (Couldry 2004: 117). He argues that media practices are concerned with specific regularities in actions relating to media and regularities of context and resources that enable media-related actions. Resources include media literacy and civic agents' capacity for navigating the possibilities and challenges that social media provide, e.g. in terms of technology, norms, and regulation (Livingstone 2008). In that sense, media practices provide a fruitful link to questions of civic engagement. They open up consideration of issues such as skills and assumptions that activists and volunteers evoke in their uses of social media platforms for organization, coordination, campaigning, interaction, and community-building.

In our study of volunteer groups, skills were reported as extremely important to visibility. All groups either had professional social media communicators or professionalized during their operations to handle communications efficiently. Even though the initiatives analysed here all gained relatively high visibility on Facebook in a very short time, only one person expressed surprise about the fast-growing success. All other interviewees were rather conscious of the logics of visibility and power in social media that are related to the size and strength of pre-existing networks. Particularly successful – in terms of gaining followers and collecting donations – was the initiative "We do what we can". One of the initiators stated that the group consisted of volunteers with strong writing skills who could express themselves and knew the logics of social as well as mainstream media. Group members already had a rather large circle of followers including so-called influencers with equally strong positions and visibility in the network of Swedish cultural industry. The capacity for expression contributed to the fact that the initiative was perceived as comparatively professional. The Swedish volunteers' capacity for navigating the visibility logics of mainstream media and Facebook's algorithm shows how skills resulting from well-educated backgrounds and professions can facilitate visibility and benefit individuals and groups from privileged backgrounds. In this way, volunteer practices were also shaped by affordances, as groups positioned people with media skills and insights to secure visibility, illustrating the interplay between practices, power and affordances.

Investigating questions of media as practice allows for links to larger societal processes of mediatization and mediation that are crucial for political engagement aimed at social change. Mattoni and Treré (2014) show how media practices are intertwined with questions of power in complex media ecologies that go beyond media as texts and media as industries and have come to include formats such as social media. While social media provide new platforms for expressing various forms of civic engagement, they privilege formal modes of civic engagement (e.g. major NGOs) over informal modes of civic engagement (small NGOs, networks and informally organized groups) such as bottom-up volunteering and anti-systemic activism (Van Laer & Van Aelst 2010); they also privilege individual over collective participation (Bennett & Segerberg 2012; Fenton & Barassi 2011). For example, increasing surveillance from government and business has led many activists to avoid social media for uses that relate to organizing protests (Gerbaudo 2012). Activists and volunteers with insight into online surveillance risks and possibilities for circumventing surveillance (i.e. a high degree of media literacy, see Livingstone 2008) instead use alternative social media platforms such as Crabgrass and RiseUp, or they use social media platforms in alternative ways (Uldam 2016). While face-to-face meetings remain crucial in organizing protests or volunteering, this highlights the interplay between media practices in terms of literacy and power relations.

These dynamics of transparency and practices also emerged in our study of volunteer groups. Here, a distinction between inbound and outbound communications is important. While the volunteer initiatives appear curated and professional in their outbound communication, there is always a messier backstage. "We do what we can" started out with two secret groups – one for the steering committee and one for the volunteers already engaged. The latter was only open for those approximately 20 people travelling to Lesvos. For raising additional funds, the public page was started and attracted much attention. Only later, internal communication was moved from Facebook to Slack in the process of professionalizing the organization. Having both internal and external communications on one platform makes the initiatives very vulnerable. For example, Facebook pages or groups being taken down because of trolling from right-wing groups and coordinated reporting to Facebook have been successfully employed to silence earlier campaigns (see Dencik 2014). Since there are potential dangers for both volunteers and migrants connected with visibility in social media, openness was in some cases regulated externally. The management of the shelter in Stockholm implemented a strict media protocol including restricted access for media to the building as well as posts in social media. This had implications for outreach and possibilities to engage broader publics in *Al Tadamon*'s relief work as they were not allowed to post pictures of the building, the clothes shop or residents in the public group on Facebook.

Discourses

While we believe that studying content related to civic engagement such as campaign material or interactions in social media platforms is an important contribution, we propose a shift in focus to discourse. Discourse encompasses textual acts in the broadest sense and as inherently connected to power (following Chouliaraki 2006, and Vestergaard 2008; see also Chouliaraki & Vestergaard forthcoming). The discourse dimension in our framework enables researchers to pay attention to aspects of civic engagement such as campaigns and interactions in social media platforms (Madianou 2013), while also acknowledging their constitutive and performative power which stresses ethics. From this vantage point, discourses condition our understanding of the world, and thus importantly also our possibilities to act in that world. In that sense, discourses have performative power to condition civic engagement, including volunteering. However, for discourses to be given a kind of reality that they would not have otherwise, they need to be seen and heard by others in the space of appearance (Arendt 1958). The rival discourses of hospitality and hostility that characterize debates and coverage of refugees entering Europe condition the possibilities and predispositions of publics in responding to the situation and taking responsibility (Chouliaraki 2016). Social media can potentially help civic actors access this space of appearance.

We therefore need to pay attention to the discourses and counter-discourses that circulate in social media – and the ways in which they are facilitated and constrained by social media affordances, power relations and practices. One of the key democratic potentialities of social media platforms relates to their capacity for circulating counter-discourses to wider publics (Dahlberg & Phelan 2013). It is not only the affordances, power relations and practices that situate possibilities for gaining visibility for discourses that are important, but also the discourses for which social and political actors struggle to gain visibility and support (Chouliaraki 2006). For example, competing discourses establish different causes, and identify different villains and different solutions to the Euro crisis (Kyriakidou et al. 2018). Other discursive struggles and representations include climate change (Uldam & Askanius

2013), corporate responsibility (Etter & Vestergaard 2015) and movements of the dispossessed (Kaun 2015). Specifically, in relation to the influx of migrants in Europe, counter-discourses of hospitality attempt to challenge dominant discourses of fear, financial constraint and nationalism (Dahlgren 2016), while discourses of rights, policy mandates, solidarity and management circulate and compete at the site of reception, as migrants arrive in Europe in the Greek island Chios (Chouliaraki & Georgiou 2017). Social media have become a key arena for these struggles.

In our illustrative case study, volunteers not only wanted to help migrants with the practicalities and logistics of arriving unsettled in a new country. They also challenged discourses of security and nationalism that dominated the debate on migrants in mainstream media (Dahlgren 2016). The group "We do what we can" considered their work explicitly as political and in support of pro-migration politics. As one of the main initiators told us: "We also had an opinion-building role. For example, we invited different politicians to follow with us to Lesvos to show them the situation" (Interview from 21 November 2016). With the changing political situation, other groups – particularly RWS – increasingly shifted their focus from relief work to promoting counter-discourses of care and human rights, especially following the closure of the Swedish border, the EU-Turkey agreement and the shrinking numbers of incoming migrants. Their engagement ranged from sharing certain articles and writing op-eds promoting safe passage for refugees to Europe, and supporting petitions against stricter migration policies, to participating in expert hearings with political decision-makers. This illustrates the significance of discourses as an aspect of the role of social media in civic engagement with constitutive and performative power.

Conclusion

Power relations, practices, affordances and discourse are the key dimensions of our model for the analysis of civic engagement in social media. As each dimension plays a vital role, research focussing on any of the four dimensions is important. At the same time, we want to stress the significance of considering their interrelations, even when highlighting one of them. It is precisely the interplay between the four dimensions that allows us to understand the conditions of possibility behind questions such as: Who participates? Who listens? It allows us to better understand phenomena such as virality and spreadability, the interplay with the mainstream press and between online/offline dynamics.

In our study of volunteers' uses of social media to assist migrants entering Sweden, this framework uncovers such issues, including questions about materiality: What different media assemblages of software, hardware, bodies, sites, and objects can we trace in civic engagement? Here, the framework we have suggested would identify specific components and consider the power relations at play in their roles in various assemblages. Facebook was reinforced as the one dominant platform used to organize migrant assistance, rendering volunteer initiatives dependent on Facebook policies and algorithmic logics of visibility. Questions of power might include: How do material resources, including digital platforms, technological infrastructures, physical places and objects, affect the power dynamics of contentious politics? The power dimension draws attention to issues such as the privileged white, middle-class, professional backgrounds of volunteer users. The practices dimension in our framework further facilitates probing questions about media literacy and assumptions of volunteers, revealing a clear tendency to critically reflect on their choices of Facebook as their central platform, even if this choice remains uncontested. The affordance dimension hints at questions of visibility and automated sorting within the infostructure that has material implications for the efforts of volunteers helping arriving migrants. The discourse dimension raises questions about what is being said about migrants and the need to help in volunteer groups and pages, but crucially, also the ways in which this challenges dominant discourses of nationalism and security on a wider societal scale.

Attending to this mix of material, discursive, practice and power configurations enables us to show that although social media have been heralded in diminishing power relations and hierarchies, Facebook reproduces existing divides and power relations. This raises questions about the ways in which Facebook establishes itself and is increasingly seen as civic infrastructure. Taken together, the four dimensions of our framework can help examine such questions, including the conditions of possibility behind social media and participation, (in)visibility, and public opinion. It is our hope that this framework's attention to the minutiae of the workings of social media materialities in relation to their interplay with discourse, power relations and practices can help researchers capture the possibilities in and constraints to using social media for civic engagement and activism – both at the level of everyday organizing and on a wider societal scale.

References

Andrejevic, M. (2013). *Infoglut. How too much information is changing the way we Think and know*. New York, London: Routledge.

Arendt, H. (1958). *The Human Condition*. Chicago, IL, London: The University of Chicago Press.

Baines, J. (2015). Nurturing dissent? Community printshops in 1970s London. In: J. Uldam, & A. Vestergaard (Eds.). *Civic engagement and social media: Political participation beyond protest* (pp.174–193). Bainsgstoke: Palgrave Macmillan.

Bennett, L., & Segerberg, A. (2012). *The Logic of Connective Action. Digital Media and the Personalization of Contentious Politics*. New York: Cambridge University Press.

Brighenti, A. M. (2010). *Visibility in social theory and social research*. Basingstoke: Palgrave Macmillan.

Bucher, T., & Helmond, A. (2017). The affordances of social media platforms. In: J. Burgess, T. Poell, & A. Marwick (Eds.). *SAGE handbook of social media*. London: Sage.

Cammaerts, B. (2009). Community radio in the West: a legacy of struggle for survival in a state and capitalist controlled media environment. *International Communication Gazette*, 71 (8), pp. 635–654.

Castells, M. (2012). *Networks of Outrage and Hope: Social Movements in the Internet Age*. Cambridge: Polity Press.
Chouliaraki, L. (2006). *The spectatorship of suffering*. London: Sage.
Chouliaraki, L. (2016). Authoring the self: Media, voice and testimony in soldiers' memoirs. *Media, War & Conflict*, 9(1), pp. 58–75.
Chouliaraki, L., & Georgiou, M. (2017). Hospitability: The Communicative Architecture of Humanitarian Securitization at Europe's Borders. *Journal of Communication*, 67(2), pp. 159–180.
Chouliaraki, L. & Vestergaard, A. (forthcoming). *Handbook of Humanitarian Communication*. London: Routledge.
Collister, S. (2016). Algorithmic public relations. In: J. L'Etang, D., McKie N. Snow, & J. Xifra (Eds.) *The Routledge Handbook of Critical Public Relations* (pp. 360–371). New York: Routledge. Couldry, N. (2004). Theorising media as practice. *Social Semiotics*, 14(2), pp. 115–132.
Couldry, N. (2012). *Media, Society, World: Social Theory and Digital Media Practice*. Cambridge: Polity Press.
Curran, J., Fenton, N., & Freedman, D. (2012). *Misunderstanding the internet*. 1st Ed. New York: Routledge.
Dahlberg, L. (2015). Expanding digital divides research: A critical political economy of social media. *The Communication Review*, 18(4), pp. 271–293.
Dahlberg, L., & Phelan, S. (Eds.) (2013). *Discourse Theory and Critical Media Politics*. London: Palgrave Macmillan.
Dahlgren, P. (2009). *Media and Political Engagement*. Cambridge: Cambridge University Press.
Dahlgren, P. (2016). Moral Spectatorship and Its Discourses: The "Mediapolis" in the Swedish Refugee Crisis. *Javnost-The Public*, 23(4), pp. 382–397.
DeLuca, K., Lawson, S., & Sun, Y. (2012). Occupy Wall Street on the Public Screens of Social Media: The Many Framings of the Birth of a Protest Movement. *Communication, Culture & Critique*, 5(4), pp. 483–509.
Dencik, L. (2014, 17 January). From breastfeeding to politics, Facebook steps up censorship. The Conversation. Retrieved from https://theconversation.com/frombreastfeeding-to-politics-facebook-steps-up-censorship-22098.
van Dijck, J. (2013). *The Culture of Connectivity*. New York: Oxford University Press.
van Dijck, J., & Poell, T. (2013). Understanding Social Media Logic. *Media and Communication*, 1(1), pp. 2–14. DOI: doi:10.17645/mac.v1i1.70.
Dobusch, L., & Schoeneborn, D. (2015). Fluidity, identity, and organizationality: The communicative constitution of Anonymous. *Journal of Management Studies*, 52(8), pp. 1005–1035.
Etter, M. A., & Vestergaard, A. (2015). Facebook and the public framing of a corporate crisis. *Corporate Communications: An International Journal*, 20(2), pp. 163–177.
Feigenbaum, A., Frenzel, F., & McCurdy, P. (2013). *Protest camps*. London: Zed Books.
Fenton, N., & Barassi, V. (2011). Alternative media and social networking sites: The politics of individuation and political participation. *Communication Review*, 14(3), pp. 179–196.
Flyverbom, M. (2016). Digital Age| Transparency: Mediation and the Management of Visibilities. *International Journal of Communication*, 10(13), pp. 110–122.
Flyverbom, M., & Murray, J. (forthcoming). Datastructures – organizing and curating digital traces into action. *Big Data & Society*.
Forsberg, U. (2015). 60 miljoner på flykt – den högsta siffran någonsin [60 million refugees – the largest number ever]. Retrieved from https://sverigeforunhcr.se/blogg/60-miljoner-pa-flyktden-hogsta-siffran-nagonsin.
Fuchs, C. (2015). *Culture and economy in the age of social media*. New York: Routledge.

Fuchs, C. (2017). From digital positivism and administrative big data analytics towards critical digital and social media research! *European Journal of Communication*, 32(1), pp. 37–49.

Gerbaudo, P. (2012). *Tweets and the Streets. Social Media and Contemporary Activism*. London: Pluto Press.

Gibson, J. (2015[1979]). *The ecological approach to visual perception*. London: Routledge.

Gillespie, T. (2010). The politics of 'platforms'. *New Media & Society*, 12(3), pp. 347–364.

Gillespie, M., Ampofo, L., Cheesman, M., Faith, B., Iliadou, E., Issa, A., Osseiran, S., & Skleparis, D. (2016). Mapping Refugee Media Journeys: Smartphones and Social Media Networks. Project Report. The Open University/France Médias Monde.

den Hond, F., de Bakker, F. G., & Doh, J. (2015). What prompts companies to collaboration with NGOs? Recent evidence from the Netherlands. *Business & Society*, 54(2), pp. 187–228.

Kaun, A. (2015). Regimes of time: Media practices of the dispossessed. *Time & Society*, 24(2), pp. 221–243.

Kaun, A., & Stiernstedt, F. (2014). Facebook Time: Technological and Institutional Affordances for Media Memories. *New Media & Society*, 16(7), pp. 1154–1168.

Kavada, A. (2015). Creating the collective: social media, the Occupy Movement and its constitution as a collective actor. *Information, Communication & Society*, 18(8), pp. 872–886.

Kyriakidou, M., Olivas-Osuna, J. J., & Hanska-Ahy, M. (forthcoming). The Indignados in the European press. In: J. Wimmer, C. Wallner, R. Winter, & K. Oelsner (Eds.). *(Mis) Understanding political participation: Digital practices, new forms of participation and the renewal of democracy*. London: Routledge.

Livingstone, S. (2008). Engaging with media—a matter of literacy? *Communication, Culture and Critique*, 1(1), pp. 51–62.

Lotan, G. (2011, 12 October). Data Reveals that Occupying Twitter Trending Topics Is Harder Than It Looks. Social Flow. Retrieved from http://blog.socialflow.com/post/7120244374/data-reveals-that-occupying-twitter-trending-topics-is-harder-than-it-looks.

Lovejoy, K., & Saxton, G. (2012). Information, Community, & Action: How Nonprofit Organizations Use Social Media. *Journal of Computer-Mediated Communication*, 17(3), pp. 337–353.

Madianou, M. (2013). Humanitarian campaigns in social media: Network architectures and polymedia events. *Journalism Studies*, 14(2), pp. 249–266.

Mattoni, A., & Treré, E. (2014). Media Practices, Mediation Processes, and Mediatization in the Study of Social Movements. *Communication Theory*, 24(3), pp. 252–271.

McVeigh-Schultz, J., & Baym, N. K. (2015). Thinking of you: Vernacular affordance in the context of the microsocial relationship App, Couple. *Social Media + Society*, 1(2), DOI: doi:2056305115604649.

Papacharissi, Z., & Fernback, J. (2005). Online privacy and consumer protection: An analysis of portal privacy statements. *Journal of Broadcasting & Electronic Media*, 49(3), pp. 259–281.

Rieder, B., Abdulla, R., Poell, T., Woltering, R., & Zack, L. (2015). Data critique and analytical opportunities for very large Facebook Pages: Lessons learned from exploring "We are all Khaled Said". *Big Data & Society*, 2(2), DOI: doi:2053951715614980.

Uldam, J. (2010). Fickle Commitment: Fostering Political Engagement in 'the Flighty World of Online Activism'. Doctoral thesis. Frederiksberg: Samfundslitteratur.

Uldam, J. (2016). Corporate management of visibility and the fantasy of the post-political: Social media and surveillance. *New Media & Society*, 18(2), pp. 201–219.

Uldam, J. (2018). Social media visibility: challenges to activism. *Media, Culture & Society*, 40 (1), pp. 41–58.

Uldam, J., & Askanius, T. (2013). Political identity and radical politics: mediating COP15 activism on YouTube. In: B. Cammaerts, A. Mattoni, & P. McCurdy (Eds.). *Mediation and protest movements* (pp. 159–178). Bristol: Intellect Books.

Uldam, J., & Vestergaard, A. (Eds.) (2015). *Civic engagement and social media: Political participation beyond protest*. Bainsgstoke: Palgrave Macmillan.

Van Laer, J., & Van Aelst, P. (2010). Internet and social movement action repertoires. *Information, Communication & Society*, 13(8), pp. 1146–1171. DOI: doi:10.1080/13691181003628307.

Vestergaard, A. (2008). Humanitarian branding and the media: The case of Amnesty International. *Journal of Language and Politics*, 7(3), pp. 471–493.

Youmans, W. L., & York, J. C. (2012). Social media and the activist toolkit: User agreements, corporate interests, and the information infrastructure of modern social movements. *Journal of Communication*, 62(2), pp. 315–329.

8

THE MATERIALITY OF CLOUDS

Beyond a platform-specific critique of contemporary activism

Stefania Milan

Introduction

Commercial social media of the likes of Facebook, Tumblr and Twitter support most contemporary socio-political mobilizations, from campaigning to street demonstrations, from online expressions of public outrage to the occupation of parks and squares. They have become crucial tools for activism for their ability to "host public expression, store it on and serve it up from the cloud [...] without having produced or commissioned it" (Gillespie 2017). They are said to amplify marginalized voices (Freelon, McIlwain, & Clark, 2016) and to facilitate the connection between otherwise dispersed individuals (Lim, 2012). What's more, mobilizations, collectives, and crowds increasingly appear to be *modelled after* social media platforms. Think, for example, of how one available app, FireChat, structured the exchanges within the "Umbrella movement" of Hong Kong (Lee & Man Chan 2016), or of the extent to which the "human microphone" adopted in the #Occupy general assemblies mirrored the individualized modes of interaction typical of social media (cf. Daubs & Wimmer 2017). While social media allow for the personalization of mobilizing messages (Bennett & Segerberg 2011), they impose their "logic" on social interactions (van Dijck & Poell 2013). Indeed, as I argued elsewhere (Milan 2015c, 2017), social networking platforms and applications, and the algorithms animating them, alter and structure activist agency. As "meta-infrastructure" (Sandvig, 2013: 91) without which much of the internet as we know it would not function, they have become essential components of our sociality.

Technical jargon like algorithm, interface, platform, and cloud has entered both the language of advertisers and the layman's vocabulary. Amongst the many "elemental media" (Durham Peters 2015: 2) that structure the ways in which meaning is communicated, distributed and shared today, the cloud – a "bundle of experimental algorithmic techniques acting upon the threshold of [human] perception"

(Amoore 2016) – is perhaps the most evocative and fuzzy of all. It is commonly understood as "the place where data lives until it is called up on the computer, tablet or smart phone—or, in the case of a malfunction, the place where data goes to die" (Mosco 2014: 1). Indeed, computing the cloud indicates the mainstream organizational, spatial and commercial model for sharing configurable resources, such as storage space or software, amongst users not necessarily connected to each other. At the same time, in layman's language the cloud is often evoked as a general metaphor for the internet as whole. Boasting its own aesthetics, this metaphor helps users to come to terms with some of the less tangible features of the infrastructure, namely its impalpability and invisibility. It is imbued with a specific aura of inevitability and neutrality, which prompts users, including activists, to take its "free" tools at face value, only rarely questioning their set up, functioning, and political economy.

This theoretical chapter converses with platform studies and social movement studies to explore, through the lenses of the cloud, the tension between activist agency and digital infrastructure. It considers the materiality of platforms in view of understanding how infrastructure shapes identities, narratives and the organizing strategies of contemporary movements. Focussing on the cloud as both (infra) structure and metaphor, rather than on the discrete platform services that animate it, has three main advantages. First, it allows us to move beyond the specifics of particular social networking, messaging or storytelling platforms, addressing social media *as a whole* rather than a series of separate services. This choice recognizes that social media apps are now hosted in the cloud and share some of the resources such as user authentication – and, most importantly, user data. It reflects the political economy and the interpenetration of many of the present platforms, which sees, to name but a few, Google/Alphabet, Facebook and Twitter in a quasi-monopolistic configuration.[1] Furthermore, it acknowledges the ongoing platformization of the web, whereby social media platforms extend their functioning into the general web to make data from third parties "platform ready" thus more easily monetizable (Helmond 2015). For example, Facebook has become an identity provider for third-party services that have little to do with social networking. Second, moving beyond a platform-specific critique of social media allows us to avoid the reductionist, here-and-now approach that makes single "evil" platforms stand out. While mega corporations like Alphabet and Facebook are indeed driving innovation in the sector, a holistic infrastructure perspective helps us to identify general trends as opposed to focussing on their contingent, time-limited implementations. Third, the explicit and controversial reference to cloud computing, with its corollary of environmental degradation and privacy threats (Mosco 2009), exposes a fundamental yet generally ignored ambivalence within contemporary activism: while claiming to distance themselves from the values and exploitative dynamics of neoliberal capitalism, protesters significantly rely on its products to assemble and mobilize (Dencik & Leistert 2015; Lovink 2016). Unpacking the materiality of the cloud as a holistic infrastructure and a "key force in the changing international political economy" (Mosco 2014: 1) of our times, will help us understanding how relations are shaped, reproduced and kept alive within contemporary mobilizations – and how they uphold activist agency.

The chapter is structured as follows. The next section briefly illustrates the main features and properties of the meta-infrastructure activists use today, and their nature of powerful metaphors for the "programmed sociality" (Bucher 2013) they support. The essay then moves to investigate the consequences of the cloud as a metaphor for organizing, followed by a reflection on how meaning-making and identity unfold in the cloud. Finally, it reflects on three dichotomies that allow us to investigate the question of activist agency *vis-à-vis* increasingly intertwined digital infrastructures.

Of platforms and clouds: The materiality of a metaphor

"Platforms are what platforms do," Benjamin Bratton claims with a seemingly tautological argument in *The Stack* (Bratton 2016: 41). The core feature of platforms is indeed to be found in their programmability, which resides in the numerical representations that characterizes all "new" media (see, e.g., Chun 2011). In essence, platforms offer users the possibility to customize uses, services, and interpretations. Away from being merely a technical feature, such programmability takes on a sociological meaning, as it embeds within its ostensibly fixed technical protocols-specific social affordances, that is to say defined "possibilities [...] for social relations and social structure" (Wellman 2001: 228). We thus ought to take into account the social relations associated with the manufacture and use of digital infrastructure (Thomas & Wyatt 1999) in order to understand its consequences for social actors. Dictating the conditions of engagement and participation, platforms de facto "govern through material intervention" (Bratton 2016: 44). Similarly, while yielding the promise of dematerializing the computing experience (Berry 2011), the cloud composes novel spaces, societies, and economies in its own image (Bratton 2016).

"Platforms" and "clouds" are politically charged terms: as Tarleton Gillespie claimed about the former, they are strategically mobilized by tech intermediaries to invoke "open, neutral, egalitarian" apparatuses (Gillespie 2010: 352). Yet, the virtues implied in the terminology, coupled with a narrative that emphasizes frictionless support and user empowerment, tends to downplay the inherent political nature of technology (see, e.g., Feenberg, 2002). It also hides the underlying materiality of digital infrastructure – like if the physical reality of data centres and optical cables, of designers, engineers and marketing campaigns, had mysteriously evaporated. Mosco (2004) referred to "the digital sublime" to indicate the tendency of digital technology to assume a transcendent role detached from its (often banal) role in the everyday. Technology is the product of a particular political system, and as such it perpetuates the power structures within which it is developed (Feenberg 2002). As Hayles (1999) argued in relation to the written word, information – here the content posted by users on social media – is not to be separated from the material conditions of its creation, namely the platforms' algorithmic environment.

Much has been written within academia on the materiality of the software and hardware that mediates our actions and interactions (see, e.g., Bucher & Helmond 2017; Gillespie 2010). José van Dijck, for example, argued that platforms have to be understood "as techno-cultural constructed and as organized socio-economic structures" (van Dijck 2013: 25), which propagate specific cultures of connectivity shaping people's interactions. "Platforms", "interfaces", and "clouds" do not solely constitute the nebulous groundwork subtending to our online exchanges. They can be seen as powerful metaphors, contributing to shape people's understanding of their social world, and heavily influencing the conditions of possibility for collective action.

Metaphors are a way of thinking about the invisible when it generates visible consequences (Chun 2011). The focus is on the interaction between words, emotions, ideas, the perception of oneself and of others and the "inscription technologies" shaping them (Hayles 2002: 24). The power and function of the metaphors describing our ordinary technology is not merely descriptive: rather, metaphors carry a normative connotation (Wyatt 2004). Frequently used to reduce the instability and the uncertainty of our technological present, they "convey what the Internet is or might be"; most importantly, "sometimes today's imaginary becomes tomorrow's lived reality" (ibid: 244).

I argue that metaphors of contemporary meta-infrastructure harbour – and provide social actors with – specific socio-cultural forms and practices after which to model sociality within an instance of collective action (cf. Turner 2009). While simplifying and trivializing the functioning of current technology, these metaphors paradoxically contribute to bring into vision the materiality of the infrastructure, making it explicit and – to a certain degree – intelligible. They reflect and enact the materiality by offering clues that move from designers, makers, producers and marketers to users, and that can shape the relationships funnelled through them. In addition, the clues provided by the imaginaries enshrined in tech metaphors become mainstream thanks to the widespread diffusion of a handful of dominant social media platforms. Prompted by the modes of interaction written in the software and widely shared by users, these clues about how to structure sociality turn into known, familiar ways of interacting with each other. In a nutshell, influencing the way people think of their communication tools, metaphors are likely to shape also people's behaviours on said platforms. As Taina Bucher uncovered, "Users' perceptions about what the algorithm is and how it works shape their orientation towards it" (Bucher 2017: 40). Hence, looking at what metaphors might not say outright but evoke and what they represent for the users, is one way of getting closer to the intrinsic materiality of digital artefacts. In so doing, we can investigate the interplay between the structural, the symbolic, the interpersonal and the organizational layers, accounting respectively for the digital infrastructure, the activists' meaning attribution processes, their relations and networking strategies. In other words, not only infrastructure *strictu sensu* but the associated metaphors, too, are deeply material in their consequences. The next section explores this claim.

Organizing in the cloud: The meta-infrastructure of sociality

As we have seen, the cloud is both an essential component of the contemporary internet (Mosco 2014) and a metaphor for the dematerialization of computing (Berry 2011). As "agencies of order" (Durham Peters 2015: 1–2), clouds are situated at the level of the fundamental media that "have meaning but do not speak". They do, however, help structure the meaning-making activities of users. The cloud has material consequences insofar as it functions as a productive metaphor that can "help the imaginary become real or true" (Wyatt 2004: 244). More specifically, it inspires a particular way of connecting individuals in an instance of collective action, while excluding other potential ways of doing things. Moving between the material of how-it-works and the symbolic of what-people-do-with-it, this section reflects on what I call the social cloud – broadly conceived to include social media platforms and the data-and-relationships universes they identify – as the main meta-infrastructure of sociality for contemporary movements.

Social movement scholars have long acknowledged that organizations are the propulsive kernel of organized collective action. Until recently, however, they have failed to recognize the influence of communication technology on organizing patterns. Yet, from the affinity groups of the 1990s (McDonald 2006) to today's ephemeral assemblages clustered around social media "groups", "pages" or even hashtags (see, e.g., Bennett & Segerberg 2011), digital technology has represented the backbone of many mobilizations worldwide. Organizing forms have been largely inspired to what we may think of as the changing "digital toolbox" of social movements.

The idea that communication technology inspires and moulds ways of organizing is not new in the sociology of the web: for example, the advent of the internet, "network of networks", is credited with stirring up global movement networks (see, e.g., Castells 1996). Stretching this line of reasoning to the present day, we can see how social media represent an allegory of a certain way of organizing, manifested in informal groups and networks *with consequences*, no matter how short-lived they often are. It is what I have termed "cloud protesting", "a specific type of mobilization that is grounded on, modelled around, and enabled by social media platforms and mobile devices and the virtual universes they identify" (Milan 2015c: 1). Cloud protesting brings to the fore the interplay between the productive mediation of meta-infrastructure and the protesters' sense-making capabilities. It points to the role of tech metaphors in supplying activists with a ready-to-use and convenient organizational model with specific, familiar instructions for action.

The metaphor of the cloud emphasises exciting possibilities such as creativity, cost reduction, speed, and on-the-move connectivity. It downplays the centralized and privatized nature of the infrastructure, which would be at odds with the distributed character of many contemporary mobilizations, while implying the values and tech ideals (cf. English-Lueck 2002) of sharing, accessibility and – paradoxically – horizontality. Similar to the computing notion of "platform as a service", whereby cloud computing provides the environment that allows users to create and/or run applications without having to set up and sustain complex, costly infrastructure, the social cloud – with its myriad channels, pages, groups, walls, "hashtag publics" (Rambukkana 2015) – provides the meta-infrastructure for "engineering sociality" (van Dijck 2013). What do organizations look like in the social cloud?

The material realities shaped by the cloud as meta-infrastructure support the adoption of specific logics of aggregation (Juris, 2012) and particular types of relations at the micro level, with their own "distinctive cultures of interaction and shared trajectories of mobilization" (Clemens & Minkoff 2004: 158). These cultures of relation building tend to mirror the instructions of use of social media. They are likely to spill over to face-to-face exchanges and to instil also messages of political nature with affectivity (see also Papacharissi 2015). With one-to-one and multidirectional one-to-many exchanges becoming the norm, more and more people potentially communicate directly with each other with the sole mediation of the platform and of its invisible algorithms – as opposed to the mediation of a movement organization or leader. The frequency of interactions has changed, too, as social media and mobile devices have stretched the protest experience to the spheres of the intimate and the quotidian. Information sharing and optimization of the self-presentation are fundamental drivers of participation (see Ellison & boyd 2012). The boundary between the private and the political has lost relevance (van Dijck 2013). The platform-enabled visibility of the micro-interactional level to participants and audiences alike can cultivate solidarities across various sectors of the population and accelerate the diffusion of the protest, also globally.

With social media providing both the main coordinating platform and the organizational principles for the action, groups increasingly identify a "dispersed and individualized constituency" (Gerbaudo 2012: 5). These transient micro-organizations of variable geometry build largely upon established interpersonal connections and networks. They are modelled after and transcend familiar assemblages like the friends' clique, the peer group, or the community of interest. They are grounded on flexible individual commitment and multiple, temporary affiliations. The group dynamics mimic those of social media platforms. In turn, the group is mirrored in said platforms, where political and non-political content in equal measure finds a sounding board; presence of the group on social media becomes the *sine qua non* condition for its existence. Similar to cloud computing, these evanescent clusters can be mobilized ad hoc. They can be quickly repurposed at need – and equally rapidly dismissed. They emphasize the freedom that comes from the flexibility of affiliation and from the possibility of multiple belonging, the reduced costs of engagement, and the ease of access. They give participants the possibility to experience the group anytime – at least online, in a sort of illusion of "perpetual participation" (DeLuca, Lawson & Sun 2012: 483). Participants pursue idiosyncratic "grammars of action" such as healing, hearing, feeling, seeing, moving (McDonald 2006: 37), whose enjoyment is amplified by social media. These grammars of action substitute the manifestation and reproduction of a monolithic group identity, as we shall see next.

The rise of cloud-specific identities

The materiality of the cloud alters the "discursive terrain in which meaning contests occur" (Snow 2004: 405). It captures, filters and turns into platform-ready data the content, relations, and emotions volunteered by the user. In so doing, it plays a distinctive broker role in the meaning-making processes of protesters (Milan 2015b), altering it significantly. In the previous section, I hinted at how participants are after specific grammars of action, which substitute the exercise of a cohesive, univocal collective identity. The resulting mobilization trajectory is one that begins and ends with(in) the individual and its mediated self-representation. But how do social media interfere with the individual/collective nexus? Here we get closer to observing the way in which meaning is mediated by and within the social cloud.

There is in fact a second connotation to the cloud as a metaphor with material consequences. It identifies the virtual place where meaning "lives until it is called upon" by social actors, to paraphrase Mosco (2014: 1). Meaning-making, or the interactive process through which social actors construct the cognitive interpretations of their universe and their actions, is a crucial stage and resource of social movements (Gamson 1992; Melucci 1996). Objects of meaning-making are the activists' grievances and demands, the socio-political context in which they operate, their feelings, values, and identities. I contend that meaning-making in the social cloud is largely the work of individual, networked participants rather than a collective endeavour. The direct contribution of each member to meaning construction results in the downsizing of the guiding role of movement leaders, which end up acting merely as coordinating "choreographers" (Gerbaudo 2012). Moreover, the large majority of said meaning-making takes place within social media platforms, as opposed to other traditional venues like the square. The cloud then becomes the computer-generated imagined universe – the "space between" devices, to paraphrase Bruce Sterling's definition of cyberspace (Sterling 1993) – where the meanings associated with collective action come to life, are enacted, accessed, and stored. These soft, immaterial resources take the shape of, for example, mobilizing slogans (e.g. "We are the 99%", "No one is illegal"), cognitive frames (e.g. "global justice", "white supremacy"), snippets of identities (e.g. the "Black Block", the defenders of the Western identity) and the associated values (e.g. solidarity, horizontality, exclusion), which act as carriers of meanings. These resources are critical to the emergence and endurance of collective action variably organized. Stored in the cloud, both actually and metaphorically, they can be accessed, mobilized and altered at will. They are rarely entirely invented from scratch, as movements continuously build on a repertoire of available meanings accumulated over time by distinct groups. Social media allow for this process of accumulation and sharing to take global proportions, which results in emulation and the repurposing of movement ideas and tactics – think, for example, of the diffusion of Occupy-like protests and their sizing of public space (Feigenbaum, Frenzel & McCurdy 2013).

Rather than acting merely as a neutral pipe, the cloud has the ability to manipulate the meaning-making process. This manipulation is the result of the algorithms animating social media, which are typically proprietary and whose behaviour, in the realm of artificial intelligence, is inaccessible to users and sometimes hard to comprehend even to designers. The opaque ways in which content popularity is calculated and displayed on social media is a case in point, although users arguably try to make sense of the algorithm and adapt their behaviour (Bucher 2017). There is a further element to consider. If, as we have seen, identity building has become highly dependent on the social cloud, the "regimes of the production and circulation of meaning" (Langlois 2011: 3) of each commercial platform have an impact on the way meaning is produced. The emoticon, the tumblr, the tweet, and the hashtag, to name but a few, wrap content into a form that is *immanent* to the meta-infrastructure that originates them. In other words, content cannot manifest itself in the same form if separated from the specific context of a given platform.

The first-person engagement with meaning-making promoted by the social cloud has two consequences. On the one hand, it encourages the emergence of only certain types of networked political subjectivities, grounded on the mechanisms of visibility of social media (Milan 2015b). On the other, it allows for the creation and circulation of personalized yet universal narratives, which hook up individual experiences into a broader context that gives them meaning. These narratives are flexible, real-time, and crowd-controlled (Milan 2015a). The collective identity, no matter how loose, is the result of the incremental juxtaposition of discrete meanings and is built on minimum common denominators particularly permeable to interpretation. It is therefore inclusive and flexible. If a collective identity is "constructed and negotiated through a recurrent process of activation of the relations that bind actors together" (Melucci 1996: 70), then the social cloud magnifies the interpersonal interaction element. It makes the process fairly public and much more visible. It strengthens the voice and role of individuals, softening that of the group; yet, it allows the "sociocultural" of shared language and symbols (Gamson 1991: 41) to emerge. But while this form of self-centred communication has advantages in terms of inclusive participation, it challenges the collective creativity of movements (Fenton & Barassi 2011). It impacts negatively on the generation of group solidarity – a crucial ingredient of collective identity – and undermines a movement's sustainability over time.

Agency vs. meta-infrastructures

What are then the consequences of the materiality of the cloud for activist agency? Agency as such has received limited attention in the sociology of social movements. Typically, it is implied in the analysis of cultural aspects (see, e.g., Jasper, 1997), identities (see Melucci 1996) and emotions (Goodwin, Jasper & Polletta 2001). Generally speaking, agency is thought to involve the ability of making strategic choices (Jasper 2004), and to emerge in dialectic interaction with the social structure, i.e. the institutions and norms of our society. Structure and agency, however, are best seen as "temporary poles bracketing a continuum, with social entities moving along this continuum over time" (Fuchs 2001: 24).

To be sure, the collective action facilitated by the social cloud is a particularly suitable terrain to examine activist agency, for it allows to observe up close the "microfoundation of political action" where agency ultimately resides (Jasper 2004: 4). We can distinguish at least three dichotomies in the structure vs. agency dialectic relation at the "microsocial level" (ibid) of political action. These dichotomies can help us think about activist agency in relation to the techno-commercial strategies of tech intermediaries.

The first and most immediate dichotomy concerns the contrast between *empowerment vs. control* (Neumayer & Stald 2014), which derive from the opportunities and the threats built-in the materiality of the social cloud. Emphasizing emancipation and possibility, the cloud as a metaphor actively downplays the threats in matter of surveillance, repression, and commercialization of user data (Leistert 2013). While social media give voice to social actors, empowering them to exercise "the act of giving an account of" themselves (Couldry 2010: 3), the top-down control firmly in the hands of tech intermediaries hinders the possibility of agency at the micro level. If the awareness of the risks is still low among activists, tech-savvy activists have long argued that next "to mobile phones, Facebook is the most subtle, cheapest and best surveillance technology available" (Nadir 2012). Blanket surveillance "shape[s] the opportunities and possibilities" for activists (Dencik, Hintz & Cable 2016: 10), and may have a chilling effect on the democratic discourse (Stoycheff 2016).

The second dichotomy points to the *individual vs. collective* dimension of mobilization. As seen prior, the materiality of the social cloud explicitly privileges the former, giving voice and perceived agency to a scattered mass of self-contained entities. Instead of fashioning an oppositional mass, social media seem to merely celebrate the voice of decentralized, atomized action, where the "single player" is empowered over the "complex players" of organizations and groups (Jasper 2004: 5). Nonetheless, the collective dimension is continuously mobilized at the symbolic level: it is evoked and implied. It is an inherent component of the metaphor, and its existence is taken for granted by participants. This often translates in media attention, as the protest content in the "public screens of social media" (DeLuca et al. 2012) spills over to mainstream outlets. This mechanism, however, is potentially deceptive: social media promise a mass but do not deliver. Distinguishing between individual and collective agency, we see how the social cloud reinforces the former, but in the long run does not necessarily do good for the latter – which is the essence of solidarity within a social movement (Melucci 1989).

This brings us to the third dichotomy, *present vs. future*, concerning the evolution and sustainability of a mobilization over time. Social media promote ephemeral exchanges and subjectivities. These appear to function well at the onset of a protest, fostering media coverage, networking, and emulation, and augmenting the perceived collective agency of social actors. Their ability to "bridge personal and collective" (Gamson 1991: 44–45) is likely to be time-limited, especially if participants experience the mobilization mostly on social media. This in turn might hinder solidarity, or "the strength of our loyalties and commitment to a movement collective identity" (Gamson 1991: 45). The question concerns the ability of a mobilization to turn into a movement and be sustained over time – with a robust political trajectory and members effectively committed to responsibility towards the group. The poor solidarity binding actors together thus is likely to result in the inability to sustain a movement past the limited attention span of mainstream media.

Conclusions

This chapter set out to disentangle the materiality of "the cloud" and how this impacts on activist agency, both collective and individual. The cloud has taken on two meanings. First, we explored its role as a metaphor for a particular way of connecting individuals in an instance of collective action. Second, it has been paralleled to the virtual imagined space hosting and *shaping* individual and collective self-expression and interactions, and acting as the main repository of the meaning resources (e.g. identities, cognitive interpretations, values, etc.) of contemporary mobilizations. The social cloud, as I have termed it, results in a novel mobilization dynamic dubbed cloud protesting, where the cultures of relation building tend to emulate the instructions of use of social media. By becoming the predominant meta-infrastructure of sociality for present-day activism, the social cloud brokers the meaning-making activities of participants. It shapes the relations channelled through it, promoting flexible groupings mimicking familiar modes of affiliation such as the peer group. The individual takes centre stage, and her/his self-representation is the origin and the end point of the mobilization. However, the social cloud also manipulates meaning-making, attributing to content not only forms that are immanent to the meta-infrastructure that brings them to life, but also altering its fruition by the public. These mechanisms encourage the surfacing of just a restricted set of networked political subjectivities, modelled after the mechanisms of visibility of social media. The consequences for the emergence and sustainability over time of activist agency are better understood through three dichotomies: empowerment vs. control, the individual vs. the collective dimension, and present vs. future. In the three instances, the ephemerality of relations and subjectivities promoted by social media result in transient mobilizations that hardly translate into sustainable movements.

Note

1 Among others, Google acquired the video-sharing platform YouTube; Facebook owns the messaging service WhatsApp and the photo-sharing application Instagram; and Twitter secured the video-sharing app Vine and the live video-streaming platform Periscope. However, users can access with Facebook credentials other services, like the streaming service Spotify, provided the accounts are connected ("single-sign on").

References

Amoore, L. (2016). Cloud geographies. Computing, data, sovereignty. *Progress in Human Geography*, DOI: doi:10.1177/0309132516662147.

Bennett, L. W., & Segerberg, A. (2011). Digital Media and the Personalization of Collective Action. *Information, Communication & Society*, 14(6), pp. 770–799.

Berry, D. M. (2011). *The Philosophy of Software. Code and Mediation in the Digital Age*. New York: Palgrave Macmillan.

Bratton, B. H. (2016). *The Stack. On Software and Sovereignty*. Cambridge, MA: MIT Press.

Bucher, T. (2013). The Friendship Assemblage: Investigating Programmed Sociality on Facebook. *Television & New Media*, 14(6), pp. 479–493.

Bucher, T. (2017). The algorithmic imaginary: exploring the ordinary affects of Facebook algorithms. *Information, Communication & Society*, 20(1), pp. 30–44.

Bucher, T., & Helmond, A. (2017). The Affordances of Social Media Platforms. In: J. Burgess, T. Poell, & A. Marwick (Eds.), *The Sage Handbook of Social Media* (pp. 233–253). London, New York: Sage Publications.

Castells, M. (1996). *The Rise of the Network Society*. Oxford: Blackwell.

Chun, W. (2011). *Programmed Visions. Software and Memory*. Cambridge, MA: MIT Press.

Clemens, E. S., & Minkoff, D. C. (2004). Beyond the Iron Law: Rethinking the Place of Organizations in Social Movements Research. In: D. A. Snow, S. A. Soule, & H. Kriesi (Eds.), *The Blackwell Companion to Social Movements* (pp. 155–170). Oxford: Blackwell.

Couldry, N. (2010). *Why Voice Matters. Culture and Politics After Neoliberalism*. Thousands Oaks, CA: Sage.

Daubs, M. S., & Wimmer, J. (2017). Forgetting History: Mediated Reflections on Occupy Wall Street. *Media and Communication*, 5(3), pp. 49–58. DOI: doi:10.17645/mac.v5i3.979.

DeLuca, K. M., Lawson, S., & Sun, Y. (2012). Occupy Wall Street on the Public Screens of Social Media: The Many Framings of the Birth of a Protest Movement. *Communication, Culture & Critique*, 5(4), pp. 483–509.

Dencik, L., Hintz, A., & Cable, J. (2016). Towards data justice? The ambiguity of anti-surveillance resistance in political activism. *Big Data & Society*, 3(2), pp. 1–12.

Dencik, L., & Leistert, O. (Eds.). (2015). *Critical Perspectives on Social Media and Protest. Between Control and Emancipation*. London: Rowman & Littlefield.

van Dijck, J. (2013). *The Culture of Connectivity: A Critical History of Social Media*. Oxford: Oxford University Press.

van Dijck, J., & Poell, T. (2013). Understanding Social Media Logic. *Media and Communication*, 1(1), pp. 2–14.

Durham Peters, J. (2015). *The Marvelous Clouds. Toward a Philosophy of Elemental Media*. Chicago, IL: University of Chicago Press.

Ellison, N., & boyd, D. M. (2012). Sociality through Social Network Sites. In: W. H. Dutton (Ed.), *The Oxford Handbook of Internet Studies* (pp. 151–172). Oxford: Oxford University Press.

English-Lueck, J. A. (2002). *Cultures@SiliconValley*. Stanford, CA: Stanford University Press.

Feenberg, A. (2002). *Transforming technology: A critical theory revisited*. New York: Oxford University Press.

Feigenbaum, A., Frenzel, F., & McCurdy, P. (2013). *Protest Camps*. London: Zed Books.

Fenton, N., & Barassi, V. (2011). Alternative media and social networking sites: The politics of individuation and political participation. *Communication Review*, 14(3), pp. 179–196.

Freelon, D., McIlwain, C. D., & Clark, M. D. (2016). *Beyond the Hashtags: #Ferguson, #Blacklivesmatter, and the Online Struggle for Offline Justice*. Washington, DC: School of

Communication, American University. Retrieved from http://cmsimpact.org/resource/beyond-hashtags-ferguson-blacklivesmatter-online-struggle-offline-justice.

Fuchs, S. (2001). Beyond Agency. *Sociological Theory*, 19(1), pp. 24–40.

Gamson, W. A. (1991). Commitment and Agency in Social Movements. *Sociological Forum*, 6(1), pp. 27–50.

Gamson, W. A. (1992). *Talking Politics*. Cambridge: Cambridge University Press.

Gerbaudo, P. (2012). *Tweets and the Streets Social Media and Contemporary Activism*. London: Pluto Press.

Gillespie, T. (2010). The Politics of 'platforms'. *New Media & Society*, 12(3), pp. 347–364.

Gillespie, T. (2017). Regulation of and by platforms. In: J. Burgess, T. Poell, & A. Marwick (Eds.), *The Sage Handbook of Social Media* (pp. 254–278). Thousand Oaks, CA: Sage.

Goodwin, J., Jasper, J. M., & Polletta, F. (Eds.). (2001). *Passionate Politics: Emotions and Social Movements*. Chicago,IL: Chicago University Press.

Hayles, N. K. (1999). *How We Became Posthuman: Virtual Bodies in Cybernetics, Literature and Informatics*. Chicago, IL: University of Chicago Press.

Hayles, N. K. (2002). *Writing Machines*. Cambridge, MA: MIT Press.

Helmond, A. (2015). The Platformization of the Web: Making Web Data Platform Ready. *Social Media + Society*, 1(2). Retrieved from http://sms.sagepub.com/content/1/2/2056305115603080.full.

Jasper, J. M. (1997). *The Art of Moral Protest: Culture, Biography, and Creativity in Social Movements*. Chicago, IL: Chicago University Press.

Jasper, J. M. (2004). A Strategic Approach to Collective Action: Looking for Agency in Social Movement Choices. *Mobilization*, 9(1), pp. 1–16.

Juris, J. S. (2012). Reflections on #Occupy Everywhere: Social Media, Public Space, and Emerging Logics of Aggregation. *American Ethnologist*, 39(2), pp. 259–279.

Langlois, G. (2011). Meaning, Semiotechnologies and Participatory Media. *Culture Machine*, 12. Retrieved from http://www.culturemachine.net/index.php/cm/article/view/437.

Lee, F. L. F., & Man Chan, J. (2016). Digital media activities and mode of participation in a protest campaign: a study of the Umbrella Movement. *Information, Communication & Society*, 9(1), pp. 4–22.

Leistert, O. (2013). *From Protest to Surveillance - The Political Rationality of Mobile Media. Modalities of Neoliberalism*. Frankfurt am Main: Peter Lang.

Lim, M. (2012). Clicks, Cabs, and Coffee Houses: Social Media and Oppositional Movements in Egypt, 2004–2011. *Journal of Communication*, 62(2), pp. 231–248.

Lovink, G. (2016). *Social Media Abyss. Critical Internet Cultures and the Force of Negation*. Cambridge: Polity Press.

McDonald, K. (2006). *Global Movements: Action and Culture*. Malden, MA, and Oxford: Blackwell.

Melucci, A. (1989). *Nomads of the Present. Social Movements and Individual Needs in Contemporary Society*. London: Hutchinson Radius.

Melucci, A. (1996). *Challenging Codes. Collective Action in the Information Age*. Cambridge: Cambridge University Press.

Milan, S. (2015a). From Social Movements to Cloud Protesting: The Evolution of Collective Identity. *Information, Communication & Society*, 18(8), pp. 887–900.

Milan, S. (2015b). Mobilizing in Times of Social Media: From a Politics of Identity to a Politics of Visibility. In: L. Dencik & O. Leistert (Eds.), *Critical Perspectives on Social Media and Protest. Between Control and Emancipation* (pp. 53–70). London: Rowman & Littlefield.

Milan, S. (2015c). When Algorithms Shape Collective Action: Social Media and the Dynamics of Cloud Protesting. *Social Media + Society*, 1(2).

Milan, S. (2017). Political agency, digital traces and bottom-up data practices. *International Journal of Communication*, 12, pp. 507–527.
Mosco, V. (2004). *The Digital Sublime: Myth, Power, and Cyberspace*. Cambridge, MA: MIT Press.
Mosco, V. (2009). *The Political Economy of Communication* (2nd ed.). London: Sage.
Mosco, V. (2014). *To the Cloud: Big Data in a Turbulent World*. New York: Paradigm Publishers.
Nadir (2012). We need to talk about Facebook. nadir.org. Retrieved from http://www.nadir.org/txt/We_need_to_talk_about_Facebook.html.
Neumayer, C., & Stald, G. (2014). The mobile phone in street protest: Texting, tweeting, tracking, and tracing. *Mobile Media & Communication*, 2(2), pp. 117–133.
Papacharissi, Z. (2015). *Affective Publics Sentiment, Technology, and Politics*. Oxford: Oxford University Press.
Rambukkana, N. (Ed.). (2015). *Hashtag Publics: The Power and Politics of Discursive Networks (Digital Formations)*. New York: Peter Lang.
Sandvig, C. (2013). The Internet as Infrastructure. In: W. H. Dutton (Ed.), *The Oxford Handbook of Internet Studies* (pp. 86–106). Oxford: Oxford University Press.
Snow, D. A. (2004). Framing Process, Ideology, and Discursive Fields. In: D. A. Snow, S. A. Soule, & H. Kriesi (Eds.), *The Blackwell Companion to Social Movements* (pp. 380–412). Oxford: Blackwell.
Sterling, B. (1993). *The Hacker Crackdown: Law and Disorder on the Electronic Frontier*. New York: Bantam.
Stoycheff, E. (2016). Under Surveillance. Examining Facebook's Spiral of Silence Effects in the Wake of NSA Internet Monitoring. *Journalism & Mass Communication Quarterly*, 93(2), pp. 296–311.
Thomas, G., & Wyatt, S. (1999). Shaping Cyberspace—interpreting and transforming the Internet. *Research Policy*, 28, pp. 681–698.
Turner, F. (2009). Burning Man at Google: A Cultural Infrastructure for New Media Production. *New Media & Society*, 11(1/2), pp. 73–94.
Wellman, B. (2001). Physical place and cyberplace: The rise of personalized networking. *International Journal of Urban and Regional Research*, 25(2), pp. 227–252.
Wyatt, S. (2004). Danger! Metaphors at work in economics, geophysiology, and the Internet. *Science, Technology & Human Values*, 29(2), pp. 242–261.

9

"PLEASE LEAVE MY NEWS FEED ALONE"

Exploring user protest against algorithmic personalization

Martina Skrubbeltrang Mahnke

Introduction

On 15 May 2017 an upset user writes on Facebook's public profile page: "Please, leave my news feed preferences alone".[1] He demands that Facebook refrain from changing the algorithms underlying Facebook's News Feed and explains that Facebook's selection of "top stories" does not "even come close to being interesting" to him. Facebook's top stories, that is, algorithmically personalized information, was introduced in September 2011 in order to replace the chronological order of Facebook's News Feed. Since then, algorithmic personalization has become a crucial factor of social media platforms; users have continually protested against the idea and voice their opinion whenever the possibility arises.

User protest against algorithmic personalization, that is to say individual users expressing their dissatisfaction with algorithmic performance, emerges often, albeit irregularly and rather spontaneously, across social media platforms. When a social media platform announces major changes via a press release, user protest revolves typically around a particular hashtag (see, e.g., Mahnke, Grunnet & Tarp 2017; DeVito, Gergle & Birnholtz 2017). This chapter, however, focusses on the sporadic but consistent protest raised by individual users, as shown above. Although algorithmic personalization has been around for more than 15 years, user protest continually emerges, making it an interesting phenomenon to explore further. What constitutes user protest against algorithmic personalization and how is it tied to the materiality of social media platforms?

This chapter tackles these questions through the analytical lens of "communicative materiality", which will be developed in the first part of the chapter. Drawing primarily on the work of Dourish (2017) and Gunkel (2012), the lens is developed with respect to the complex algorithm-user relationship that lies at the centre of algorithmic personalization. The empirical data this chapter draws on have been collected through the procedure of (1) "diving into", (2) "travelling through" and (3) "tracing" user comments on social media platforms. As a first step, I will now present and discuss selected studies on algorithms in order to shed light on the complex entanglement of algorithms and their users.

Untangling the algorithm-user relationship

Algorithms as mathematical entities have a long and extensive history and they earned their name from Muhammad ibn Mussa Al-Khwarizmi, an Arab mathematician, who lived in the 9th century CE (Chabert & Barbin 1999). Although a basic mathematical concept, the very term algorithm has recently gained public popularity in media discourse (see among others Sisario 2018), certifying algorithms' strong influence in the information realm, if to the extent media discourse proposes is, however, still subject to academic discussion (Kitchin 2017). Not least, therefore, Barocas, Hood and Ziewitz (2013: 1) postulated in a provocative piece that algorithms have developed into "somewhat of a modern myth". More humorously, users have also described algorithms on Twitter as "a word used by programmers when they do not want to explain what they did".[2] Irrespective of how algorithms should be precisely defined, it is clear that the majority of social media platforms currently employ algorithms as a means to create a selection of personalized information for their users.

When Google first introduced algorithmic personalization in 2009, wide public discussion with regard to so-called filter bubbles and echo-chambers arose. When, seven years later, in 2016, Instagram announced it was also implementing an algorithmically-curated feed, criticism erupted once again, this time especially from dedicated users. They started to express their discontent using the hashtag #RIPInstagram (read: Rest In Peace Instagram). An analysis of the tweets related to the hashtag shows that users were primarily protesting against the perceived ruling nature of algorithms (Mahnke, Grunnet & Tarp 2017). Users further felt that the process of algorithmic personalization violated their autonomy to select relevant information for themselves. Looking more closely at user comments, it becomes clear that most users were of the belief that it was solely the algorithm that "decided" whether specific information became visible or not and that they had little or no influence.

A study investigating a similar hashtag, namely #RIPTwitter (read: Rest In Peace Twitter) shows similar results. The hashtag was created right after Twitter announced alterations to their algorithmic performance (DeVito, Gergle & Birnholtz 2017). The authors identified a total of 11 distinct reasons for user resistance to algorithmic personalization. The study names general anger and frustration with algorithms as one of the major reasons for user resistance. The authors write: "The user is expressing a simple disapproval, admonishment, accusation, or other expression of anger or frustration" (DeVito, Gergle & Birnholtz 2017: 5). While many users seem to experience frustrations, the question as to why algorithmic performance provokes such strong emotions remains unclear. Although the authors of the study conclude that the "non-chronological algorithmic apocalypse prophesied by the community" (DeVito, Gergle & Birnholtz 2017: 12) did not occur, the emotional outcry of users still shows how affected they are by changes made to algorithmic performance.

On a more general level, algorithms are said to strongly influence culture, politics, and everyday practices (Kitchin 2017). Gillespie (2014) and Bucher (2017) argue that algorithms have far-reaching social consequences that we are only beginning to understand. Studying "algorithmic imaginaries", Bucher (2017) describes different kinds of experiences users have when encountering algorithms. One example of such an experience is what Bucher (2017: 35) calls the "whoa moment", that is to say when people feel that the algorithmic system has figured them out. Gillespie (2014) investigates on a more structural level how algorithms shape and re-shape culture. He concludes that algorithms create patterns of inclusion and exclusion through the construction of (hierarchical) relevance in the digital realm. Willson (2017) in turn looks at the role algorithms play in shaping and engaging with the contemporary everyday and raises questions regarding how to conceptualize issues such as agency and power in technologically mediated environments. She makes an especially strong argument for looking at and understanding algorithms as technology-in-flux due to their ever-changing nature.

Although studies on algorithms generally acknowledge their complexity, only few engage in the actual algorithm-user relationship. Bozdag (2013) was one of the first. He demonstrated that algorithms do not operate independently but in strong relation to user behaviour. He writes: "Humans not only affect the design of the algorithms, but they also can manually influence the filtering process" (Bozdag 2013: 209). Furthering this line of research, Neff and Nagy (2016) have illustrated the complex entanglement of the algorithm-user relationship. Drawing on the example of Microsoft's chat bot "Tay", they trace how agency is formed and co-created through socio-technological interactions. Their case shows that users were quickly able to reverse good design intentions. Within only 16 hours, chat bot Tay had turned into a racist commentator, having learned from interactions with users employing offensive and ambiguous language. Neff and Nagy (2016) conclude in their study that technology is inseparable from the ways users imagine it could be used.

The highlighted studies show that algorithms and their societal ramifications are manifold and still subject to discussion. While they are technically advanced in the field of computer science, critical studies on algorithms try to fathom out their broader societal, cultural, and political implications. In relation to this chapter, algorithms are investigated as a means of personalizing information on social media platforms. Here the algorithm-user relationship plays a crucial role because it is the basis on which information gets personalized on social media platforms. User behaviour feeds into so-called user profiles, which in turn serve as the basis for the selection of relevant information. Algorithmic performance is hence strongly related to user behaviour and therefore needs to be studied from the basis of the algorithm-user relationship. The analytical lens of "communicative materiality", which will be developed in the following section, is hence an attempt to acknowledge this complex entanglement of algorithms with their users.

Communicative materiality as an analytical lens

When acknowledging that algorithms are strongly entangled with user behaviour the question arises of how to grasp this relationship analytically. In this regard, Willson (2017: 148) offers a comprehensive definition, describing algorithms as "dynamic processes designed and implemented by humans in conjunction with technical affordances and with broader political, social and cultural environments that are shaped by the continual interactions of strategies, structures and tactics". Two pivotal points in her definition are (1) technological affordances, and (2) user interaction. Baym (2010: 44) argued prior to Willson for a similar perspective, which is not caught in traditional deterministic views but understands that "the consequences of technologies arise from a mix of 'affordances' [...] and the unexpected and emergent ways that people make use of those affordances". Neff and Nagy (2016: 4915), already mentioned in the section above, suggest in this relation the term "symbiotic agency", which points towards how technological affordances are intertwined with the way users perceive and imagine the use of technology. To reiterate, even though users might not be aware of the fact that their behaviour is related to algorithmic performance from a theoretical perspective, it is crucial to account for this complex socio-technical relationship.

Not least, therefore, the term "affordances" is an oft-used term when studying algorithms (see, among others, Bucher & Helmond 2017). According to Gibson (2015[1979]), who originally coined the concept of affordance, it is the perceived physical properties of an object, which depends on their observer. This means that, depending on the observer, the affordance of an object can be perceived differently. To illustrate his idea, Gibson draws on the example of a fly, to which water may have the affordance of "support". A heavier animal, however, does not perceive water in the same way. By highlighting how the perception of the physical affordance depends on the observer, Gibson was one of the first to underline the importance of the object-observer relationship.

Even though the term affordance is often used in relation to algorithms, Dourish (2017: 27) criticizes the term as charged and states that "the language of affordance might actually be counterproductive". He argues that, despite the fact that digitality is a human achievement, many aspects of digital information still lie in its own structure. With this, Dourish advocates for perceiving of social media platforms as material objects that are continuously evolving. As algorithms continuously change and, as Willson (2017) suggests, can be understood as technology-in-flux, the developed analytical lens needs to account for this evolving material structure. In order to account for this, I therefore follow the notion of "materiality" as Dourish suggests and further add a relational dimension. The research presented in the section above has shown how influential user conceptions and user behaviour are in relation to algorithmic performance. The term "materiality" hence stands for algorithmic materiality entangled with user behaviour.

Moving from the structural aspects to the communicative level, Gunkel's (2012) work offers some interesting perspectives. His philosophical work inquires mainly into the question of how to understand digital media technology. The starting point for his work is the observation that technology no longer merely mediates communication but functions as an active participant in the communicative exchanges taking place on social media platforms. Building up a theoretical argument that is based on the Turing test as well as natural language processing application ELIZA, he advocates for "communication" being the decisive element in the digital realm. Rather than understanding intelligent technology, such as algorithms, as instruments or even mediators, he offers the concept of the "communicative other" (Gunkel 2012: 21) as a way of understanding such technology. He advocates:

> [I]t is clear that it is no longer accurate to define the computer exclusively as an instrument that is to be animated and used, more or less effectively, by a human being. The computer is beginning to be understood as an Other – another kind of communicative Other – who *confronts* human users, *calls* to them, and *requires* an appropriate response.
>
> *Gunkel 2012: 21 (emphasis added)*

Following the development of digital technology from mechanical to intelligent machines, Gunkel argues that traditional approaches overlook the intelligent nature of modern technology and understand them to be too instrumental.

Building on Gunkel's thoughts, algorithmic performance can then be understood as algorithms *communicating* with their users. Having specified the algorithm-user relationship as a *communicative* relationship bound to the *material* structure of the algorithm-user relationship, I propose the concept of "communicative materiality" as an analytical lens for this chapter. To sum up, the concept of communicative materiality comprehends the complex entanglement of algorithmic structure with user behaviour and thereby allows an analysis from a relational-structural standpoint. Instead of either looking at user behaviour or algorithmic performance, the analytical lens of communicative materiality takes an observational perspective.

A note on methodology

Studying user protest against algorithmic personalization on social media platforms is an ambiguous venture as it is hard to recognize, identify, and follow. As stated in the introduction, the protest as such is not organized or coordinated but is first and foremost individual users stating their objection to algorithmic personalization. In order to collect data from these individual users when they are not gathered in a specific place, I am using the following steps to collect and simultaneously analyze user protest against algorithmic personalization: (1) diving into and (2) travelling through social media platforms, and (3) tracing the results.

In order to dive into and travel through social media platforms, netnography provides a valuable methodological framework. Netnography draws on digital ethnographic fieldwork, typically studying consumer communication. Kozinets (2012: 101) defines netnography as "participant-observational research based in online fieldwork". As such it is based on Geertz's (1973: 3) proposal of ethnographic fieldwork, which is meant to create a "thick description" of culture, cultural artifacts and lived experience. Geertz (1973: 89) thus defines culture as "a system of inherited conceptions expressed in symbolic forms by means of which men communicate, perpetuate, and develop their knowledge about and attitudes toward life".

For me, it was a difficult undertaking to carry out traditional ethnographic fieldwork on social media platforms, especially because their content is so tremendous yet highly fragmented. Elliott and Jankel-Elliott (2003: 218) therefore suggest classifying the digital method of netnography as "quasi-ethnographic", which allows for a more exploratory approach, and this is what I then started to use. Following this perspective, netnography can then be viewed as "a written account that results from fieldwork studying online, computer-mediated or Internet-based communications" (Beckmann & Langer 2005). In terms of diving into and travelling through social media platforms in search of user protest against algorithmic personalization, I was present on the various social media platforms over a period of two months and I collected data via copy and paste and taking screenshots, when the opportunity arose. As I was mainly interested in user comments, I consequently collected data as text and also analyzed the collected data as such. To contextualize the collected material, I further scribbled notable observations and immediate insights down.

The first step of "diving into" helped me to gain a comprehensive overview of social media platforms with a specific focus on user protest against algorithmic personalization. Here, I looked generically at well-known social media platforms, such as Facebook, Twitter and Reddit. This step provided me with the necessary contextual knowledge and allowed me in the following to make statements across platforms. In the following description, however, I will use user comments from Facebook as illustrative examples, because they are the most meaningful material I collected.

In the second step, "travelling through", I followed specific users and looked at whether their protest emerged across platforms. With regard to the data collection, however, I did so anonymously, which means I only collected the comment itself and not the username or profile, so no generic information would lead immediately back to the user. Throughout the process, it became clear that protest often emerged on Facebook's own profile page. I therefore looked deeper into how users comment on Facebook's public posts and how users comment on each other's posts. As such, I studied user protest in the form of semi-public communication. The form of communication is semi-public, because the comments analyzed for this study were subject to the common password protection of social media platforms; they were not, however, subject to private communication channels. All text collected was freely available after entering the social media site using the search function and tracing communication activities among users on public sites.

The third and final step of "tracing the results" involved composing the analysis. This meant going back and forth between the collected texts, the specific space in which they had been collected, and the notes made in this regard. The chosen methodological steps of diving into and travelling through social media, and tracing the results are fruitful and original insofar as they allowed me to uncover individual user protest that would otherwise have remained invisible. I stopped collecting data following the notion of theoretical saturation, that is to say, when user comments were very similar, I stopped collecting them and looked for examples that provided a substantive difference.

The three steps described provide a structured yet explorative approach to studying user protest against algorithmic personalization. It allows user protest to be uncovered via the content of a comment rather than a pre-defined description. As objections towards algorithmic personalization are mostly made by individual users, it is hard to identify at first glance, and a longer presence is advisable. A method such as netnography turned out to be useful because it allows the researcher to really "dive into" the hundreds of individual comments users make on a post or in relation to a topic.

"Please leave my news feed alone"

This chapter started out with an illustrative example of user protest against algorithmic personalization. The user comment reads in full as follows:

> Please, leave my news feed preference alone. I select "Most recent" for a reason. Your "Top Stories" doesn't even come close to being interesting to me, what my friends have going on in their lives right now does. I think it's completely asinine that I have to make the change over and over again. Is it really so difficult to let me choose my preference, and leave it alone??
>
> *(User comment on Facebook's official page, 15 May 2017)*

This comment was posted among 432 other comments under a public Facebook announcement and serves as an excellent example of how users protest against algorithmic personalization. The user is obviously frustrated; he cannot make the technology work for his own purpose. Apparently, he has changed the News Feed preferences several times, but every time he goes back to Facebook, the default setting – Top Stories – overrides his personal choice. For the user this is frustrating because he does not see the advantage of the default setting "Top Stories" and further does not think that the stories algorithmically presented to him are of interest. An obvious reading of the comment would be through the lens of power, on two levels: (1) the individual, and (2) the organizational. On the individual level, it seems as if the user is resigned to the choices being made for him and, on the organizational level, that this single user's protest is marginal in the face of Facebook's forceful presence.

The tone and content of the above user comment corresponds with several other comments I found when travelling through the digital realm. Overall, it can be stated that user protest against algorithmic personalization is highly emotional and a loss of control is expressed, especially in relation to feelings of powerlessness. Users state their convictions with passion and to the point, very often using upper case letters and exclamation marks, while at the same time suggesting practical solutions, as the following two examples show:

> Facebook: Please give an option to keep others from seeing a person's "likes" and "comments" so it doesn't fill up their Newsfeed!"
>
> *User comment on Facebook's official page, 13 May 2017*

> Why do those annoying comment threads keep popping up? I HATE THAT. HOW DO I TURN IT OFF?
>
> *User comment on Facebook's official page, 13 May 2017, emphasis in the original*

Many of the protesters ask implicitly *"How can we solve this problem?"* and many of them even offer hands-on solutions. For example, they suggest how features on social media platforms can be organized so they can use social media platforms according to their own ideas. In this regard, user protest against algorithmic personalization can be described as solution-oriented. Even though driven by emotions, the solutions proposed by users are practical. From the user perspective, it seems like a simple problem to solve and why is Facebook not doing it? This type of protest shows deep user immersion. They feel ownership of their information feed and they feel they have the right to control it. Facebook is thus not only a service they are using but it can be argued that algorithmic personalization has turned Facebook's News Feed into a personal and intimate space, which users now claim control of.

Looking through the analytical lens of "communicative materiality", further questions arise: How does the ever-evolving material structure of social media platforms provoke and shape user protest? And how is it possible for users to "play" if not "manipulate" algorithmic performance? Neff and Nagy's (2016) study has shown in this regard that users can manipulate good design intentions, so why does that not seem possible when it comes to algorithmic personalization? The collected material suggests that the idea of "chronological order" gives users the idea of power because they understand what it means – even though they cannot rely on Facebook actually showing all information. The idea of "algorithmic personalization", however, leaves people with a sense of powerlessness because they do not understand how their behaviour is tied to algorithmic performance.

Instead of looking at their behaviour, what they are trying to do is to adjust the various settings given; these do not, however, fulfil their personal needs. This demand for personal use and the ability to completely be in charge of the information feed runs through almost all comments. This points to the fact that users generally like the idea of personalization but distrust algorithms. Users want to decide themselves how to organize their stories and, in this regard, as mentioned above, chronology is a crucial factor. Users seem to get the feeling that they are missing out on interesting stories when they need to rely solely on algorithmic personalization. The nature of user protest can then be boiled down to the question of who or what is in control.

As stated earlier, user protest against algorithmic personalization arises spontaneously and is driven by individuals. During the process of data collection, I did not come across any systematically organized protest. This does not mean that such protest does not exist; it just shows that it was not prevalent at the time of research. Protests similar to the comment below underline that users have individual requirements:

> @Facebook, I would love a streamlined mode where I can just log in and scroll through ALL of my friends in chronological order. I don't care what they like or what they commented on, and I certainly don't care if they commented on their own post from eight days ago. I would also like a tab at the top to switch to a news feed of only pages I have liked and in chronological order. I used to use the custom feed filters, which was especially nice during inclement weather. I could click on News Pages and get only a feed of the news pages I added to the list for immediate updates on the weather from various sources in order. It was perfect – and then you removed that feature! I'm still very, very bitter about that. Now I'm starting to feel like Facebook is becoming unusable. I just want to see recent news without going through hundreds of individual pages every day. Come on.
>
> *User comment on Facebook's official page, 13 May 2017*

The comment above is another excellent example of how users protest and as pointed out earlier, users typically express rather strong emotions from an individual and personalized perspective. The question it raises is how this kind of highly individualized user protest can be understood on a more conceptual level, especially in relation to its communicative materiality. Bennett and Segerberg (2013) introduced the term "connective action", which is fruitful in this context. Their work looks at how digital media mobilize and organize protest movements. They argue that the rise of digital media led to the rise of more highly individualized publics and that individuals experiencing common problems in such publics are inclined to seek common solutions. Individuals thereby enter a form of protest, even though they would not join any traditional form of protest movement. In relation to this chapter, it can thus be argued that although users have highly individual experiences, on the broader level they are connected through their actions, namely expressing their discontent of algorithmic personalization. Even though they are not formally organized, they still raise their voices and, in rare cases, they find other users that share their frustrations.

Having explored the users' sites, the question is now what the organizational response to such a protest is. Social media platforms, and especially Facebook, which stands behind a number of social media applications, argues primarily for improving the user experience. User comments, such as the ones presented above, are typically answered by professional communication employees. Their main argument is that algorithmic personalization needs to work for the majority of users and hence make it into an individual user's problem. They state that their research shows that the majority of users do not wish to have chronological order but rather a selection of information that is relevant to them. Whom they are referring to by the "majority of users" remains unclear. A communication professional from Facebook answers one user's comment as follows:

> We're sorry you feel that way, Shirley. We're constantly working to improve the Facebook experience for everyone and if there's something we can do to improve yours, please let us know at: https://www.facebook.com/help/feedback/?ref=gfmod. – Aurora

This rather general comment does not engage in the user's actual individual wish but addresses the user's feelings and points to the general direction Facebook is heading in, i.e. creating an experience that works on a general level. The problem thus turns into an individual user problem, indeed an emotional problem rather than a structural one. While Facebook might "feel" for the user, they use their power to impose their choice of technology on users. The question that is left open is why it seems so impossible to offer a variety of options for organizing an information feed and leaves users suspicious that it has something to do with how revenue is created.

In sum, it can be stated that user protest takes its starting point in the experience of individual users. On a higher level, it turns into connective action as users share similar experiences and, as such, frustrations. On the level of materiality, social media platforms provoke and shape user protest and it is, as such, subject to the platform's structure. That which has materialized in terms of user protest is not easily recognized and, as such, is non-systematic. User protest mostly stands alone among many other comments and therefore loses momentum on a collective level. This might also explain why social media organizations typically react in the same way and with the same tone of voice: when responding to a protest, organizational employees either point out the help function or explain that the user has a number of different options to adjust their feed. It seems that social media organizations are convinced that user algorithmic personalization is the best way of presenting content to make profit; otherwise one would assume that they would engage with user protest more seriously.

Concluding remarks

This research explores the nature and materiality of user protest against algorithmic personalization. Algorithms have been disputed ever since they were introduced in the digital realm and researchers in various fields are still debating their social implications. It can generally be observed that a significant number of users are continuously dissatisfied and keep on raising their voices. What they call for is the chronological order of information as the default option on social media platforms, which gives them the feeling of being in control over the way information is presented to them. As the analysis suggests, loss of control and powerlessness as an outcome to algorithmic personalization, result in emotional responses.

The empirical analysis showed further that user protest against algorithmic personalization is sporadic and highly individual. While some users suggest practical solutions, others express their concerns highly emotionally, using expressive uppercase letters and exclamation marks. No matter how the protest is communicatively expressed, however, the analysis showed that users seem to become personally attached to the specific service they are using and are hence severely affected when changes are made. In that regard the question of power is discussed, especially based on the idea that algorithmic personalization has turned a rather abstract information feed into a highly personalized space, which users now claim power over.

While it is important that social media platforms take the protest seriously, the analysis also shows that users do not take the opportunity to engage in the matter more systematically. User protest is currently highly individual and also treated as such from the organizational side. If users were to start protesting more systematically and in organized communities, they could become powerful. As such user protest against algorithmic personalization can be observed as a form of "connective action" as no collective is gained at the moment. In this regard, Beer (2009: 997) pointed out that "individuals are unable to reflexively play with algorithmic power to their own advantage". From a user perspective, it therefore seems desirable to find a more independent and somewhat playful way of engaging in algorithmic personalization. This could give users the feeling of empowerment to use algorithms in a way that is beneficial to them.

Through the lens of communicative materiality, we can observe that algorithms shape, if not provoke, user protest. Every change made in relation to algorithms is experienced as an intrusion into the personal sphere of the user. This could indicate that users do not use social media platforms simply as tools but are highly connected, in other words, related to them. The lens of communicative materiality is therefore valuable because it allows for a relational perspective. Looking at the algorithm-user relationship will become even more important as social media platforms continue to be personalized, and social media corporations maximize profit from personalized user data.

With regard to future research, this work raises the question of how algorithms are able to shape emotional reactions and, more specifically, "emotional connections". What unites users right now is a common contradictory, in other words, negative experience of algorithmic personalization. Can this turn into technological resistance at some point? Current research has looked at how algorithms shape information diets and thus how users may perceive the world (Willson 2017; Wolf 2016). What current researchers may overlook, however, is the strong emotional reaction users have with social media platforms. In other words, algorithms may be influential in the way people think about the world but also in how they feel about the world (see, among others, Eslami et al. 2015, Bucher 2017). This chapter, and the developed conceptual lens of communicative materiality, aims to provide a valuable starting point for further thought in this regard and deeper engagement in such questions.

Notes

1 https://www.facebook.com/facebook/posts/10155804112131729 (accessed 22 June 2018)
2 https://twitter.com/sambehnam/status/503964792974233600?lang=en (accessed 22 June 2018)

References

Barocas, S., Hood, S., & Ziewitz, M. (2013, March 29th). Governing Algorithms: A Provocation Piece, SSRN. Retrieved from https://ssrn.com/abstract=2245322 or http://dx.doi.org/10.2139/ssrn.2245322.

Baym, N. (2010). *Personal connections in the digital age*. Cambridge: Polity Press.

Beckmann, S., & Langer, R. (2005). Netnography: rich insights from online research. *Insights at CBS*, 14(6). Retrieved from https://stosowana.files.wordpress.com/2010/10/670005_beckmann_langer_full_version.pdf.

Beer, D. (2009). Power through the algorithm? Participatory web cultures and the technological unconscious. *New Media & Society*, 11(6), pp. 985–1002.

Bennett, W., & Segerberg, A. (2013). *The Logic of Connective Action*. Cambridge: Cambridge University Press.

Bozdag, E. (2013). Bias in algorithmic filtering and personalization. *Ethics and Information Technology*, 15(3), pp. 209–227.

Bucher, T. (2017). The algorithmic imaginary: Exploring the ordinary affects of Facebook algorithms. *Information, Communication & Society*, 20(1), pp. 30–44.

Bucher, T., & Helmond, A. (2017). The Affordances of Social Media Platforms. In: J. Burgess, T. Poell, & A. Marwick (Eds.). *The SAGE Handbook of Social Media*. London, New York: Sage.

Chabert, J.-L., & Barbin, E. (Eds.) (1999). *A history of algorithms: From the pebble to the microchip*. Berlin, Heidelberg: Springer.

DeVito, M., Gergle, D., & Birnholtz, J. (2017). "Algorithms ruin everything": #RIPTwitter, Folk Theories, and Resistance to Algorithmic Change in Social Media. In: *Proceedings of the 2017 CHI Conference on Human Factors in Computing Systems* (pp. 3163–3174). New York: ACM. DOI: doi:10.1145/3025453.3025659.

Dourish, P. (2017). *The stuff of bits, an Essay on the materialities of information*. Cambridge, MA: MIT Press.

Elliott, R., & Jankel-Elliot, N. (2003). Using ethnography in strategic consumer research. *Qualitative Market Research*, 6(4), pp. 215–223.

Eslami, M., Rickman, A., Vaccaro, K., Aleyasen, A., Vuong, A., Karahalios, K., Hamilton, K., & Sandvig, C. (2015). "I always assumed that I wasn't really that close to [her]": Reasoning about Invisible Algorithms in News Feeds. *33rd Annual ACM Conference on Human Factors in Computing Systems* (pp.153–162). Retrieved from http://www-personal.umich.edu/~csandvig/research/Eslami_Algorithms_CHI15.pdf.

Gibson, J. (2015[1979]). *The ecological approach to visual perception*. London: Routledge.

Gillespie, T. (2014). The relevance of algorithms. In T. Gillespie, P. Boczkowski & K. Foot (Ed.), *Media technologies: Essays on communication, materiality, and society* (1st ed, pp. 167–194). Cambridge, MA: MIT Press.

Geertz, C. (1973). *The interpretation of cultures: Selected essays*. New York: Basic Books.

Gunkel, D. J. (2012). Communication and Artificial Intelligence: Opportunities and Challenges for the 21st Century. *communication +1*, 1(1), pp. 1–25.

Kitchin, R. (2017). Thinking critically about and researching algorithms. *Information, Communication & Society*, 20(1), pp. 14–29, DOI: doi:10.1080/1369118X.2016.1154087.

Kozinets, R. (2012). The method of netnography. In: J. Hughes (Ed.). *SAGE Internet Research Methods* (pp. 101–118). London: Sage.

Mahnke, M. S., Grunnet, J. & Tarp, N. (2017). #RIPINSTAGRAM: Examining user's counter-narratives opposing the introduction of algorithmic personalization on Instagram. *First Monday*, 22(4). DOI: doi:10.5210/fm.v22i4.7574.

Neff, G., & Nagy, P. (2016). Automation, Algorithms, and Politics. Talking to Bots: Symbiotic Agency and the Case of Tay. *International Journal of Communication*, 10(17), pp. 4915–4931.

Sisario, B. (2018). Facebook's New Political Algorithms Increase Tension With Publishers. *The New York Times*. Retrieved from https://www.nytimes.com/2018/06/14/business/media/mark-thompson-facebook-algorithm.html (accessed 22 June 2018).

Willson, M. (2017). Algorithms (and the) everyday. *Information, Communication & Society*, 20 (1), pp. 137–150.

Wolf, C. (2016). DIY videos on YouTube: Identity and possibility in the age of algorithms. *First Monday*, 21(6), DOI: doi:10.5210/fm.v21i6.6787.

10

EVOLVING DIGITAL REPERTOIRES OF CONTENTION IN TRANSITIONAL SOCIETIES

The case of China

Jun Liu

Introduction

The adoption and appropriation of social media for contentious collective action has recently become an exciting focus in studies of information and communication technologies – ICTs (e.g. Bennett & Segerberg 2013; Castells 2012; Howard & Hussain 2013; Zayani 2015). In such studies, the interrogation of social media materialities and affordances has emerged as a relevant issue for shedding light on the usage of communication technologies in contention (e.g., Bennett & Segerberg 2013; Lane et al. 2017; Lim 2012; Poell 2014). While existing scholarship has contributed to a fruitful discussion on social media materialities and contention, few studies have elaborated upon the crucial process of the *actualization* of social media materialities in political contention, i.e. the process by which agents engage with and are constrained and enabled by social media materialities for political contention. This chapter seeks to gain a deeper understanding of this topic by examining the case of social media use for political contention in China.

The use of social media for political contention in China – the world's largest authoritarian state with the largest social media population (CNNIC 2016) – has attracted enduring attention over the past decade (e.g. Chan et al. 2013; deLisle, Goldstein & Yang 2016; Poell, de Kloet & Zeng 2014; Yang 2009, 2015). Nevertheless, existing scholarship is largely dominated by case studies of singular, discrete, or isolated contentious events and is thus unable to identify the possible long-term effect of social media on political contention and broader transitional society (for a detailed critique, see Liu 2017a). To fill this gap, the present study employs the concept of "repertoires of contention" (Tilly 1986) to examine how people perceive and actualize social media materialities as sets of means for making political claims against powerful authorities and how social media have become integral to the various forms of contentious collective action in contemporary

Chinese society. The term "social media" is used in a broad sense, referring to any digital environment that fosters communication and involves social interaction among participants (Papacharissi 2015). It includes, for instance, Weibo, WeChat, mobile phones, and online encyclopaedias. By taking a series of environmental activism against petrochemical plants in six cities from 2007 to 2014 as a case study, this chapter dissects people's experience and perception of social media use for contention and the evolving role of social media as repertoires of contention in society.

I first present a critical review of current studies of social media and contention in China. Given the argument, I suggest using the concept of repertoires of contention to understand the evolving role of social media in contention. Second, I elaborate upon case selection, data collection, and analysis methods. Third, I examine various uses and perceptions of social media as repertoires of contention in the context of a specific form of environmental activism that arose in six cities between 2007 and 2014. The conclusion moves beyond the specific cases and suggests that further research needs to scrutinize the evolving role of social media as repertoires of contention and its political implications in contemporary China.

Considering repertoires of contention: Social media and contentious collective action in China

There has been growing discussion concerning social media use in a variety of contentious collective actions in China (e.g. Bondesa & Schuchera 2014; deLisle, Goldstein & Yang 2016; Huang & Sun 2014; Yang 2009, 2015). While existing studies have usefully contributed to our understanding of social media use in contentious activities, most scholars depart from what I term an "an event-based approach" (Liu 2017a) to interrogate the antagonistic use of social media in discrete, isolated contentious events (e.g. Hassid 2012; Huang & Sun 2014; Zhu, Skoric & Shen 2017). Such an approach has at least two limitations. First, an exclusive focus on media (technologies) in contention risks "technological-fascination bias," in which use of media technologies is treated as "movement in *itself*", oversimplifying "the complexity of social movement practices in the use of technologies and [...] overestimat[ing] the role played by the media [technologies]" (Mattoni & Treré 2014: 255, emphasis in original). Second, because it focusses on a single, isolated event, the event-based approach cannot recognize the historicity – and thereby possible changes across time and place – of (digitally mediated) political contention, which may help reveal the potential long-term effect of social media on contention and broader society (Yang 2011: 1044).

To fill this gap, I deploy the concept of "repertoires of contention" (Tilly 1986, 1995) in the discussion concerning social media and contention in China. A repertoire of contention, as Tilly (1995: 42) defines it, is "a limited set of routines that are learned, shared, and acted out through a relatively deliberate process of choice". The term suggests that the array of contentious claim-making and performance is always situated in prior societal experience. People learn from the history and experience of contention and "often find inspiration elsewhere in the ideas and tactics espoused and practiced by other activists" (McAdam & Rucht 1993: 58). They then employ the "learned conventions of contention" (Tarrow, 2011: 29) in later struggles. Most importantly, as Tarrow (1993: 70, emphasis in original) stresses, "the repertoire is not only what people *do* [...] it is what they *know how to do* and what others *expect* them to do". Here, contentious repertoires allow us to scrutinize the actualization of social media materialities in situated contention, as the concept offers a practice-based understanding of the recursive interaction between people and (the affordance of) social media materialities in political contention over time. In some cases, social media materialities – i.e. the material infrastructures and business interest of social media platforms – may constrain or even sabotage the unfolding of contention (e.g. Uldam 2016; Youmans & York 2012). King, Pan, and Roberts (2017), for instance, identify the Chinese government's attempt to distract the public from contentious collective action by fabricating social media posts. Furthermore, while people engage with and are constrained and enabled by social media materialities as pre-existing technological conditions, they remain capable of modifying understandings of material properties and, in some cases, introducing new understandings of existing materialities for political contention. The discussion of social media as repertoires of contention hereby entails careful consideration of social media materialities and the culturally available tactics in a specific context.

Methods

This study examines seven anti-petrochemical protests in six cities from 2007 to 2014. China's demand for a petrochemical feedstock, also known as para-xylene (i.e. a petrochemical feedstock used in plastics, polyester, and other synthetic manufacturing, hereafter "PX"), has been soaring over the past few years to satisfy growing demand for polyester production. However, most of the proposed PX projects have been forced to suspend and close operations due to strong public opposition to the construction of PX plants. After the first protest against the PX project in Xiamen (Xie & Zhao 2007), anti-PX protests have broken out in several cities, including Chengdu (Huang 2008), Dalian (BBC 2011), Ningbo (South China Morning Post 2012), Kunming (Chang 2013), Chengdu (Staff Reporter 2013), and Maoming (BBC 2014). Social media have emerged as a key means of contentious collective action within the anti-PX protests. In 2007, people relied primarily on mobile phone text messages to organize the anti-PX protest. The protest has consequently been labeled as "The Power of Mobile Messaging" (Xie & Zhao 2007). In later contentions, citizens employed various social media such as internet forums, blogs, the internet-based instant messaging platform QQ, weibo, mobile texting, and the mobile messaging app WeChat to share information and protest plans as well as to facilitate protest participation and mobilization (e.g., Goldkorn 2008; Sevastopulo 2014; *South China Morning Post* 2013). The anti-PX protests hereby allow us to observe the integration of social media into contention, particularly environmental activism, and its possible contribution to long-term structural change in a transitional society like China.

I used snowball sampling and in-depth interviews with participants to explore both their practice and perception – including experience and knowledge – of (the use of social media in) contention over the course of anti-PX protests. Of the initial 85 participants contacted for the study, 54 agreed to be interviewed. All were Internet users who were familiar with social media in various forms (i.e. mobile phones, Weibo, WeChat, etc.). Although the interviewees had diversified backgrounds in education, profession, and geographical location, all shared a firm understanding of social media as means of contentious collective action.

Semi-structured in-depth interviews were conducted, allowing the researcher to maintain the general direction and framework of the interview while eliciting detailed responses and permitted more detailed probing when clarification was necessary (Lindlof & Taylor 2010). The interviews began by reconstructing the interviewee's personal background, experience of use of various social media, and knowledge of contention, before moving on to his or her description of the selected event, perceptions and uses of social media in the event, and self-reflections on the opportunities and risks involved in the usage. Usage and evaluation of social media as repertoires of contention were probed during the interview, with the result that the discussions, based on interview subjects' experiences and practices in protests, are particularly relevant for considering how social media materialities might both enable and constrain contentious practices.

The interviews typically lasted 1.5 hours. All interviews were conducted in Chinese and in person, then transcribed and translated by the researcher. Thematic analysis and cross-case synthesis (Yin 2009: 18) were employed after data collection to assess the possible changing role of ICTs in the selected events.

Evolving repertoires of contention in anti-PX protests: Findings and discussions

Interview findings demonstrate that, in an atmosphere in which both mass media and social organizations are under highly repressive control, social media acts as a crucial part of repertoires of contention by facilitating alternative information diffusion, encouraging collective action mobilization, and engendering discourse competition and legitimation. While social media materialities – e.g. rapid diffusion, social networking, and real-time location-based information – encourage the development of contentious collective action, official media coverage legitimizes earlier collective action, which plays a key role in shaping the (innovative) understanding of social media materialities for contention and driving political participation and mobilization. This section starts by considering social media as the means of contentious information diffusion among citizens, describing their various roles in three stages of contentious collective action. This is followed by a discussion of mobilization and coordination of collective action on the basis of existing social networks and an examination of the deployment of social media to compete with authorities and legitimize activism.

Diffusion of alternative information

The interviews indicate that the use of social media for diffusion of alternative information relative to official sources became an important aspect of social media's role during three different stages – i.e. before, during, and after – of contentious collective action. In the initial stage, social media materialities afford channels for distributing alternative, contested information that contradicts the authorities, thereby laying the foundations for follow-up online or offline collective action. In the second stage, or during the period of offline political contention, social media enable people to disseminate various kinds of information regarding protests. Such dissemination not only expands the influence of protests but also encourages more engagement and participation. In the final stage, after the contention, social media allow the storage and retrieval of protest information, which promises subsequent visits and extends the long-term influence of contention as *knowledge* in society.

In the case of the anti-PX protest, digital technologies played a key role *before* political contention in making people aware of the project despite censorship or silence from the authorities. In the Xiamen case, a petition against the PX project, which called for its relocation, had been proposed three months prior to the protest. Nevertheless, local media kept silent about both the project and the petition in order to conceal the argument. The project instead came to the public's attention when a popular text message was circulated via mobile phones and later proliferated via the internet in mid-March 2007. The text-message read:

> The Xianglu Group has invested in the project in the Haicang District. When this massive toxic chemical product goes into production, it will mean an atomic bomb has been released all over Xiamen island. The people of Xiamen will live with leukaemia and deformed babies. We want to live, and we want to be healthy! International organizations require these types of projects to be developed at least 100 kilometres away from cities. Xiamen will be only 16 kilometres away [...] For the sake of future generations, pass this message on to all your Xiamen friends!

This message argued that the PX project would be detrimental to the environment and public health. It triggered furious redistribution and public opposition against the project. The pinnacle of the anti-PX movement occurred after "millions of Xiamen residents forwarded the [above] same text message around their mobile phones" (Lan & Zhang 2007, personal communication with residents in Xiamen) from 28 May 2007 urging each other to join a street protest opposing the government's chemical plant.

Similarly, forwarding the alternative information via social media to generate a counter-authority initiative became a key part of activism in the follow-up protests. For instance, the anti-PX tweets abruptly rose through the ranks and topped the list of trending tweets on Weibo before the local government ordered its removal from the list. Many interviewees described how they had distributed the alternative information via either their mobile phones, WeChat, or Weibo accounts to express discontent with the local government censorship.

Social media also enable people to broadcast the real-time situation they have witnessed or in which they engaged *during* contentious activities. Given the real-time, location-based information enabled by social media platforms like Weibo, the continuously uploaded, on-the-spot photos and videos not only breached the censorship blockade but also helped maintain sustained attention on the protest both online and offline. Such real-time messages also encouraged people in the same city to assemble as soon as possible at the site at which the protest was taking place in order to join or cover these collective actions.

For instance, in the Kunming case, several interviewees recalled that on the morning of 4 May 2012, as soon as people updated the Weibo homepage or glanced at their Weibo feeds, they received photos that not only demonstrated the existence of the protest but also included detailed locational information. As a 35-year-old engineer recalled of the anti-PX protest:

> I read several tweets with photos of the demonstration and detailed locational information. [...] I thought I should join them, be part of this event, reinforce our power, and make our voice louder. I also quickly forwarded this message through my Weibo account as well, set out, and went to join the demonstration.

Social media's real-time messaging function thereby affords and shapes information on contention as a mobilizing "call" beyond its immediate content dimension, drawing more residents to participate in protest activities, increasing the number of participants, and contributing to greater societal influence and visibility.

Even *after* the protest, the internet functions as a crucial platform on which people can retrieve information about previous protests and learn from them. Interviewees reported that they read a lot of information about anti-PX protests in other cities as soon as they searched for keywords such as "PX" via social media. These messages allowed them to learn from previous experiences. A 33-year-old clothing storeowner from Ningbo described it thus:

> You can find webpages, online forums, and tweets including photos and videos of the anti-PX protest in Xiamen, the very first one in 2007. This material expands our awareness of the PX project. [...] It shows to us how we can adapt to stop the project.

While the protest in Xiamen remained "the most famous anti-PX protest", according to a 27-year-old mobile phone salesperson from Chengdu, people can also easily track news, photos, and videos about later protests in Kunming, Dalian, and so on from webpages, Weibo, blogs, and online forums, despite censorship. The mobile phone salesperson said:

> After checking the internet, we saw several anti-PX protests around the country. If the project isn't toxic or problematic [as the government claimed], why would people in other cities oppose it? Why do we need a project that people elsewhere discarded? If they succeeded in forcing the government to give up on the project by protesting, we should also do the same!

This statement exemplifies how accessible and retrievable information on social media represented an essential source for establishing long-term knowledge about anti-PX protests.

To conclude, social media acts as a crucial information resource against authorities' attempts at information control. Various social media platforms became a crucial channel for diffusing alternative information, including both contested messages regarding the highly controversial project and experiences from the protests. Moreover, the on-site storage of information on social media materialities enables the searchability and availability of information on previous political contention as learnable experiences, even in the face of censorship. The rapid diffusion furthermore greatly shaped people's perceptions about the PX project and laid the foundations for later contention.

Collective action mobilization and legitimacy

Social media not only allow people to identify and circulate alternative information but also offer possibilities for movement mobilization. The interviews demonstrate that people deliberatively adopted social media to organize and coordinate protests in the anti-PX events.

In the anti-PX protest in Xiamen, mobile communication functioned as "the only way" (in the words of a 28-year-old consultant) for citizens to engage with their friends, classmates, colleagues, and so on regarding their shared environmental concerns. More importantly, mobile communication largely exists within a person's social ties and network, which embeds trust, obligation, reciprocity, and reliability (Chu et al. 2012; Liu 2017b). Apart from allowing people to inform each other about collective action, the embeddedness of social ties in mobile communication processes encourages people to join protests to fulfil their social obligations within their networks. The mobile phone-mediated social network thus formed the basis for protest mobilization (for a detailed discussion, see Liu 2017b). The fact, however, that mobile communication was frequently the *only* communicative channel available to residents played a crucial, if accidental, role in proliferating text messages that mobilized for the anti-PX protest in Xiamen.

Social media use for protest mobilization and coordination is also common in follow-up protest events. Nevertheless, people's perception and use of social media in later protests served a more straightforward purpose: to organize and facilitate offline protest against a PX plant, as citizens had done in other cities. According to the interviews, a popular understanding among participants was that they could use "the mobile phone, the internet, WeChat, and Weibo to organize demonstrations

[...] as citizens did in earlier anti-PX protests in other parts of the country [e.g. Xiamen]." Here, the understanding of using social media as "legitimate" repertoires of contention significantly encourages the adoption of social media in later contention.

On the basis of the interviews, this understanding generally seemed to emerge from the traditional media coverage of the protests. That is, traditional media coverage of the anti-PX protest encouraged people to learn from and imitate earlier collective actions – in particular, the successful protest in Xiamen – against the project. The anti-PX protests were covered by official media such as *People's Daily*, the official newspaper of the Communist Party of China; *China Newsweek,* published by China News Service, the second-largest state news agency; and national and regional newspapers such as *Southern Metropolis Daily*. For participants, such coverage implied that "the [central] government had accepted street protest as a legitimate way of opposing the PX project" (according to a 36-year-old taxi driver from the Chengdu case). As an authorized symbol (O'Brien 1996: 37) from the central government, the coverage became not only a benchmark of anti-PX protest but also a successful, politically accepted example that people elsewhere could later learn from, follow, and duplicate. A 42-year-old university lecturer from the Kunming case explained:

> The media would not be allowed to cover the protest in Xiamen if it was an illegal act. Now it appears in the news, which means the government recognized this activity as a legitimate form of public participation in the PX issue. [...] We can take to the streets as people did in Xiamen.

The above statement suggests that official media coverage plays a key role in influencing the adoption of social media as contentious repertoires for protest mobilization. The way in which official media covered anti-PX protests underlined the relevant role of digital technologies in initiating and organizing protests, serving as examples by which people could learn from the past regarding the adoption and appropriation of various social media for collective action organization and mobilization. Interviewees also mentioned a report by *China Newsweek*, titled "The Power of Mobile Messaging" (Xie & Zhao 2007), which detailed how Xiamen residents used text messaging to organize the anti-PX protest. People treated this report as a signal from the authorities giving *tacit consent* for the use of mobile phones for successful protest organization. Similarly, in later coverage of anti-PX protests, traditional official media reported the use of various social media as a means of protest. Such reporting inspired and encouraged the "replication" of past successful examples of the deployment of digital media in protests.

To summarize, perception and knowledge of social media as organizing repertoires arise mainly from official media coverage. Even though none of the official media stated that the protests were legal, this official media coverage was regarded as signifying the withdrawal of censorship of opposition to PX, as a go-ahead signal for using social media for protest mobilization. In this process, coverage of social media use was perceived as an encouragement to follow "the successful model" of the past by adopting social media for political contention, which has accordingly sustained its mobilizing role in later anti-PX protests. The relevance of official media in this process necessitates an analysis of the complex media ecosystems of political contention in authoritarian regimes such as China. In practice, social media alone is insufficient for making possible political activism. Different types of media contribute to different elements of the protest mechanism. While social media play a key role in informing the public about the contention and mobilizing established with social network resources, in the case of the anti-PX protests, it was the official media that legitimized contention and encouraged the emergence of repeated patterns of collective action. In this sense, the intertwining of social media and official media generates a new understanding of social media materialities as repertoires of contention and sustains the long-term influence of political activism in society.

Struggles over online encyclopaedias and legitimation of contention: Innovative repertoires

In addition to alternative information distribution and digitally mediated mobilization, the study also observes the emergence of innovative repertoires (McAdam, Tarrow & Tilly 2001: 49) at individual anti-PX protests. Repertoires evolve in moments of contention, and new repertoires emerge as innovative tactics adopted by protesters. Consequently, the most successful and transferable innovative tactics will be integrated into future repertoires, generating long-term changes in the form of contention. I present here an analysis of the virtual battle over the description of PX's toxicity in *Baidu Baike*, the most popular Chinese-language encyclopaedia, during the anti-PX protest in Maoming in 2014.

In addition to alternative information diffusion and protest mobilization, Chinese internet users launched a running battle over the entry on PX's toxicity in *Baidu Baike* during the protest in Maoming, struggling to shape the popular understanding of PX. After the anti-PX protests erupted, on 30 March 2014 an internet user reportedly (Ma et al. 2014; Wang 2014) changed the toxicity of PX from "low" to "high" on *Baidu Baike*, an open internet encyclopaedia that allows all users to write, revise, and edit its contents. After realizing that this had occurred, some university students majoring in chemistry changed the entry back to "low", declaring that PX was less toxic than people thought and suggesting that people needed to acquire accurate knowledge about the petrochemical. One of the internet users, reportedly from Maoming, then repeatedly changed PX's toxicity to "high" in the encyclopaedia listing. The university students engaged in an online battle, keeping an eye on the *Baidu Baike* definition of PX 24 hours and day and correcting it as soon as it was modified. This went on until *Baidu Baike* locked the entry from further change. The toxicity of PX had been rewritten 28 times in a five-day period after the anti-PX protest broke out. On the evening of 2 April the entry for PX was revised every half an hour.

The interviews showed that the *Baidu Baike* entry for PX played a role in shaping popular understanding of PX. Although none of the interviewees had engaged in the "battle" over the entry, all had searched for keywords such as "PX", "the toxicity of PX", and "petrochemical" on *Baidu Baike* and had read the entry several times before and during the protest. The censorship of Google made this the dominant source of information about the chemical. A 34-year-old civil servant stated:

> The first reaction of almost all my friends [after they had heard about the PX plant] was to search and read the entry on *Baidu Baike*. They also cited the information from the entry in their conversations [...] instead of from media reports.

Here, people treated online encyclopaedia entries as their primary source of information, paying less attention to reports in official media, which sought "to de-demonize the PX plant" (e.g., the tweet from the official Xinhua News Agency, see Xinhua Viewpoint 2014). The interviewees rarely mentioned or read media reports because, as a 42-year-old sales representative said, "there are – and will be – only positive propaganda stories about the PX plant in the media".

Most interestingly, the PX entry became a key resource from which people could learn about arguments and protests against the PX plants. The structure of *the Baidu Baike* online encyclopaedia allows users to locate and link to other related entries containing the same keyword (in this case, PX). Within the entry for PX, interviewees also found links to, for instance, "PX projects" (http://baike.baidu.com/view/978818.htm), "Xiamen PX incident", and "Chengdu PX project" – entries that describe a series of protests against PX plants, dating back to 2007. Such information strengthens people's resolve to protest against the plants. One example is given by a 29-year-old consultant:

> I realized that there had been so many protests against the [PX] project over the past several years. People in different cities were against it and succeeded. We should do that as well. If they can succeed, we can do that, and we should do that as well.

In summary, this section identifies an emerging, innovative tactic in anti-PX protests targeting national attention. Protest participants sought to shape the popular understanding of issues in the dispute by modifying information about the issue in an online encyclopaedia. This move attempted to leverage domestic public opinion, which could force the government to review its stance. Most importantly, this tactic demonstrated a new direction in using social media as repertoires of contention beyond information diffusion and action mobilization. The struggle over the encyclopaedia entry entailed an attempt to legitimize environmental activism beyond specific, individual protests as such. In this sense, the attempt to change the entry and influence public understanding of contentious issues demonstrates a new purpose for environmental activism – utilizing and manoeuvring social media materialities – beyond a particular geographical location. In this sense, the participants seek not only to legitimize their present activism but also to generate a long-term influence on PX projects by influencing public understanding. Such an initiative accordingly manifests the fact that participants have moved beyond the local scope and begun employing digital media to gain more national resources and generate large-scale, long-term political influence. Repertoires are always situated in the sense that contentious repertoires are dependent upon an interpretation of how materialities will be used in a specific context. The material aspects of social media enable and restrain the contentious performances and repertoires, while performances and repertoires reproduce and further alter understandings concerning the actualization of materialities. Nevertheless, although it may be too early to draw conclusions regarding the potential sustainability of this innovative tactic, it provides a few hints regarding how repertoires evolve on the basis of social media materialities within a societal range of contention.

Conclusion

This study investigates repertoires of contention to understand the evolving role of social media in contention in contemporary China. First, the initial anti-PX protest features the use of social media mainly to disseminate alternative information within China's highly controlled media environment. By embedding existing social ties and networks, social media act as key channels to rapidly receive and distribute protest information and to successfully recruit protest participants. Social media also allow the storage and retrieval of protest information after the protest. These materialities enable people to easily identify and imitate previous events by learning from their practices and legacies.

Second, social media act as fundamental repertoires of mobilization, while official media function as a legitimate source of learning and duplication of previous contention. Reciprocity, embedded in social media, not only encouraged people to disseminate alternative messages within their social networks but also facilitated movement participation and mobilization. Furthermore, reliability introduces mutual trust and obligations, which further consolidate protest initiatives and generate solidarity for activist practices in an authoritarian regime. More importantly, the mobilization process shows how engagement by official media plays a crucial role in legitimizing the perception of social media as organizing repertoires of contention. The specific role of official media as mouthpieces of the government contributes to the public understanding that the activism is no longer sensitive and that authorities have begun taking a more tolerant position toward the protest. Consequently, such understanding legitimizes the move toward environmental activism and further encourages the emergence of similar actions. In this sense, social media alone are insufficient for mobilizing contention. Instead, the intertwining of social media and official media establishes a complex media ecology that drives and legitimates the (re-)emergence of contentious collective action.

However, as we also see in other cases, authorities may utilize social media to hinder or sabotage the evolution of contentious collective action (e.g. Neumayer, Rossi & Karlsson 2016).

Third, the later anti-PX protests have involved the use of social media to gain national resources and legitimize contention by shaping popular understandings of the contested issue. This innovative initiative is capable of generating large-scale, long-term political influence beyond a local, specific scope. It also exemplifies a strategic deployment of social media materialities not only to distribute protest information but also to legitimize contention *per se* with potential long-term political implications for society. By taking anti-PX protests as a case, this study suggests the need for further research to go beyond individual cases to scrutinize the changing role of social media as repertoires of contention and the long-term influence of ICTs in political contention. I argue that the exploration of social media materialities and affordances as repertoires of contention can play an important role in understanding social media in contention. Most existing studies simply consider the use of social media in movements and actions. However, social media are not "born" to be used in and for political contention (e.g. Zuckerman 2015). Instead, people appropriate and manoeuvre them for such purposes in a specific context. Exploring the reasons behind people's strategic or tactic understandings, choices, and uses of (specific) social media as repertoires of contention *outside* their materialities thereby reveals "the micro-foundations of political action" (Jasper 2004: 4) by introducing an agency perspective.

Funding

This work was supported by Dr.phil. Ragna Rask-Nielsen Grundforskningsfond.

Acknowledgements

The author expresses appreciation for comments from the editors for improving the manuscript.

References

BBC (2011). China Protest Closes Toxic Chemical Plant in Dalian. Retrieved from http://www.bbc.co.uk/news/world-asia-pacific-14520438, 12 March 2017.

BBC (2014). China Maoming environmental protest violence condemned. Retrieved from http://www.bbc.com/news/world-asia-china-26849814, 12 March 2017.

Bennett, W. L., & Segerberg, A. (2013). *The Logic of Connective Action: The Personalization of Contentious Politics*. Cambridge: Cambridge University Press.

Bondesa, M., & Schuchera, G. (2014). Derailed Emotions. *Information, Communication & Society*, 17(1), pp. 45–65.

Castells, M. (2012). *Networks of Outrage and Hope*. Cambridge: Polity Press.

Chan, M., Wu, X., Hao, Y., Xi, R., & Jin, T. (2013). Microblogging, Online Expression, and Political Efficacy Among Young Chinese Citizens: The Moderating Role of

Information and Entertainment Needs in the Use of Weibo. *Cyberpsychology, Behavior, and Social Networking*, 15(7), pp. 345–349.

Chang, M. (2013, May 17). Thousands protest Kunming PX plan. *Global Times*. Retrieved from http://www.globaltimes.cn/content/782252.shtml, 18 September 2018.

Chu, R., Fortunati, L., Law, P.-L., & Yang, S. (2012). *Mobile Communication and Greater China*. London: Routledge.

CNNIC (2016). The 38th China Internet Development Statistics Report. Retrieved from https://www.cnnic.cn/gywm/xwzx/rdxw/2016/201608/W020160803204144417902.pdf, 12 March 2017.

deLisle, J., Goldstein, A., & Yang, G. (2016). *The Internet, Social Media, and a Changing China*. Philadelphia, PA: University of Pennsylvania Press.

Gerbaudo, P., & Treré, E. (2015). In Search of the "We" of Social Media Activism. *Information, Communication & Society*, 18(8), pp. 865–871.

Goldkorn, J. (2008). NIMBY protest hits Chengdu. Retrieved from http://www.danwei.org/environmental_problems/nimby_protest_hits_chengdu.php, 12 March 2017.

Hassid, J. (2012). Safety Valve or Pressure Cooker? *Journal of Communication*, 62(2), pp. 212–230.

Howard, P. N., & Hussain, M. M. (2013). *Democracy's Fourth Wave?* New York: Oxford University Press.

Huang, R., & Sun, X. (2014). Weibo Network, Information Diffusion and Implications for Collective Action in China. *Information, Communication & Society*, 17(1), pp. 86–104.

Huang, Z. (2008, May 6). Chengdu People Walk to Express Environmental Concerns. *China Daily*, p. 4. Retrieved from http://www.chinadaily.com.cn/china/2008-05/06/content_6662940.htm, 18 September 2018.

Jasper, J. (2004). A Strategic Approach to Collective Action: Looking for Agency in Social-Movement Choices. *Mobilization: An International Quarterly*, 9(1), pp. 1–16.

King, G., Pan, J., & Roberts, M. E. (2017). How the Chinese Government Fabricates Social Media Posts for Strategic Distraction, not Engaged Argument. *American Political Science Review*, 111(3), pp. 484–501.

Lan, Y., & Zhang, Y. (2007, May 29). Millions of Xiamen Residents spread crazily the same SMS to Against High-Pollution Project. *Southern Metropolis Daily*.

Lane, D. S., Kim, D. H., Lee, S. S., Weeks, B. E., & Kwak, N. (2017). From Online Disagreement to Offline Action. *Social Media + Society*, 3(3), pp. 1–14. DOI: doi:10.1177/2056305117716274.

Lim, M. (2012). Clicks, Cabs, and Coffee Houses. *Journal of Communication*, 62(2), pp. 231–248.

Lindlof, T. R., & Taylor, B. C. (2010). *Qualitative Communication Research Methods*. Thousand Oaks, CA: Sage.

Liu, J. (2017a). From "Moments of Madness" to "the Politics of Mundanity". *Social Movement Studies*, 16(4), pp. 418–432.

Liu, J. (2017b). Mobile Phones, Social Ties, and Collective Action Mobilization in China. *Acta Sociologica*, 60(3), pp. 213–227.

Ma, L., Liu, X., Lv, Y., & Li, G. (2014, 6 April). PX, a special "defense of science". *People's Daily*, p. 4.

Mattoni, A., & Treré, E. (2014). Media Practices, Mediation Processes, and Mediatization in the Study of Social Movements. *Communication Theory*, 24(3), pp. 252–271.

McAdam, D., & Rucht, D. (1993). The Cross-national Diffusion of Movement Ideas. *The Annals of the American Academy of Political and Social Science*, 528(1), pp. 56–74.

McAdam, D., Tarrow, S. G., & Tilly, C. (2001). *Dynamics of Contention*. New York: Cambridge University Press.

Neumayer, C., Rossi, L., & Karlsson, B. (2016). Contested Hashtags: Blockupy Frankfurt in Social Media. *International Journal of Communication*, 10(22) pp. 5558–5579.
O'Brien, K. J. (1996). Rightful Resistance. *World Politics*, 49(1), pp. 31–55.
Papacharissi, Z. (2015). We Have Always Been Social. *Social Media + Society*, 1(1), pp. 1–2.
Poell, T. (2014). Social Media and the Transformation of Activist Communication. *Information, Communication & Society*, 17(6), pp. 716–731.
Poell, T., de Kloet, J., & Zeng, G. (2014). Will the Real Weibo Please Stand Up? *Chinese Journal of Communication*, 7(1), pp. 1–18.
Sevastopulo, D. (2014, April 1). China PX plant protests spread to provincial capital Guangzhou. *Financial Times*. Retrieved from http://www.ft.com/intl/cms/s/0/cf6594fa-b98d-11e3-957a-00144feabdc0.html-axzz3ZeGWgZ3k, 12 May 2015.
South China Morning Post (2012). Ningbo PX Project. Retrieved from http://www.scmp.com/topics/ningbo-px-project, 12 November 2016.
South China Morning Post (2013). Governments toughen stance on environmental protesters amid Kunming, Chengdu actions. Retrieved from http://www.scmp.com/news/china/article/1241474/governments-toughen-their-stance-towards-environmental-protesters, 22 December 2016.
Tarrow, S. G. (1993). Cycles of Collective Action. *Social Science History*, 17(2), pp. 281–307.
Tarrow, S. G. (2011). *Power in Movement* (3rd ed.). New York: Cambridge University Press.
Tilly, C. (1986). *The Contentious French*. Cambridge: Harvard University Press.
Tilly, C. (1995). *Popular Contention in Great Britain, 1758–1834*. New York: American Mathematical Soc.
Tong, J., & Zuo, L. (2014). Weibo Communication and Government Legitimacy in China. *Information, Communication & Society*, 17(1), pp. 66–85.
Uldam, J. (2016). Corporate management of visibility and the fantasy of the post-political: Social media and surveillance. *New Media & Society*, 18(2), pp. 201–219.
Wang, W. (2014, April 8). Wiki edit battle microcosm of Maoming PX protests. *Global Times*. Retrieved from http://www.globaltimes.cn/content/853057.shtml, 12 November 2016.
Xie, L., & Zhao, L. (2007). The Power of Mobile Messaging. *China Newsweek*, 326(20), pp. 16–17.
Xinhua Viewpoint (2014). De-demonizing the PX plant. Retrieved from http://www.weibo.com/1699432410/AEBydslL4?from=page_1002061699432410_profile&wvr=6&mod=weibotime&type=comment-rnd1430836924445, 12 November 2016.
Yang, G. (2009). *The Power of the Internet in China*. New York: Columbia University Press.
Yang, G. (2011). Technology and Its Contents. *The Journal of Asian Studies*, 70, pp. 1043–1050.
Yang, G. (2015). *China's Contested Internet*. Copenhagen: Nordic Institute of Asian Studies Press.
Yin, R. K. (2009). *Case Study Research: Design and Methods* (4th Ed.). London: Sage.
Youmans, W. L., & York, J. C. (2012). Social media and the activist toolkit: User agreements, corporate interests, and the information infrastructure of modern social movements. *Journal of Communication*, 62(2), pp. 315–329.
Zayani, M. (2015). *Networked Publics and Digital Contention*. Oxford: Oxford University Press.
Zhu, Q., Skoric, M., & Shen, F. (2017). I Shield Myself from Thee: Selective Avoidance on Social Media During Political Protests. *Political Communication*, 34(1), pp. 112–131.
Zuckerman, E. (2015). Cute Cats to the Rescue? In: D. Allen & J. S. Light (Eds.), *From Voice to Influence* (pp. 131–154). Chicago, IL: University of Chicago Press.

AFTERWORD

Lessons and puzzles in studying social media materialities and protest

Alexandra Segerberg and W. Lance Bennett

This volume applies welcome attention to the role of materiality in protest. Contemporary activism and civic engagement frequently intertwine with social media, and the latter are not neutral intermediaries in this interaction. Important work has started to clarify how social media business models, policies, technologies, and discourses shape activism in various ways. The authors show how platforms and their cultures enable and constrain, but also monitor and moderate action, how algorithmic regimes primed for acceleration, attention, commodification, datafication and personalization inform protest practices, and how this produces a series of tensions, and indeed dilemmas, for activists. Yet there is still much to understand about the relationship between social media materialities and protest, and its broader implications.

The question at the heart of the book is how we should conceptualize the tension between activist agency and the techno-commercial infrastructures of social media. When social media shape protest, what happens to activist capacities to develop ideas and act, and to do so autonomously, effectively, and with critical insight into the conditions for their doing so? This is a tricky area, both because the notion of agency tends to be conceptually ambiguous and because studying the mutual articulation of social media and protest is empirically challenging. The overarching inquiry raises the question of how we catch sight of the ways in which social media materialities shape protest. This is not a trivial task. The starting point is plural, encompassing many social media (not all commercial) and kinds of activism (not all contentious). These processes are obscure and hard to pin down. The challenges with respect to agency might be expected to take similarly varied or unexpected form.

The core question is not something that can be settled in one book, but the volume offers inspiring grounds for a collective push in this direction, and it is worth thinking carefully about the ways in which it does so. This afterword highlights four key lessons shared across the contributions: the relational starting point, the beyond-technology focus, the idea that infrastructures reveal themselves in breakdowns, and, finally, how all of these factors shape the researcher's attention. Each of these lessons provide useful guides for research, but they also combine to suggest at least three critical puzzles. First, since many cases of technology-enabled activism depend on peripheral networks for the scale and the visibility of the action, it is not clear how to select an analytical focus among various actors and levels of analysis. Secondly, the continuing call from both scholars and activists for non-commercial, open access technologies is understandable in light of many of the concerns raised in this volume, but it is not clear that non-commercial technologies are likely to reach the broader networks of supporters and publics who continue to engage through commercial social media. Finally, the first two puzzles are complicated by disputes among activists themselves over the appropriate roles for communication technologies. Following our discussion of the analytical lessons we will address the puzzles that they present.

Four constructive lessons for research

Several assumptions from across the volume are helpful for teasing out the issues involved around social media materialities and protest, and might be taken as lessons for going forward.

1. The importance of relational dynamics

A key starting point is the assumption of a relational emphasis in the study of social media materialities and protest. This is not just a matter of preferred approach, it does significant work in this context. In many ways, attention to fine-grained relational dynamics helps unfurl both the subtle processes and the sudden game changes. Most of the authors focus on the relationships among protesters, with an eye to how social media platforms, with their own embedded values, interact with activist ideas and practices. Neither the activist nor the technology elements in most cases can be assumed to be homogeneous. Protesters may include organizers and different kinds of participants, from diverse coalition partners to engaged publics. Social media may encompass multiple platforms that interact with each other, along with the corporations that own them, the designers and third-party developers that work on them, and the government actors that monitor them. Surrounding these core relationships, there are many others involved, such as journalists, antagonists, police, bots, and spectator publics. All of these factors can produce diverse forms of activism with varying kinds of impact. Depending on the type of activism, the different networks involved, and the forms of media used, the nexus of social media materialities and protest is a moving target: something that needs to be studied in action and with respect for how components change.

One strategy for designing analyses in such complex mediated political ecologies is to sort out the various types of agency. There are clearly differences between activist organizers and leaders, and various networks of less committed supporters, opponents attempting to disrupt online activism, and the potentially large spectator publics who can variously amplify or modify activist messages. In addition, technology introduces its own agency into political situations, be it in the programmable capabilities of bots, or the ways in which the kinds of information carried by different media affect human engagement. Importantly, the human and technological forms of agency also interact, as when people discovered they could improvise Twitter messages by adding #hashtags that enabled different kinds of network formation and communication monitoring. A further step toward developing a framework for comparing relational dynamics is to recognize that agency can also operate at different levels – from the individual level, to identifiable groups and networks, to complex networks of networks such as large protest crowds – and that each level of analysis can tell us different things about the organization and impact of activism. The significance of refining agency and identifying related units and levels of analysis has been noted in several contexts. Mattoni (Chapter 1) unpacks the emergence of stratified "infrastructures of participation" within an occupied protest space. Kavada and Poell (2017) suggest that social media materialities may shape the "trajectories of publicness" stretching beyond a protest in interestingly distinct ways from the event itself. Likewise, tracking the multilayered flow of ideas from core to peripheral networks across digital intermediaries helped shed light on how the public legacy of the national Occupy Wall Street protests ended up "being about" issues that reflected the different situations of actors and spectators and the mediated relations among them (Bennett, Segerberg & Yang forthcoming). Reflecting carefully about which levels and units of analysis can help answer what research questions will be important for continuing to move the field towards more general theoretical understandings of how social media materialities shape political organization and outcomes.

2. Take media and technology seriously but do not fetishize it

A second key point developed by several authors here is to take media and technology seriously but to reject a technology-centric focus. This outlook counters the tendency to fetishize the particular technological development of the moment, such as talking about "Facebook Revolutions", which has little explanatory power and often freezes analyses in time. Instead, it brings to the fore the questions about agency and levels of analysis raised above, and focusses on actor-network dynamics (Latour 2005) that may yield more enduring empirical findings and theoretical generalizations. A general value of this starting point lies in the ways it directs analytical focus to the often dense relationships that are lodged in complex political, social, discursive and material contexts. Locating both human actors and their technologies in context in turn makes it possible to trace how social media materialities incorporate and affect political, economic and socio-cultural power – such that, for example, it becomes clearer how and why activists may have varying degrees of success using the same platforms to achieve very different outcomes, from effectively communicating their positions to silencing or harassing others (Uldam & Kaun, Chapter 7; see also e.g. Massanari 2017).

3. Track disruptions and breakdowns

Several of the contributions track disruptions and breakdowns, a classic and instructive way of catching sight of infrastructure at work. The deeply felt and ingrained platformization of daily life makes the processes defining the relationship between social media materialities and protest even harder to pin down. Yet tracking breakdowns can still reveal dynamics around both processes and tensions that arise despite, and sometimes even because of, that ingrained quality. To the extent that social media are swords with many edges (bringing advantages as well as vulnerabilities), they also spark reactions and present opportunities for negotiation. While the most obvious breakdowns revolve around disrupted service, other kinds of disruption present themselves in the ways activists engage in micro-negotiations such as avoidance, anonymity, self-censorship, deliberate miscommunication, or navigate the fault lines through strategies of remediation and "hybrid materiality as resistance" (Treré, Chapter 3). Different, but equally revealing, are the conflicts that emerge within groups in the course of action, whether in the disconnects between what activists plan and what is programmatically produced, or what different parts regard as desirable organization and legitimate participation.

4. Acknowledge how social media materialities shape research

Finally, as several of the contributions suggest, social media materialities shape researcher practices in analytically and methodologically important ways. On the one hand, social media are rife with gaps and silences, as a result of design choices that over-represent certain content and activist strategies of self-censorship and avoidance. On the other, platform business models lead to "regimes of access" (Burgess & Bruns 2015) through which social media companies regulate the data researchers can collect and use. The terms for data access issued by media companies are not only often prohibitive, it is also important to take into account how they change. The political investigations of Facebook's role in hosting fake news and disinformation in the 2016 US elections led Facebook to restrict data access in ways that limited research. It is ironic that these restrictions may have more to do with hiding the dark side of Facebook's business model than with protecting privacy of user accounts. While Facebook has agreed to discuss making data available to trusted third parties (e.g., The Social Science Research Council in the US), many questions remain about how the data would be archived, tagged, hosted, and served to the research community.

Such conditions shape scholarly attention and preferred methodologies, often exaggerating focus on relatively open platforms (e.g. Twitter) and on collectible (real-time) and trackable data (e.g. collection strategies that follow the specific structuring affordances of particular platforms such as hashtags). The problem is not primarily that social media collections are imperfect mirrors or that we have imperfect ways of getting at the world. Analysis is always a matter of judicious isolation, and the analytic use of media material has long been subject to methodological debate and refinement, as exemplified in the tradition of protest event analysis. What this starting point instead highlights is the need to retain a sober view of limitations and to leave connective traces for others in conceptual and methodological terms. Connective traces are important for piecing together our analytical slices – for example, showing how a particular level or unit of analysis connects with others. More fundamentally, they also help to distinguish shifts in researcher focus from the empirical developments that we are trying to trace in the world, which are crucial for developing critical oversight and reflection in the field (Neumayer & Rossi 2016; Mattoni & Pavan 2017).

Three Critical Puzzles

These four lessons about the politics of technological materiality are excellent starting points for further research. At the same time, when taken together, they also highlight critical puzzles that pose dilemmas for research design and analysis.

A first puzzle is how to decide where to focus analytical attention on complex assemblages of activist networks: on core actors who control "official" media accounts; on more peripheral but engaged supporter networks that may carry news about the action from the activist core to spectator publics; on the digital intermediaries; or on those monitoring and/or intervening from potentially more critical standpoints (from government surveillance agencies, to opponents, to the legacy media)? Ideally, the answer is "all of the above". It is understandable that the limited capacity of most researchers results in putting the focus on one or another of these political actor and technology clusters. Nevertheless, we should spend more time discussing these choices, because the organization and impact of political action often depends on the interactions among these different types of agents. Moving among the levels and units of analysis, as discussed above, often requires introducing variable frameworks into the analysis. The challenge is that performing this kind of analysis is similar to solving a complex puzzle composed of parts that each provide separate but incomplete understandings.

A second puzzle emerges in tensions between commercial and custom technologies. The problems associated with dominating commercial platforms make it pertinent to explore alternatives. However, while there are many reasons to worry about the limitations and security issues associated with opaque commercial social media platforms that harvest personal information and were not built for the purpose of political organization, there are also limitations to custom designed open source technologies (see Croeser, Chapter 2). For example, to the extent that engaging publics is a goal, a significant problem remains that of broad access to custom-built political platforms. Most citizens will not be reached by those technologies, and many will not find them convenient to learn. Indeed, experiments with "connective parties" or "net parties" suggest that custom technologies limit both growth and participation due to problems with coding online deliberations and curating large volumes of input (Bennett, Segerberg & Knüpfer 2017; Haberer 2017; Husted & Plesner 2017).

Relatedly, a third puzzle presents itself in conflicting views on the appropriate role of technology in protest. While some activists deliberately drill into digital media for the purposes of organizing and publicizing protest, for others the extensive reliance on technology conflicts with other values of political participation, such as the personal commitment and face-to-face relationships that are often associated with practices of direct, deliberative democracy. From this perspective, even if problems such as those of designing complex participatory processes and organizing large volumes of inputs are solved, substantial focus on online relationships and mediated attention risks undermining efforts to build strong political communities. This is surely an interesting challenge produced by technological materiality, and it is not easy to resolve. It is clear that many networks fracture along identity and issue differences, suggesting the paradox that strong face-to-face relationships may limit the scale of sustainable and focussed action, yet the technological networks that enable action to scale often result in short-lived and unstable politics (Bennett & Segerberg 2013; see also Milan, Chapter 8, and Coretti & Pica, Chapter 5).

A research challenge with respect to the latter two points is the possibility that these puzzles may look different from other empirical angles. The question needs to be considered whether some of the key findings and generalizations to have emerged in the field thus far in fact apply mainly to the better-studied cases, such as particular platforms or protest on the progressive left with strong underpinnings in direct participatory democracy, as opposed to, for example, contemporary activism on the right that assigns different roles and values to technology and participation. This possibility suggests a more mundane collective challenge for us working in the area, namely that of facing up to the streetlight effect – a reminder not to look only in the lighted areas for lost keys.

Building a field beyond the streetlight

In any field, it is important to avoid studying only the parts of the street that are best lit at the expense of other areas that might be more relevant and revealing. Making a deliberate effort to pursue theoretical nuance and empirical breadth is particularly important at a time in which social media pervade ever more dimensions of social life, the role of popular protest is becoming increasingly ambiguous, and both are the objects of attention across disciplines with very different analytical concerns.

In the present context, avoiding the streetlight effect as a field entails expanding on several obvious but important points. For example, to be able to isolate and understand the implications of techno-commercial materialities in the context of activism, we also need to include in our analytical remit a range of non-commercial and non-social media, and the hybrid dimensions in media ecologies. We need comparative research, including observing highly commercial media ecologies embedded in different political systems. Similarly, understanding the implications of social media materialities and protest in the big picture requires extending analysis beyond the better-known case types. It is important not to miss what is happening where the going is smooth as well as rough, and to gain oversight of the broader landscape of political action and activism.

It follows from the discussions here and in this volume that pursuing the nexus of social media materialities and protest requires effort that stretches across several analytical and methodological dimensions. The high degree of sophistication required in analytic expertise invites a division of labour based on extant skills. While deep specialization is sometimes the strongest and most relevant strategy, here it would be a mistake to stay too much in the light. A relevant way forward would instead seem to be to work more deliberately to widen the scope of the spotlight by joining efforts across specialities. This presents a true challenge, as it makes high demands on expansive thinking. It is not just about skills and sources, but also about conceptualizing other analytical dimensions. All this demands interdisciplinary collegiality and innovation – a demanding but worthy path the editors have rightly opened up in this book.

References

Bennett, L., & Segerberg, A., (2013). *The Logic of Connective Action: The Personalization of Contentious Politics*, Cambridge: Cambridge University Press.

Bennett, L., SegerbergA., & Knüpfer, C., (2017). The democratic interface: technology, political organization, and diverging patterns of electoral representation. *Information, Communication & Society*, 21(11), pp. 1655–1680. DOI: doi:10.1080/1369118X.2017.1348533.

Bennett, L., SegerbergA., & Yang, Y., (forthcoming). The Strength of Peripheral Networks: Negotiating Attention and Meaning in Complex Media Ecologies. *Journal of Communication*.

Burgess, J. & Bruns, A., (2015). Easy data, hard data: The politics and pragmatics of Twitter research after the computational turn. In: G. Langlois, J. Redden, & G. Elmer (Eds.) *Compromised data: From social media to big data* (pp. 93–111). New York: Bloomsbury Academic.

Haberer, M. (2017). The birth of the net party: Political party commitments responding to citizen demands. Unpublished manuscript.

Husted, E., & Plesner, U. (2017) The spaces of open-source politics: Physical and digital conditions for political organization. *Organization*, 24(5) pp. 648–670.

Kavada, A. & Poell, T., (2017). Trajectories of Publicness and Contestation. Paper presented at ECPR Joint Sessions, 25–30 April, Nottingham, UK.

Latour, B. (2005). *Reassembling the social: an introduction to actor-network-theory*. Oxford: Oxford University Press.

Massanari, A. (2017). #Gamergate and The Fappening: How Reddit's algorithm, governance, and culture support toxic technocultures. *New Media & Society*, 19(3), pp. 329–346.

Mattoni, A. & Pavan, E. (2017). Information, Communication, Digitization, and Datafication: Four Analytical Stages in Researching Social Movements and Media. Paper presented at ECPR General Conference, 6–9 September, Olso, Norway.

Neumayer, C., & Rossi, L. (2016). 15 Years of Protest and Media Technologies Scholarship: A Sociotechnical Timeline. *Social Media + Society*, 2(3). DOI: doi:10.1177/2056305116662180.

INDEX

Made in the USA
Monee, IL
12 November 2026

694b40b6-c1cf-4d13-baab-06598994b3caR01